Christian America?

Christian America?

What Evangelicals Really Want

Christian Smith

UNIVERSITY OF CALIFORNIA PRESS
Berkeley • *Los Angeles* • *London*

University of California Press
Berkeley and Los Angeles, California

University of California Press, Ltd.
London, England

Library of Congress Cataloging-in-Publication Data

Smith, Christian (Christian Stephen), 1960–
    Christian America? : what evangelicals really want / Christian Smith.
      p.   cm.
    Includes bibliographical references (p.)and index.
    ISBN 0-520-22041-2 (cloth : alk. paper).
    1. Evangelicalism—United States—History—20th century. 2. Christianity
and culture—United States—History—20th century. 3. Christianity and
politics—United States—History—20th century. I. Title.

BR1642.U5 S623 2000
277.3'0829—dc21

                                      99-048340

Manufactured in the United States of America

09 08 07 06 05 04 03 02 01 00
10 9 8 7 6 5 4 3 2 1
The paper used in this publication meets the minimum requirements of ANSI/NISO Z39.48-1992 (R
1997) (Permanence of Paper). ∞

For Caroline

Contents

Acknowledgments   ix

Introduction: The Big Evangelical Question   1

1 Making Sense of "Christian America"   21

2 The Problem of Pluralism   61

3 The Limits of Politics   92

4 Evangelicals on Education   129

5 Male Headship and Gender Equality   160

Conclusion: Demythologizing the Angel/Demon   193

Appendix: What Surveys Tell Us   197

Notes   229

References   243

Index   253

Acknowledgments

MANY PEOPLE AND INSTITUTIONS deserve thanks for helping bring this book to publication. Recognition and gratitude must go first and foremost to Joel Carpenter and The Pew Charitable Trusts, for their interest and confidence in this research project. Needless to say, none of the publications from this project would have been possible without Joel and the Trusts' generous support of my research.

I am also grateful for the semester-long Junior Faculty Study Leave provided by the University of North Carolina at Chapel Hill to complete work on this book.

I am appreciative of both the American Jewish Committee and the University of North Carolina at Chapel Hill Institute for Research in Social Science, for the use of their Religious Right Survey and Southern Focus Poll datasets, respectively, which I analyzed for the appendix.

Thanks to Jim Moody for his work on the religious traditions diagram in the introduction; to Keri Iyall for her work on the interviews map in the introduction; and to Jenifer Hamil-Luker for her preliminary analysis of interviews on education. Finally, I am grateful to Stan Gaede, Mark Noll, Rod Stark, John Tyson, Tom Tyson, Bob Woodberry, David Sikkink, Mark Regnerus, Melinda Lundquist, Brad Wilcox, Jenifer Hamil-Luker, and Amy Argue for feedback on earlier drafts of some or all chapters. Their criticisms and advice have, I think, improved my arguments considerably.

Doug Abrams Arava and Reed Malcolm have proven engaged and supportive editors. Many thanks to them for their interest in and support for publishing this book, and for their very helpful suggestions along the way for reshaping its structure and argument.

Last, to the hundreds of evangelicals around the country with whom we conducted interviews—and in many cases, the pastors who granted us access to them—many thanks as well.

One final caveat: the analysis and interpretation expressed in this book are those of the authors, and do not necessarily reflect the views of The Pew Charitable Trusts.

The Big Evangelical Question

EVANGELICALS WERE VIRTUALLY INVISIBLE on the radar screen of American public life prior to the mid-1970s. While numbering in the tens of millions and growing in adherents and institutional strength, American evangelicals had for decades blended into mainstream American life. But the 1976 election of the "born-again" President Jimmy Carter and the rise in the late 1970s of Jerry Falwell's Moral Majority changed all of that. Evangelicals found themselves on the American cultural and political map, and they have remained conspicuous throughout the decades since then.

Today, many journalists, scholars, public leaders, and ordinary Americans are curious and concerned—sometimes frightened—about who evangelicals are and what they want. People especially wonder about the political significance of evangelicalism. Aren't evangelicals the core of the Religious Right? Don't they want to rebuild a theocratic "Christian America"? Don't they aim to legally impose their moral standards on all other Americans? Won't evangelicals come to dominate the Republican party? Doesn't evangelicalism—with its preoccupation with "Christian America," prayer and creationism in schools, male headship in the home, and so on—represent some kind of backlash that is jeopardizing the liberties and rights of other Americans who disagree with their beliefs and values?

This book attempts to answer these and similar questions in a fair and balanced manner. It explores the beliefs, values, commitments, and goals of ordinary American evangelicals, particularly as they relate to the issues of pluralism and politics. I ask how much, in what ways, and for what reasons evangelicals are tolerant and intolerant of other groups of Americans who differ from them, and I investigate how ordinary evangelicals view politics and political activism—and what that means for American democracy. I also analyze evangelical approaches to specific issues—such as religion in education, "family values," and gay rights—to illuminate the motivations and goals of evangelical public influence. My primary goal is neither to defend nor to attack evangelicals, but to understand them better.

This book focuses on the social and political orientation of the tens of millions of *ordinary* American evangelicals in this country.[1] Some books attempt to examine the views of evangelicals by focusing on the beliefs and goals of the Religious Right[2] or by profiling certain conservative Protestant organizations, popular authors, and outspoken leaders.[3] Still other books look at ordinary evangelicals, but are less concerned with pluralism and politics than with the theoretical issues of cultural accommodation and secularization.[4] What is needed, in addition to these, is an analysis of evangelicals' opinions specifically on pluralism and politics that explores the actual views of the mass of ordinary American evangelicals, not merely the official positions of some of their more well-known, vocal organizations and proponents.

The data this book analyzes were collected as part of a massive scholarly research project on American evangelicals carried out by a team of twelve sociologists from around the United States over a three-year period, from 1995 to 1997.[5] This research included personal, two-hour interviews with 130 churchgoing Protestants in six different locations around the United States. Of these, 65 were conducted with white Christians who attend churches in evangelical denominations or who clearly identify themselves as "evangelical"; 27 were conducted with members of theologically conservative black churches; and the rest were conducted with mainline Protestants. The project also entailed a 1996 national telephone survey of 2,591 Americans, with a large oversample of churchgoing Protestants, which asked detailed questions about faith, morality, pluralism, Christian social activism, and other issues of religion and public life. And this research involved a second wave of face-to-face two-hour personal interviews with 187 evangelical Christians (as well as some self-identified Protestant fundamentalists and liberals) in twenty-three different states around the country.[6] Figure 1 shows where we conducted our 187 interviews with

Fig. 1. Locations of Personal Interviews with Evangelicals

evangelicals. In addition, this study reports evidence from a variety of other relevant national telephone surveys, such as the 1996 General Social Survey and the 1996 Religious Right Survey commissioned by the American Jewish Committee (see appendix). This book's findings, then, are based on data of great scope, depth, and richness. With these data we can be confident that we are accessing the actual views on pluralism and politics of ordinary evangelicals across the nation.

WEIGHTY MATTERS

The issues addressed here are no trivial matters. At stake are important issues of fundamental freedoms, intense cultural conflicts, the healthy functioning of American democracy, and the basic identity of the United States as a nation.

Recently I attended a professional conference on religious pluralism and higher education held at a leading Ivy League university. During a break between talks, I met a leader of a major evangelical para-church ministry devoted to Christian evangelism and discipleship on university campuses. He described how he and his ministry have been completely excluded from his own campus ministry association. He said the ministers from the more mainline, "respectable" denominations, who together control the association, have denied his group recognition and access to resources, without any explanation or chance for appeal. They simply don't like his conservative evangelical brand of Christian ministry, he said, and wish to marginalize him. Furthermore, he reported that every week he receives two or three phone calls from other evangelical campus-ministry leaders around the country asking for his help in dealing with similar cases of religious discrimination.

Five minutes later, during the same break, I talked with another conference participant, a university professor from a different Ivy League school, who insisted that evangelicals should not be allowed to proselytize on college campuses. Evangelicals, she argued, have tremendous power in society at large ("Just look at Newt Gingrich!" she exclaimed), are promoting creationism in the curricula of most public schools, and are seeking to marginalize if not eradicate those with whom they disagree ("First it will be the homosexuals, next it will be the Jews"). Furthermore, she claimed, evangelicals leverage their broad social influence on campuses in order to pressure confused college students into converting to their religion. To create a level playing field, she declared, evangelicals must be restricted, disempowered.[7]

So, in less time than it took me to finish my Coca-Cola, I was presented with many of the key issues in a nutshell. Evangelicals often feel excluded, marginalized, or discriminated against by secular institutions and elites.[8] And many nonevangelicals view evangelical Christians with deep suspicion, as enemies of freedom and liberal democracy. Thus U.S. Representative Vic Fazio declared that activist conservative Christians are "what the American people fear the most."[9] What is going on here? What are the deeper issues at stake? Which view of evangelicals is more accurate?

Apprehensions about the social and political influence of evangelicals appear not infrequently in popular journalism. Most often, the concerns seem to derive from evangelicalism's seemingly close connection with the Religious Right. Writing in the aftermath of the 1992 elections, for example, Ruth Walker of the *Christian Science Monitor* noted that the victors turned out to include hundreds of conservative Christians who had camouflaged their true goals and interests during the campaign. "It is troubling," she wrote, "that many of the new officials ran 'stealth' campaigns, hiding their affiliations with groups like the Christian Coalition and often, when addressing general audiences, concealing their real agendas: public prayer and creationism in the schools, restrictions on abortion rights, and opposition to laws guaranteeing women's rights." Walker expressed concern that "the agenda of these conservatives moves so deeply into areas that many of us are used to thinking of as matters of individual choice, and not political issues at all. After all, many spiritually minded individuals feel that government supports them best in their practice of their religion by leaving them alone."[10]

Concerns about evangelicalism's excessive influence within the Republican party and general intolerance toward out-groups also surface in the mass media. For example, Curtis Wilkie reported in October 1995 in the *Boston Globe* that "the takeover of the Republican Party in Iowa by forces of the religious right is . . . complete." Citing candidates' complaints that "an 'intimidating' climate was created by religious conservatives, 'motivated by one or two issues,'" Wilkie reported that nearly one-half of those who planned to attend the Iowa caucuses were "born-again" or fundamentalist Christians, an "invisible army" that had seized control of the party's state central committee. Other Republican party leaders, he reported, opposed their "effort to impose their religious agenda through the party system. It's a hard-line, doctrinaire adherence to religious beliefs."[11]

Even articles that seek to commend some aspect of evangelicalism often convey similar concerns. In an article in *U.S. News and World Report* intended to defend as legitimate some of the concerns of the Christian Right, John Leo nevertheless points out in the article's second sentence that "parts of conservative Christianity are indeed tainted by intolerance, antisemitism, racial bigotry, and dreams of theocracy."[12] Likewise, simply equating "conservative evangelicals" and the "Religious Right," as many commentators do, Harvard University Chaplain Peter Gomes, in a 1996 article in *Harvard Magazine*, recognizes activist evangelicalism as an expression of a legitimate hunger for a "virtuous life and culture." However, he says, "the spiritual values of the republic and their relation to citizenship are too important to be left to the special interests of religious partisans"—especially those of a movement Gomes sees as "ham-fisted," "irritating [in] . . . moral arrogance," and defined by a "paranoia . . . from which it derives much of its energy." Indeed, Gomes notes, "to many . . . the rise of a self-consciously religious political movement with savvy and clout is the same nightmare that brought us Prohibition and sustained racial segregation, and now promises an Islamic-like revolution of the fundamentalists." Gomes's alternative solution is "religious education . . . that incorporates duty and reverence [and] . . . instruction in the art of life."[13]

Serious concern about the social and political significance of American evangelicals is also evident in more scholarly works by academic writers, published by academic presses. For example, in her University of Chicago Press book, *The Antigay Agenda: Orthodox Vision and the Christian Right*, Didi Herman describes the Christian Right as "one of the most vibrant and effective social forces in the United States." She counsels that the Christian Right represents more than a politically activist minority: "It should at all times be remembered that the Christian Right has a huge potential constituency of Christian orthodox believers"—by which she means "primarily conservative evangelical Protestant[s]." "The opposition to gay rights comes from much wider quarters than [active political operatives]." Herman concludes with the observation and warning that these Christian activists "look forward to a 'new heaven and a new earth' (Rev 21:1), where they are not simply the most prosperous, but the only people who exist. It is one thing to have faith that this utopia is inevitable; it is another to impose its imperatives in the here and now."[14] And, according to Sara Diamond's 1995 Guilford Press book, *Roads to Dominion: Right-Wing Movements and Political Power in the United States*, evangelical churches are "the organizational bastions for the Christian Right's political mobilization." "Concerned about the declining prestige of its belief system," she writes, conservative evangelical activists have united with the Republican party in order to "enforce a new era of moral righteousness and economic severity, with a vengeance."[15]

These widespread concerns and alarms about evangelicals raise big questions: Are American evangelicals ultimately tolerant and freedom-loving people who actually can get along with other Americans with whom they disagree? Or are evangelicals finally intolerant absolutists who really seek to impose their morals and values upon those with whom they differ? Are American evangelicals friends or foes of diversity and pluralism? Just exactly who are these evangelicals, what do they want from America, and how do they hope to get it? These are the questions this book seeks to answer.

FOUR FALLACIES

Before undertaking our investigation, however, we must consider four analytical fallacies that so often confuse similar discussions about evangelicalism. Only by recognizing them as fallacies and avoiding them in our analysis can we answer satisfactorily the questions about evangelicals that we address.

1. The Representative Elite Fallacy

A most common error that observers of evangelicals make is to presume that evangelical leaders speak as representatives of ordinary evangelicals. In fact, evangelical leaders do not simply give voice to the thoughts and feelings of the millions of ordinary evangelicals. Nor do ordinary evangelicals simply follow whatever their leaders say—assuming that they even listen to them much. The relationship between evangelical elites and common believers is much more complex than that.

Here, of course, is a fallacy nested within a larger fallacy—the presumption of a *single* evangelical elite who speak in accord. In fact, evangelical leaders can be found spread across the political and ideological map. Theologically conservative Christians are at odds with each other in the public square, taking positions as diverse as pro-American conservativism, traditional liberalism, peace-and-justice activism, and theonomic reconstructionism.[16] Pat Robertson may indeed fling about outrageous statements that attract media attention, such as: "We have enough votes to run the country. And when the people say, 'We've had enough,' we are going to take over."[17] But other important evangelical leaders—such as James Skillen of the Center for Public Justice; Richard Mouw, president of Fuller Theological Seminary; and George Marsden, historian at Notre Dame University—strongly advocate from Christian premises for genuine socio-cultural pluralism and Christian civility.[18] Given the diversity of evangelical political thought among, say, Jim Wallis, Stephen Mott, Charles Colson, Gary North, and James Dobson, to talk about a single view among evangelical leaders is simply nonsensical.

Of course it is legitimate, and helpful, to analyze the discourse of evangelical elites. Dennis Hollinger, for example, has written an interesting analysis of evangelical social thought based on a content analysis of *Christianity Today* magazine articles over two decades. Hollinger acknowledges that his study represents "the more intellectual and articulate side of evangelicalism and not the grassroots perspective."[19] The problems come when analyses suggest, implicitly or explicitly, that the views of spokespeople represent those of their supposed constituencies. Michael Lienesch has written an insightful book, *Redeeming America*, on the "worldview" of the Christian Right, based on the works of Jerry Falwell, Pat Robertson, Anita Byrant, James Robison, Pat Boone, Jim and Tammy Bakker, and others. He states that in the New Christian Right, "because of its cultural homogeneity, the differences between those who write the books and those who read them may be considerably smaller than in other comparable groups." But he adds, "Nevertheless, a more complete understanding of rank-and-file views requires supplementing these sources by using methods such as in-depth interviews and survey questionnaires."[20] It could be, however, that the views of the Christian Right rank and file (much less, of ordinary evangelicals) are, in fact, not so culturally homogeneous, nor adequately captured by the written products of well-known leaders. Rhys Williams and Jeffrey Blackburn, for example, have shown that the ideologies and strategies of many grassroots Operation Rescue activists are actually quite different from the official rhetoric of the movement's leader, Randall Terry.[21] If so, merely supplementing the writings of Christian Right leaders with other data might be insufficient.

Nevertheless, many commentators and analysts do frequently present the views of evangelical elites as if they were those of ordinary evangelical believers. Erling Jorstad's *Popular Religion in America: The Evangelical Voice*, for example, is based entirely on an examination of the writings of evangelical leaders and religion scholars.[22] Alfred Darnell and Darren Sherkat's "The Impact of Protestant Fundamentalism on Education"—which suggests that conservative Protestant beliefs discourage educational attainment—interprets its quantitative findings through the writings of authors like James Kennedy, Beverly and Tim LaHay, and theonomist R. J. Rushdoony.[23] And Marsha Witten's "'Where Your Treasure Is': Popular Evangelical Views of Work, Money, and Materialism" is based entirely on her analysis of the writings of eighteen evangelical authors.[24] This approach is valid for certain kinds of questions. But to think one can access religion at the popular level only by reading the books of religious elites implies a view of ordinary evangelicals not unlike *Washington Post* writer Michael Weisskopf's view of conservative Christian activists—as "largely poor, uneducated, and easy to command."[25] Field research with ordinary evangelicals, however, shows that they live in different worlds and have different experiences, concerns, thoughts, and goals than those journalists and scholars often take to be their leaders.

Why people would conflate the views of ordinary evangelicals with those of evangelical spokespeople is understandable. Published writings are methodologically much easier to access and analyze than the thoughts and feelings of millions of grassroots believers spread around the country. And, for journalists at least, the statements of religious elites, especially controversial political ones, attract more public attention (and therefore help to boost sales and subscriptions) than those of less flashy ordinary believers. But if we want to truly understand "evangelicals" and "evangelicalism," and not just the views of a handful of leaders, we must not conflate the two. We must listen to and observe what ordinary evangelicals say and do, on their own terms. When we do, we find more diversity, complexity, and ambivalence than conventional wisdom would lead us to expect.

2. The Factual Survey Fallacy

Another fallacy that helps to muddle other Americans' understanding of evangelicals is the general belief that public opinion surveys accurately and adequately represent the views of ordinary people. Much of what is often reported about evangelicals comes from survey research.[26] This information is helpful, but by itself is superficial and incomplete. To think that surveys alone can tell us what we need to know about evangelicals, pluralism, and politics is like believing that one can come to know New York City by flying over it in a Lear jet. To really understand evangelicals requires conducting in-depth, face-to-face interviews and, ideally, ethnographic research with real people.

Anyone who has ever felt frustrated by the forced multiple-choice answers offered by a telephone survey should appreciate this problem. It is one thing to report on a survey one's age, sex, and political party membership.[27] It is quite another to convey the richness and complexity of one's theological beliefs, spiritual experiences, social views, political positions, attitudes toward other social groups, or opinions about specific policy issues.

But the problem runs still deeper. For survey research does not merely tap into and report "objective realities" that exist out in the real world, but itself helps to create and organize that "reality." Survey results are to a large extent *academic constructions of reality*, the ordering and interpreting of "facts" generated from a relatively amorphous mass of lived feelings, ideas, impressions, beliefs, maxims, habits, hopes, and troubles. This is particularly, though not exclusively, true when it comes to more "subjective" matters. Surveys, in other words, are not passive detectors and conveyors of objective, preexistent information. Rather, they actively formulate consumable information through their own presuppositions, theoretical agendas, vocabularies, question wordings, question ordering, answer categories, and so on.[28] Surveys, in other words, help to *construct* culture and public discourse, not simply measure and report on them.

Moreover, the arbitrary nature of many survey categories—sometimes in combination with the researcher's lack of knowledge about the subject of study—can often skew findings. For example, perhaps the most widely used measure of the category "evangelical" in survey research is the "Gallup scale," which defines an evangelical as someone who (1) holds a literalistic interpretation of the Bible, (2) has had a "born-again" experience, *and* (3) has evangelized others with the Christian gospel.[29] In fact, there are many American evangelicals who do not believe in reading the Bible literally; who have not had a specific conversion experience, or may not be comfortable with "born-again" language; or who, perhaps due to shyness or fear, have never evangelized others. Yet these presuppositional criteria of inclusion and exclusion profoundly affect what "evangelicals" look like in the final analysis. Biblical literalism, for example, is negatively correlated with education. So by automatically demarcating evangelicals as biblical literalists—and so definitionally excluding the better-educated evangelicals who believe the Bible is God's true Word but should *not* always be read literally—researchers find that, lo and behold, evangelicals as a whole are less well educated than other Americans! By contrast, survey research that relies on respondents' religious self-identification finds that self-identified evangelicals are among the best-educated Americans and have enjoyed the greatest intergenerational educational mobility among all major American religious traditions.[30]

The point is not that all survey work is useless and should be disregarded. The point is that—particularly when it comes to issues like religion, pluralism, and politics—surveys can only provide superficial and incomplete pictures of reality, and that the content of these pictures is profoundly framed—and sometimes systematically misframed—by the surveys themselves. This means that we should not claim to understand the social and political significance of evangelicalism from survey data alone. We *must* rely more heavily on the qualitative methods of personal, in-depth interviews and, whenever possible, ethnographic field research.

3. The Ideological Consistency Fallacy

A third fallacy we need to avoid is assuming that people normally work out their beliefs, attitudes, and desires in an ideologically consistent fashion that reflects an internally coherent and nonparadoxical world-view. They generally do not. Most people, it appears, carry on in life with outlooks and belief systems containing significant complexity, paradox, multivocality, ambivalence, inconsistency, and sometimes confusion.[31] By assuming people's views are internally consistent and well ordered, observers think they can use known information about some views of evangelicals to make reliable inferences about other views about which they do not have data. But how people think about one issue may be logically inconsistent with how they think about another. It is impossible to determine which is their "real" position. We simply cannot approach people's viewpoints, therefore, as if they were algebraic equations through which we can calculate all possible views on issues when we plug in one known value.

Stephen Hart has shown that the Christian tradition is richly multi-vocal when it comes to ethical standpoints on social and economic issues. It does not provide one or two comprehensive, mutually exclusive, logical systems of moral reasoning (e.g., "conservative" versus "liberal"). Rather, it comprises a set of elemental moral "building blocks" of faith that Christians "assemble" in varying combinations to construct their social ethics. This creates conditions for tremendous complexity and unpredictability in the moral worldviews of religious believers.[32] In our own interviews with evangelicals, an underlying rationale for their apparent "inconsistencies" was sometimes discernible and sometimes not. We met evangelicals who were staunch pro-lifers but equally staunch opponents of the death penalty; opposed to gay rights but supportive of the environmental movement; absolute pacifists but open to abortion rights. We also found in our telephone survey, for example, that respondents whose voting is influenced by conservative Christian political organizations, such as the Christian Coalition, are—contrary to conventional wisdom about the Religious Right and compassion—significantly more likely to give money to organizations that help the poor and needy than respondents who do not.[33] It thus became apparent to us that the usual labels of "conservative" and "liberal" were overly simplistic categories for understanding evangelicals' approaches to public life.

But the messiness runs deeper. As we will see in coming chapters, the evangelical tradition (like most traditions) not only has many voices but also contains important cultural tensions and paradoxes regarding pluralism and politics, which evangelical believers work out with difficulty. For this reason, we found evangelicals affirming in the same interview that Christian morals should be common for all Americans and that Americans should be free to live as they wish, even to follow non-Christian lifestyles. We found evangelicals saying that same-sex marriages should be outlawed, and simultaneously, that laws should not try to regulate people's sexual lives and relationships. A facile explanation for these seemingly blatant contradictions is that these evangelicals are obtuse, erratic, or mentally unsteady. Certainly, evangelicals can simply be muddled about some of their most cherished views. But we also came to see that many of these contradictions often reflect cultural tensions within the evangelical subculture, and that these tensions can be explained. There is some method, or at least intelligibility, to the madness. Moreover, we will argue, evangelical approaches to the influence of religion in the public square tend to run in cycles, so the dominant evangelical worldview in one decade may be quite different from that of the previous decade or the decade to come. This, too, creates complexity and unpredictability that must be accounted for.

All of this runs against scholarly norms and expectations. Academics are trained to think and communicate consistently and coherently, and to analyze critically whether their assumptions are correct, their arguments follow their premises, their methods are appropriate, their data speak to their questions, and their conclusions can be drawn from their evidence. Scholars value and expect intellectual systems and arguments that are internally lucid, tight, consistent, and elegant. But, in actuality, this kind of thinking is unusual and unnatural in humans—which is why developing it takes years of critical training. Even then, highly educated scholars and professionals are often less consistent in their own thinking and behaviors than the norms of rationality and science prescribe (something usually conspicuous in one's colleagues, if not in oneself). But they expect the empirical world to reflect these norms.[34] That expectation can blind students of religion to the complexity, ambivalence, multivocality, and other messy inconsistencies that exist in the "worldviews" of real people. That myopia is something we must avoid in our efforts to better understand evangelicals, pluralism, and politics.

4. The Monolithic Religious Bloc Fallacy

The final misconception we need to avoid is treating conservative Protestants as a monolithic social group who can be identified as "evangelicals," "fundamentalists," "ultra-fundamentalists," "the Religious Right," or something else.[35] The broad wing of "conservative Protestantism," in fact, comprises a conglomeration of varied subgroups that differ on many issues and sometimes clash significantly. Among these are major groups that are properly known as pentecostals, fundamentalists, evangelicals, and charismatics. Cutting across these to a certain extent are the black churches, which constitute yet another major segment of conservative Protestantism. Each of these groups has its own history, formative concerns, characteristic tendencies, and organizational location.[36] Pentecostalism arose within the Holiness-Methodist wing of American evangelicalism in the 1910s, constructing a distinctive tradition centered in divine healing, speaking in tongues, and prophesy. Pentecostals emphasize personal religious experience and the authority of the Holy Spirit (over the written word of the Bible, for example). Fundamentalism emerged through a split with the modernist movement in American Protestantism in the 1920s. Fundamentalists emphasize biblical literalism, doctrinal purity, and separation from the world. Evangelicalism was an attempt by some moderate fundamentalists in the 1940s, 50s, and 60s to break away from the more separatist, defensive, and anti-intellectual tendencies of the fundamentalist movement in which they were raised. Evangelicals emphasize theological orthodoxy, personal evangelism, and the exertion of a "redemptive" influence on the culture around them. The charismatic movement swept across many sectors of Christianity—including the Catholic, Anglican, and many Protestant churches—in the 1960s and 70s, promoting informality and expressiveness in worship and the "spiritual gifts" of healing, speaking in tongues, and so on.

There is much that differentiates and divides these conservative Protestant traditions. To begin with, they are organized quite differently. Pentecostalism is denominationally based; fundamentalism tends to be found among independent churches and in small sectarian denominations; and evangelicalism and the charismatic movement are transdenominational. Furthermore, historically these traditions have generated much intergroup tension and conflict. From the 1940s through the 1970s, fundamentalists and evangelicals constructed their identities to a large degree in opposition to each other. They are historical rivals who have spilled much ink criticizing one other. And although pentecostals and charismatics both emphasize the gifts of the Holy Spirit, they represent very different social class backgrounds, hold disparate views on separation from the world, and have very little overlap in membership (only about 11 percent of charismatics also consider themselves pentecostals).[37] Fundamentalists and pentecostals differ sharply over the relative authority of the Bible and the Holy Spirit. All told, the histories and identities of American conservative Protestant traditions contain more potential for mutual antagonism and distance than for cooperation and solidarity.

The race factor also creates division within conservative Protestantism. Originally, pentecostalism was an interracial movement, but in time, black and white pentecostals separated into their own denominations. Fundamentalism has been primarily a white Protestant movement historically; and although sectors of the black church now feel comfortable with the fundamentalist label, few black fundamentalists identify with white fundamentalism's formative historical controversies of the 1920s. Black and white evangelical churches have their own national organizations, and even now white evangelicals struggle to know how to be reconciled with their black brothers and sisters. The charismatic movement has made limited inroads into the already energetic and expressive black churches. Ethnic identities, too, create further fracture lines within conservative Protestantism, as groups like the Dutch Reformed Calvinists, German Lutherans, Swedish Baptists, Swiss and Russian Mennonites retain significant ethnic-identity boundary markers.

Within the transdenominational evangelical tradition alone so many ecclesiological, denominational, theological, ethnic, and political differences exist that scholars sometimes have difficulty identifying what those who stand under the big evangelical tent actually hold in common. At best, they refer to an "evangelical mosaic," an "evangelical kaleidoscope," an "evangelical extended family." Some, such as evangelical scholar Donald Dayton, even suggest that "the category 'evangelical' has lost whatever usefulness it once might have had and . . . we can very well do without it."[38]

From the outside, the differences between the various types of conservative Protestantism may be invisible and seem trivial. What does it matter to anyone else whether it is "biblical" or not for modern Christians to speak in tongues? But such differences matter very much to conservative Protestants, and therefore profoundly shape the capacity of conservative Protestantism to think, speak, and act with one voice. This, in turn, has tremendous social and political consequences. For example, because of the historical divide between fundamentalists and pentecostals, active support for fundamentalist Jerry Falwell's Moral Majority was limited almost entirely to white fundamentalists, and active support for charismatic Pat Robertson's 1988 presidential campaign was limited almost entirely to the "Spirit-filled."[39] Because they gave little support to each other, neither ended up having much political impact. Conservative Protestants have also been split along evangelical-fundamentalist lines with regard to the Christian men's movement, Promise Keepers.[40]

At the very least, for our task at hand we should not assume that all conservative Protestants are essentially alike socially and politically.[41] Instead, we should bear in mind the differences between distinct conservative Protestant traditions and attend to possible variations in their approaches to pluralism, tolerance, and political activism. We should also consider the larger social and political consequences of the tensions and divisions within conservative Protestantism. Only through this more nuanced approach will we be able to answer adequately the questions posed above.

Singly, any one of these four fallacies can mislead us. In combination, their potential to distort is greatly magnified. Yet numerous journalistic and scholarly analyses of evangelicalism remain oblivious to these fallacies. Our task in this book will be to avoid them and thereby render a better-informed investigation of evangelicals, pluralism, and politics. But before we turn to questions of pluralism and politics, we need to clarify what we mean by the often-misused term "evangelical."

DEFINING "EVANGELICAL"

There is no single definition of "evangelical"—a fact that is largely due to the construction of "evangelical" as a useful religious category by researchers and journalists. Still, we can at least try to be clear about what we mean by the word. Sometimes people use "evangelical," along with "fundamentalist," "born-again Christian," and other terms to refer broadly to all conservative Protestants. At other times, people use "evangelical" to refer precisely to the subset of conservative Protestants whose "neo-evangelical" movement broke from fundamentalism during the 1940s and after. In this book, from here on, we will always refer to the former, broad group as "conservative Protestants," and to the latter, specific group as "evangelicals." It is important to remember that "conservative" in the phrase "conservative Protestant" means theologically, not necessarily politically, conservative. In this respect, it is also important to clarify that this book is not about the "Christian Right" political movement per se, but about conservative Protestants broadly and American evangelicals specifically, whatever their relation to the Christian Right may be.

Another issue requiring examination is how sociologists determine how to measure "evangelical" and "conservative Protestant" for empirical study. Social scientists typically employ three main measures: denominational affiliation, theological belief, and self-identification. Based exclusively on the location of individuals within different organizations, the first measure assumes that we should designate people who attend churches in conservative Protestant denominations as conservative Protestants. The second measure employs theological criteria (like the "Gallup scale" described earlier). According to this approach, we should consider as conservative Protestants those who believe the theological creeds that conservative Protestants are supposed to believe (for instance, the authority of the Bible and salvation through faith in Christ alone). The third measure, self-identification, maintains that we should presume people to be "evangelical" if they identify themselves as "evangelical," "fundamentalist" if they identify themselves as "fundamentalist," and so on.

Figure 2 depicts the sizes and overlaps of the major subgroups that comprise conservative Protestantism. Based on data from the 1996 Religious Identity and Influence Survey, this diagram is not merely an estimation for illustration's sake. The spaces shown within the circles accurately represent the proportions of these groups in relation to each other. We see here that Americans who attend churches in conservative Protestant denominations make up 21.3 percent of the population. Those who self-identify as "evangelicals" and "fundamentalists" comprise 11.2 and 12.8 percent of the population, respectively. Self-identified "charismatics" make up 4.8 percent of Americans, while those in pentecostal denominations comprise 1.7 percent of Americans. And all of these groups overlap with each other to some extent. Measured all ways and accounting for overlaps, conservative Protestants in total make up about 29 percent of the American population.

All three measurement methods are useful but imperfect ways to

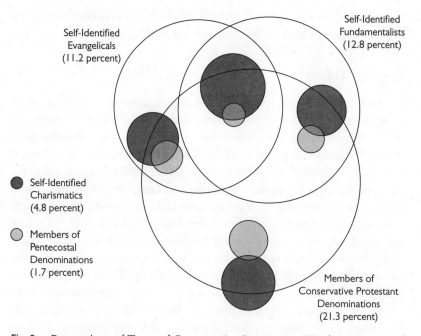

Self-Identified
Evangelicals
(11.2 percent)

Self-Identified
Fundamentalists
(12.8 percent)

● Self-Identified
Charismatics
(4.8 percent)

◉ Members of
Pentecostal
Denominations
(1.7 percent)

Members of
Conservative Protestant
Denominations
(21.3 percent)

Fig. 2.   Proportions of Types of Conservative Protestants (Total: 29 Percent of American Population)

identify these religious groups. Not all conservative Protestants, for example, attend conservative Protestant denominational churches. Many attend nondenominational churches, and others attend churches in mainline and liberal denominations. Also (as we noted with the "Gallup scale"), not all people who attend conservative Protestant denominational churches or self-identify as "evangelical" necessarily agree with all of the theological criteria that researchers establish a priori to define this group. Moreover, people who identify themselves on surveys as "evangelical" may misunderstand the label, may not attend church, or may not entirely subscribe to evangelical theology.

Each measure, then, provides one approximate and indirect means to access and label a religious group whose members we believe have some important things in common. But we must recognize that we have no direct empirical access to "conservative Protestant" or "evangelical," only proxy measures that work more or less well to mark them. Finally, we need to be alert to the fact that these different measures can often produce somewhat different results. Evangelicals measured denominationally can look different from evangelicals measured theologically or through self-identification. When possible, we should use multiple measures to corroborate our findings.

LOOKING AHEAD

In the following chapters, we undertake an intensive examination of evangelicals' approaches to pluralism and politics. I have written elsewhere showing that self-identified evangelicals are the most intensely distinctive and most publicly oriented subgroup of conservative Protestants.[42] Even more consistently than self-identified fundamentalists, they are the most religiously orthodox and committed, the most alienated from secular American institutions and movements, and the most dedicated to seeing Christian morality and values influence American culture. Evangelicals are the most likely of all major American Christian groups to believe that religion is a public matter that should speak to social and political issues.[43] They are the most likely to believe that political activism is an appropriate way to change American society to better reflect God's will. And they are the most likely to be influenced by conservative Christian political groups, such as the Christian Coalition, when it comes to voting.[44] If we are to address the concerns about conservative Protestants, pluralism, tolerance, and politics raised in the many writings cited above, then American evangelicals will be our best test case, for they appear to represent most explicitly the traits that concern so many other Americans. So, it is upon evangelicals that this book will focus its analytical attention.

Our goal will be to move beyond simple characterizations and broad generalizations about evangelicals as seen by others. Rather, we intend to examine closely the substance and texture of the views of ordinary American evangelicals by trying to "get inside" the evangelical subculture. By listening attentively to a multitude of evangelical voices speaking on a broad range of related issues, and by avoiding the four fallacies noted above, we hope to answer clearly and informatively the questions of exactly who evangelicals are, what they want for America, and how they hope to get it.

Finally, a brief word about the theoretical assumptions we bring to this kind of inquiry: This book is essentially a cultural analysis. We need to analyze evangelicalism's cultural structures to better understand evangelical discourse and practices regarding pluralism, tolerance, and politics. The social sciences have in recent years undergone a sea change in their basic assumptions about human culture and its analysis. According to theorist William Sewell, classic studies characteristically presumed that human cultures are highly integrated, logically consistent, consensual, clearly bounded, and exceptionally resistant to change.[45] Sewell points out, however, that many important contemporary studies are now turning these basic assumptions on their heads. Contemporary social scientists are much more likely to view cultures as contested, loosely integrated, internally contradictory, changeable, and weakly bounded.[46]

This theoretical change appears to be no mere academic fad. Rather, it seems to be rendering visible very real complexities, tensions, and incongruities within human cultures, which the old theoretical assumptions obscured from view. This enhances our understanding of cultures significantly. So we would be unwise to approach our analysis of evangelical culture guided primarily by older theoretical assumptions. Of course, we should be prepared to find and analyze high integration, internal consistency, unity, and resistance to change, when and where they exist in evangelical culture. But we should be equally prepared to discover and investigate the kinds of complex, contested, loosely integrated, internally inconsistent, and changeable elements that contemporary theory suggests normally characterize human cultures. Being sensitive to these kinds of complexities and tensions should significantly enhance our understanding of evangelicals, pluralism, and politics.

CHAPTER ONE

Making Sense of "Christian America"

"THERE IS NOTHING more powerful than an idea whose time has come. And the idea of reclaiming America for Christ has definitely come." Thus proclaimed Florida preacher Reverend James Kennedy, of the Coral Ridge Presbyterian Church and the "Coral Ridge Hour" television program, at a national conference on "Reclaiming America for Christ" hosted by Coral Ridge in March 1998. Standing beneath a giant American flag to address the 1,400 in attendance, Kennedy proclaimed, between choruses of "God Bless America" and "America the Beautiful," that "God's will for this nation will be done. Twenty-six other empires have risen, and all have fallen." One conference participant concurred: "We're going to self-destruct, the way I see it. [U.S.] laws have no correlation with the laws of the Creator." The only hope, according to the message of the conference, is to make America righteous again by "reclaiming" it for Christ through grassroots Christian activism.[1]

"Reclaiming America for Christ" is for many Americans a presumptuous, if not dangerous, ambition. One American Jew, for example, commented in response to Kennedy's conference: "When the language becomes exclusively Christian, Jewish groups become at best ambivalent, at worst hostile."[2] The dominant image that many nonevangelical Americans hold of American evangelicals can be characterized as contentiously exclusivist, self-congratulatory, and intolerant of diversity. And many of the spokespeople for the Christian Right certainly provide evidence to substantiate that view.

Our question is: to what extent do the views and commitments of people like James Kennedy and his conference participants actually represent those of the tens of millions of ordinary American evangelicals? Are most evangelicals really committed to defending an exclusively *Christian* America? Are American evangelicals in fact hostile to religious and cultural pluralism? How do most evangelicals think about America's past and envision its future when it comes to issues of national cultural identity and moral diversity?

A DIVERSITY OF VIEWS

Conducting more than two hundred personal interviews with evangelicals on the subject of "Christian America," and then reading and rereading the transcripts of those interviews, one is impressed by the surprisingly diverse range of perspectives on the matter. If you ask whether America ever was a Christian nation, what being a Christian nation might have meant, whether being a Christian nation was a good thing or not, and whether America today is or should be a Christian nation, you will get a variety of answers. Only on the single question of what Christians should actually *do* about a perceived loss of a Christian America are the answers relatively consistent.[3]

The first thing to know when it comes to the question of "Christian America," then, is that evangelicals are not thinking, speaking, and acting with unanimity. Enough evangelicals do think and talk sufficiently alike about "Christian America" that perhaps we can speak of a "most common" evangelical view. But this should not overshadow the fact that many other evangelicals think and talk very differently about the subject. These differences are well worth examining.

To begin, American evangelicals are not unanimous that America once was a Christian nation. About 10 percent of the evangelicals we interviewed said no, America never was a Christian nation. A Nazarene woman from California said, "I don't believe there are Christian nations, there are [only] Christian people." Some, such as one Presbyterian man from Pennsylvania, focused on the lack of faith of America's founders: "I have read Thomas Paine, *Common Sense*, and some of Ben Franklin's stuff. Those guys were some of the founders of this country and they were not Christians." Others, such as one Presbyterian man from North Carolina, contrasted biblical and American political principles: "When I think about the principles that have organized our society, no way. It's a sort of power structure, a balance of powers, an interbalancing of interests. Totally different from principles, like 'we are one Body,' which [Saint] Paul describes." A man from a Missionary church in Michigan observed, "I think we were actually based more on tolerance—allow me to do my own thing—than the parameters of scripture, than being strictly Christian. Christianity is not elective, democratic society." And a Baptist man from Pennsylvania argued: "I think it had a Judeo-Christian aura about it, but whether it was founded on Christian principles, I really don't think it was. You go back to the Constitution, the Declaration, the Articles of Confederation, they're very humanistic—nothing different from what was being produced elsewhere in the world at the same time."

Another nearly 30 percent of the evangelicals we interviewed were uncertain whether America was ever a Christian nation. In tones that revealed little nostalgic hankering for a Christian-governed past, they maintained simply that America may or may not have been Christian, depending on the definition of the word. Many interviewees focused on the percentage of true believers in the past, as did one Evangelical Free man from Minnesota: "A lot of the basic Christian beliefs were much more accepted by a broader segment of society. Was there ever a majority of Christians? I don't know. I don't think we ever were a majority Christian nation, but I think we've had a higher percentage." Others, such as a Congregational man from Massachusetts, concentrated on the genuineness of past faith: "I suspect that in the past we just had a lot more nominal Christians, and now we have [the sharper contrast of] evangelical Christians and non-Christians. That's where there is a difference." And a Baptist woman from Oregon said, "I am not sure we ever were a totally Christian nation. But I think culturally we may have had more of those boundaries." Some, like one independent charismatic man from North Carolina, doubted the Christian ethical character of America's past: "If they were Christian, there are certainly a lot of historical events, wars and lots of killings, ever since the American Revolution. I would ask, did they *call* themselves Christians, or did they actually behave in a Christian manner? Certainly a lot of the beginning documents had 'In God We Trust' and that kind of stuff, but did they *act* any more Christian than our society does today?" Still others, such as one Colorado man who attends a community church, rather matter-of-factly observed a real but limited Christian presence at the nation's founding: "I think there were some Christian men who helped start and formulate America. I don't know if I can necessarily call it a Christian nation.

But I do believe there were some Christian men who came along and helped put it together."

Between these two groups, then, nearly 40 percent of the evangelicals we interviewed either denied or somewhat doubted the idea that America was once a Christian nation—despite the fact that at least some of them answered otherwise on the Religious Identity and Influence telephone survey. Thus this significant minority of evangelicals do not possess a strong image of a Christian American past that can serve as a model for what today needs to be "reclaimed," or the supposed loss of which can be used to explain contemporary national troubles. For them, Kennedy's exhortation to "reclaim America for Christ" would not make much sense.

The message of Kennedy's conference would also not make sense to some evangelicals who *do* think that America was once a Christian nation, since they also believe that America *still is* a Christian nation. Theirs is not an image of a Christian past tragically lost through apostasy or the attack of secular humanism. They are actually quite sanguine about contemporary America's religious identity. "I still think we are a Christian nation," said a Methodist woman from Illinois, "that if we had our backs against the wall it would really come out, I really do. Most of the people are Christians; it's just that they're not very vocal about it. But like I said, if our backs were up against the wall and we had to take a stand, I think you'd see it." An independent charismatic man from Maryland focused instead on America's religious freedoms: "We are free to worship, we do have the right to go to church and to choose the church we want. So in that respect I would say, yeah, because a lot of other countries don't have that freedom." A Massachusetts woman who attends a nondenominational church said, "I don't know because I don't always read the papers, but if you look at all of the fundamentalist groups and all of the Catholic groups, yeah, I think we're pretty Christian. Our government I would guess is largely Christian, and I think the way everybody is talking these days it seems as if it's very conservative Christian actually." A nondenominational charismatic woman from Minnesota observed, "In the past, I think we were a nation with struggling Christians, that's what I believe. I think [now] we're becoming, you know, a nation of Christians, I mean, I hope that we are. I can see it happening." And an Evangelical Free man from Colorado focused on the U.S. government, noting that "Congress is opened with a prayer. Some of the things they do within the world seem like they have a Christian attitude about it, and the country seems like it is always willing to help other countries and come to their aid. It seems like there are some Christian values that are still kind of a thread going through things."

Yet other evangelicals—admittedly only a few—argued that America should definitely *not* be a Christian nation in the sense that the Christian Right often uses the term. A Baptist man from Minnesota, for example—a self-declared lifetime evangelical—argued:

> To be honest with you, I don't think I want it to be a Christian nation. I would rather have it populated by Christians who are practicing their Christianity, and then you can call it whatever you want. But again, the label of "Christian" is always frightening when you label a country, because then you are talking about cultural things. And that's a big problem, especially when one travels overseas—to recognize that the American way is not the only way practiced by Christians, like in the former Soviet Union or in the Third World. So labeling countries as Christian I think is problematic.

We asked him, problematic in what way? He replied, "If you label the U.S. as Christian, then whatever they do is Christian and biblical, and that, I think, is misleading. Many of the policies we practice are not Christian, and to say that they are is deceptive." Some Christians, we then observed, say that certain non-Christian groups are trying to turn America away from its godly heritage. Did he agree or disagree with that? "Well," he answered, "I would like to know which century you're talking about in terms of a godly heritage. There has always been sin in this country and corruption, so I've always been bothered by people who talk about the good ole days and going back. We live in the present, and need to do what we can do in the present."

Nevertheless, the majority of the evangelicals we interviewed did believe that America was once a Christian nation. And many of them conveyed that they wish it somehow still were. What is most interesting, however, is to pay close attention to what these evangelicals mean by "Christian nation." For when one hushes the rhetorical echoes of the James Kennedys and Pat Robertsons, and refrains from projecting Christian Right discourse onto the speech of ordinary evangelicals, one notices a tremendous variety of meanings attached to the phrase "Christian America," many of which have little if anything to do with organizing a Christian control of American culture and society.

WHAT "CHRISTIAN AMERICA" ACTUALLY MEANS

Six principal meanings of "Christian America" emerged from our interviews.

Religious Freedom.   The meaning that evangelicals most frequently gave to the idea that America was once a Christian nation was that it was *founded by people who sought religious liberty and worked to establish religious freedom.* Nearly 40 percent of the evangelicals we interviewed discussed this while describing what "Christian America" meant to them.[4] A nondenominational Bible church woman from Illinois, for example, explained, "It was a Christian nation. They came to worship God in their own way. It was founded on the right to worship as you wanted to, and not in a state-mandated manner." We asked one Congregational man from Massachusetts to elaborate when he said that Christian beliefs had helped found the nation, and he said, "That we're created equally and have the basic right to express our point of view, the right to choose whether to believe in God or not, a choice of whether to go to church or don't go to church." One Colorado man who attends a community church argued that the U.S. Constitution contains a lot of biblical themes. When we asked him to explain, he said, "Freedom, the concept of freedom. Freedom of religion. That is one of the reasons why America was started: a lot of these men were saying that biblically they believed differently than the British."

Two things are worth observing about this definition of "Christian America." First, most of the evangelicals who subscribed to this definition were simply pointing out that America was started by people with religious motives—that the initial impetus behind America's colonization by Europeans had to do with religious interests. This is just a descriptive way of recognizing that many of America's earliest colonists were committed Christians—a simple empirical fact. (More subtly, it also legitimizes the presence of religious concerns in American public culture, which most evangelicals think is important.) A second, more striking implication of this definition is the importance it places on religious pluralism and toleration. When evangelicals think of "Christian America" this way, they are not laying the discursive groundwork for the legitimation of Christian social domination. If anything, they are tapping a historical tradition of freedom and choice that reinforces the value of religious pluralism and liberty. Perhaps ironically, this meaning of "Christian America" functions more to bolster liberal toleration than religious dominion.[5]

A Majority of Faithful Christians. The second most frequently mentioned meaning of "Christian America" was that *the majority of Americans of earlier generations were sincere Christians who put their beliefs and morals into practice more faithfully than Americans do today.* This meaning is somewhat related to the "religious freedom" definition, and evangelicals mentioned it nearly as frequently—about 35 percent of the time. Usually these responses were based on fairly romanticized views of history. One Presbyterian woman from Maryland observed, "Just reading history, I believe that everything was done in prayer and under God's influence, rather than a personal interest." A Presbyterian man from South Carolina said, "I think the majority of people in the past were Christians and everybody kind of had the same values." "Everyone was churchgoing people," claimed an Assemblies of God woman from Texas. "At one point, we all talked about God," mentioned a woman from Michigan attending a nondenominational church.

Some, such as one Lutheran man from Oregon, focused on the centrality of church life in the past: "People looked to God and recognized God as their supreme being. More people were into God's Word and the church, you know, before television. Your whole social life centered around church activities." Others, like one Presbyterian woman from Ohio, focused on common Christian practices: "The stores weren't open on Sundays, and the people went to church. They did their chores on Saturday night, and Sunday was the Lord's day. Sunday had a true meaning." The overall sense of this definition was that Christian faith and morals were normal and pervasive. As a Baptist woman from Massachusetts explained, "We were in the early days much more religious and devout and clean-living than we are today."

Like the "religious freedom" definition, the definition of "Christian America" as a majority of faithful Christians in America's past does not necessarily support a Christian Right agenda. For some evangelicals, it does do this. Especially when it is linked to a belief that contemporary national problems (drugs, crime, school failure, etc.) are due to a loss of national religious commitment, this second meaning can serve as a premise for the argument that America needs to "reclaim" its godly heritage.[6]

But for many other evangelicals, the "majority of faithful Chris-

tians" definition does not recommend a Christian Right agenda. They
offer it simply as a matter-of-fact, empirical description of the past.
They have no intention to use it to build a case to re-Christianize
America; they are only answering an interview question with what they
consider a factual answer. Probably the majority do recall fondly a bygone era of simple faith and moral consensus—whether with historical
justification or not—and in an ideal world they would like to have that
again. But very few evangelicals are this naive. Even the more roman-
ticizing ones know full well that the past cannot be resurrected, that
the world is different now. As a nondenominational woman from
Michigan observed:

> The people who founded this country believed there was a Creator God,
> and many of the institutions—Harvard, Princeton, and so on—were started
> by Christian people. Not that everyone who has immigrated here is a Chris-
> tian. Now we've become more of a melting pot. To try and go back and to
> force Christianity upon these institutions I don't believe can occur now.

Even among the evangelicals for whom the "majority of faithful
Christians" definition of "Christian America" does logically support a
Christian Right agenda, not many are seriously prepared to act on that
idea for very long. For a more basic and compelling evangelical logic
inevitably intervenes. In the evangelical worldview, the *only* valid way
to regenerate that bygone Christian era—for more people to become
devoted Christians and practice their beliefs and morals in a way that
will revive America—is for more people to decide personally and voluntarily to follow Christ. No evangelical thinks you can externally
manufacture faithful Christian living, especially not through political
means. They maintain, rather, that Christian faithfulness only comes
through believing the gospel and "committing one's life to Christ as
personal Lord and Savior," and that this is accomplished through conversion of one individual at a time. In the evangelical worldview, the
logical consequence of this meaning of "Christian America" is that
Christians must invest in more evangelism, revivalism, and church
planting. For political activism can never produce a majority of faithful Christians; only an individual and personal "saving knowledge of
Jesus Christ" can. This helps to explain why, although Christian Right
rhetoric does hold a certain initial appeal for some evangelicals, in the
long run it cannot and does not mobilize strong, sustained evangelical
political activism.

Principles of Government.   The third most regularly mentioned meaning of "Christian America" was the belief that the basic laws and structures of the U.S. government reflect or embody important Christian principles. About 30 percent of the evangelicals we interviewed suggested this meaning. Though people often were not particularly articulate about *which* laws and structures embody *which* principles, the view was somewhat widespread and similarly articulated nonetheless. A Presbyterian woman from North Carolina, for example, noted, "America was established as a Christian nation; politically the foundation was to be a Christian nation. We were established to have the Bible as the center, as our guidebook, and to recognize it as an important part of our country's life." "Was America ever a Christian nation?" asked one Community church man from Georgia. "Yeah, I think there is a great deal found in the Constitution and the Bill of Rights." A pentecostal man from Wisconsin agreed: "The Bill of Rights and those things were all founded on the Bible. The first leaders of this country were Christian, and [so were] the things that they wrote."

At face value, this view certainly seems to champion a Christian Right perspective on America. Isn't this an unvarnished admission that what evangelicals want is essentially a Christian-based state? But though this interpretation may be accurate in the case of some, most evangelicals do not even want Christianity to be America's established religion—much less want America to be a formal Christian state. They fully believe in the American system of liberal, representative democracy. A careful reading of our interview discussions reveals that many interviewees defined "Christian nation" in terms of representative government and the balance of powers. A Bible Fellowship man from Pennsylvania, for example, claimed that "The idea of having a balanced government with the three branches—the executive, legislative, and judicial—that original theory was something that was derived from a scriptural passage." We asked one Nazarene woman from California, who had said that America was founded on Christian principles, exactly what she meant. She answered, "Biblical principles on right and wrong, our judicial system—just the whole idea of democracy and republican form of representative government. It was pretty radical back then, and a lot of it came straight out of the Bible." Some, like one Presbyterian man from Georgia, gave very general explanations: "If you look at the Constitution and a lot of the laws, you get the idea of Christian beliefs." Others, such as one California woman from a Congregational church, tried to link American government to specific theological points, such as the doctrine of sin:

> The people who began the country set it up under the principles of the Bible, which is a very good heritage and legacy to pass down. It allows us to have, for one thing, an understanding that people are evil, so we need other people to help kind of keep us on track. So there's checks and balances established on a real good foundation. Because there was an understanding that there should be no king but Jesus, they set it up so that any person would have a difficult time taking over. So [it was Christian] I think from the standpoint of the setup of government.

Most of these evangelicals, then, appear to be baptizing the American system of government with Christian legitimacy more than seeking to reconstruct American government according to specific and exclusionary Christian principles—whatever those might be. Even so, we should remember that not all conservative Protestants agree with this idea either. More than a few evangelicals would concur with the self-identified fundamentalist man from Oregon who said:

> I don't consider Christianity to be a governmental form. Not all of our forefathers were Christians. They were setting up a country that allowed people of different belief systems a place to live. No, I don't think the United States is a Christian country. It wasn't set up to be that. It was set up to be a free country where people of all beliefs could come.

Theistic Founding Fathers.   The fourth most frequently mentioned meaning of "Christian America"—the last quote notwithstanding—was that *most if not all of America's "founding fathers" were theists who prayed and sought God's will for the nation.* Slightly less than 30 percent of the evangelicals we interviewed offered this as evidence that America was once a Christian nation. As with the preceding meaning, most evangelicals who mentioned this were not very specific about details. They often mentioned it as if it were folk wisdom that they assumed was widely known and understood. At the same time, of all of the meanings of "Christian America" offered in our interviews, this one seemed the most closely connected with the information outlets of conservative Christian activists. Interviewees often mentioned that they had heard this idea taught by James Dobson, James Kennedy, Peter Marshall, or others through a Christian radio program, television program, video, or book.

"Just listening to Jay Seculo or Focus on the Family and stuff in talking about some of the original documents and their intent makes me think that it was a Christian nation," said one Presbyterian woman from Maryland. "And reading some of the quotes from past presidents, some from Washington and Jefferson seem to be Christian. Some of the other leaders were not Christian, but they believed in biblical values." One Baptist woman from California claimed, "The founders were mostly if not all Christians. I've been reading Dr. Kennedy's book about the founding fathers, and it seems to me they all sound like they are all Christian." A Presbyterian man from South Carolina agreed: "I'm getting my information from summaries I've heard on the radio program. You look at all of our founding fathers, and they admitted that if our government wasn't founded on Jesus Christ, on him being Lord and Savior, that this land wouldn't survive, it wouldn't work. All of them believed that. It's in their writings."

Who exactly are thought of as "founding fathers" is not always clear. Many, such as one woman from California who attends an independent charismatic church, mixed together the Pilgrims and key Revolutionary War leaders: "When the people got off the Mayflower, they fell on their knees on the beach and dedicated this land to God, and they lived their Christianity. And all of the great leaders of this nation—George Washington and all of those—were Christians. It's proven by their own letters and statements. Even Thomas Jefferson in his writings—he said he believes in God." Others, such as a Baptist woman from New Jersey, sometimes added Abraham Lincoln to the list of venerable founders: "A lot of our forefathers, their personal writings and even public documents, mention God and Jesus Christ. George Washington, Abraham Lincoln talked about depending on the wisdom of the Lord and so forth. I think it was intended to be a nation under God." One man even counted Christopher Columbus among the godly founding fathers. Some pointed to the founding fathers' devotional piety,[7] others to their biblical erudition,[8] and yet others to their dedication to the idea of a public role for religion.[9] But the common theme was the once-legitimate public character of Christian religion as expressed through the pantheon of America's national heroes.

Anyone familiar with evangelical beliefs cannot help but notice the "curve" by which evangelicals grade many of these founding fathers spiritually. In other contexts, there is a clear and firm standard for defining who is a Christian: an individual must repent their sins and accept Jesus Christ as their personal Lord and Savior by faith. Neither a general belief in God, nor a moral lifestyle, nor public church attendance, nor external expression of religiosity alone is good enough for evangelicals to count someone as a real Christian. Yet when it comes to America's founding fathers, many evangelicals become uncharacteristically lenient, willing to share their bed, for example, with Enlightenment deists. They are impressed that Jefferson believed in a supreme being. They are satisfied that some otherwise morally questionable founders at least apparently believed in "biblical values." They find it significant that the founding fathers as a group were concerned with religion and morality. For the company of revered forefathers, many evangelicals considerably lower the bar in determining genuine Christian faith.

At the same time, some evangelicals are more discriminating. For example, a Congregational man from Massachusetts argued:

> Some Christians rant and rave about revisionist history which says the founding fathers weren't Christians. If they weren't Christians, they weren't Christians. And a lot of the principles the country was based upon don't seem to be ones we're supposed to be really involved with anyway. It wouldn't faze me too much if I found out things weren't as Christian as we thought they were.

A Christian Reformed man from Michigan observed: "Yeah, there's a whole story about the Pilgrims leaving England. But I think a lot of our founding fathers—I think this is a misconceived idea. A lot of our founding fathers were not Christians. But that tradition has been carried on throughout generations and right up to today." And a woman from Massachusetts who attends a Congregational church said:

> No, there's a sense of belief in God. But when you look at some of these people, like George Washington, Thomas Jefferson, James Madison—I just happen to read Christian history—I mean there is some respect [for Christianity]. They wouldn't come out and say, "I don't believe." [But] you wouldn't hear Nixon say that either.

Once again, on this matter, as on most, there is a diversity of views within evangelicalism.

Christian "Principles" and "Values."   The meaning of "Christian America" that was the fifth most frequently mentioned in our interviews was an often vague reference to *the influence of Christian "principles and values" in an earlier era of American history.* The nebulous terms "principles" and "values" were used in slightly less than 20 percent of our interviews. One nondenominational man from Illinois, for example, noted that "There are certainly a lot of strong principles that the country was founded on that seem to be tied into the foundation of the country." A man who attends a nondenominational church in Minnesota observed, "I think the whole basic principle of this country was based on Christian values. They were very strong in their faith and wanted men and women to do something about it. There's a very strong background on faith for that." And a Church of God woman from Alabama simply said, "America was founded on the Christian principles."

It is difficult to pin down exactly what our evangelicals meant by "principles" and "values," since they did not often elaborate. Indeed, some seemed to studiously avoid specifying what founding Christian principles and values meant, even when we probed. One Congregational man from California, for example, argued, "It was founded on Christian principles, with a Christian mindset. I can't say it was Christian per se, but it had a Christian influence in the start, and they had Christian principles." We asked whether he could give specific examples of these Christian "principles." He only replied, "The nation was founded certainly under God, His direction, His leading. It seemed to have a moral direction from the start about what was right. The founding fathers seemed to have a real strong sense of direction—that point of view." This somewhat grandiose vagueness led us to think that, although these people really believed that these principles and values were important, they were not very sure of what they were.

Some, such as one woman attending a seeker-oriented mega-church in Georgia, spoke of principles in connection with governmental accountability to God: "America was a nation based on Christian principles. At one time, we held to a Christian standard." When we asked her what that standard was, her response was still in the abstract: "Well, just the fact that we were accountable to a higher authority. And God has said, 'This is the way I want you to live and here's how the government should be run.' I mean, all of this is in the Bible." Others, such as one Southern Baptist woman from South Carolina, linked the idea not to something specifically Christian, but to the Ten Commandments: "There were Christian principles upon which we founded our nation when they were meeting to write the Constitution and whatnot. They believed they needed to find [common moral standards]; a lot of them accepted the Ten Commandments as a basis for going on." But even in this case it is not clear how the founding fathers accepting the Ten Commandments would make America a distinctively Christian nation.

For many interviewees, the "principles and values" approach seemed to be a way to affirm the reality and importance of "Christian America" without turning to the more specific "majority of faithful Christians" or "theistic founding fathers" definitions. It allowed people to acknowledge that many early Americans and forefathers were not faithful Christians, yet still assert that in some fundamental way America was nevertheless Christian. What was Christian was not America's people or its leaders so much as its basic principles and values. A man from California who attends an independent evangelical church, for example, stated, "I wouldn't say it was ever all Christian, as I believe that is up to the individual. But it was definitely founded on Christian principles and values." And a pentecostal woman from Oregon said, "This country was founded on Christian principles, even though not everybody was a Christian." And as long as the understanding of "principles" and "values" remains at this level of abstraction, it is hard for anyone to argue with or refute this definition of "Christian America." The vagueness of the terms "principles" and "values" is actually conducive to resolving the logical dilemma of a Christian nation without a preponderance of Christian leaders and people—which would also explain why most evangelicals who used these terms had difficulty specifying what they meant by them.

Theoretically, this incongruity should be disquieting for evangelicals. One woman from Georgia attending an independent evangelical church did express ambivalence about the tension between the believed historical influence of Christian "values" and the admitted lack of personal commitment and morality in early Americans:

> I don't believe there wasn't sin going on or people weren't running around doing everything they are doing nowadays. They just pretended; it wasn't as accepted. So I think maybe Judeo-Christian values were held up more as the norm than they are now.
> *Values like what?*
> Fidelity, honesty, integrity—character qualities that nowadays we seem to overlook. [We say today,] "Well, he's had a few affairs, it's no problem; he couldn't commit to those vows, but I'm sure he will do well with these." I think we accept more [today]. I'm sure it was more hypocritical [in the past].

Here, juxtaposed, are the views that Christian moral values were normative in the past while contemporaries have abandoned these important standards, and that earlier Americans were hypocritical, merely pretending in public to live by those values. However, most evangelicals who stressed the "principles and values" meaning of "Christian America" did not express concern about this tension.

Acceptable Public Expression of Religion.   Finally, the sixth and least frequently reported meaning of "Christian America" offered by the evangelicals we interviewed was that *in America's past the public expression of religious symbols and customs was deemed normal and acceptable.*[10] This definition, like many of the others, was usually contrasted with contemporary conditions, in which these evangelicals see religion as largely excluded from the public square. This "public expression" definition of "Christian America" was mentioned in about 12 percent of our interviews. One Evangelical Free woman from Minnesota, for example, reflected, "When I think of a Christian nation, I think of one that's Bible-based, you know—the Ten Commandments on the wall of every school, you say the Pledge of Allegiance and the Lord's Prayer. You know, Laura in *Little House on the Prairie*—they read the Twenty-Third Psalm before school started, and that teacher got paid by the state." Similarly, a Baptist woman from Michigan observed:

> You used to not be able to run for political office unless you were a Christian. That was the way back when it was founded. They always started everything in prayer. They proclaimed that they were Christians. Today you can't pray or talk about God, you can't hang pictures and don't have a nativity scene, you can't have any display of religion—of Christianity, I should say. You can have displays of other religions.

Central to this definition of "Christian America" is the concept of Christian symbols explicitly displayed in or on official and public spaces, rituals, and documents. "If you look even at our money," noted one Presbyterian woman from Michigan, "'In God We Trust,' the Pledge of Allegiance, the Constitution, all those things that started way back when, were based on what I would consider Christianity and belief in God, God the Almighty." For these evangelists, the fact that key religious words are referred to in public declarations qualified the nation as Christian. One Evangelical Free man from California said, "America was probably more of a Christian nation back in the original times because of the extent that God was mentioned in things like the Constitution—things like that."

This meaning of "Christian America," like the "principles and values" meaning, functions for some as a way to establish America's original Christianness without relying on the Christian faithfulness of its early leaders or citizens. A Baptist man from New York, for example, expressed the same sort of affirmation and qualification we noted previously: "It certainly was founded by men who believed in God. Whether they actually wanted to serve Him completely or not is another question. But at the same time, certainly the founders of the Constitution included God in the preface [Preamble] and so forth." In this view, by incorporating references to God in the nation's charter, the founders, regardless of their own commitment to a Christian life, made America a Christian nation.

Summary.   What can we say about these various connotations of the phrase "Christian America"? How does this parsing of meanings help to answer the larger questions of this study? In keeping with the theme of diversity and complexity emerging in this chapter so far, we see that "Christian America" is not a single concept around which evangelicals can rally in unison. It has different meanings—or combinations of meanings—for different evangelicals, some of which are incongruous with others. For some, "Christian America" means religious freedom; for some it means a governmental structure of checks and balances; for others it means lots of faithful Christians in the population; for still others it means a small group of well-known historical leaders speaking and writing about the Creator, prayer, and morality; and for yet others it means religious references on political documents, regardless of the degree of Christian faithfulness of the authors. Two of these meanings (theistic founding fathers, public expression of religion) can lend themselves to a justification of Christian cultural hegemony; two (religious freedom, principles of government) seem to imply instead an emphasis on liberty and pluralism; and two (majority of faithful Christians, principles and values) can be interpreted variously. "Christian America" is, in sum, a concept with multiple meanings, and these various meanings have real consequences for the possibilities of evangelical political mobilization centered on this phrase.

In other words, the belief that America was once a Christian nation does not necessarily mean a commitment to making it a "Christian" nation today, whatever that might mean. Some evangelicals do make this connection explicitly. But many discuss America's Christian heritage as a simple fact of history that they are not particularly interested in or optimistic about reclaiming. Further, some evangelicals think America never was a Christian nation; some think it still is; and others think it should not be a Christian nation, whether or not it was so in the past or is so now. It is a mistake, then, to presume that all talk of a "Christian nation" is a sure rhetorical indicator of the desire or intention to reestablish Christian domination of society, culture, and politics. The reality is more complex than that.

THE ALMOST UNANIMOUS EVANGELICAL SOLUTION

Perhaps the most surprising yet most consistent theme that emerged on the topic of "Christian America" in our interviews had to do with the proper Christian response to the loss of American's Christian heritage. The almost unanimous attitude toward those who the evangelicals see as undermining this heritage was one of civility, tolerance, and voluntary persuasion. This near-consensus response can be elaborated into eight major beliefs. With regard to nonevangelicals Christians should

1. focus first on being faithful in their own lives;
2. always be loving and confident, not defensive or angry;
3. show tolerance and respect;
4. allow adversaries and antagonists to have their own opinions;
5. never force Christian beliefs on others;
6. avoid disruptive protests and hostile confrontations;
7. rely on the power of individual good examples and shared faith through personal relationships;
8. to influence others, rely on voluntary persuasion through positive dialogue and communication.

Some evangelicals clearly did not share this approach. Some thought that Christians should use the political system to marginalize secular forces in society. Others confessed to anger and hostility toward their cultural antagonists. But these were small minorities. The great majority of ordinary evangelicals we interviewed were definite in their support for these eight beliefs.

Christians should focus first on being faithful in their own lives. Primary focus on one's own integrity is linked to a number of other important evangelical beliefs. Some people, like one charismatic man from North Carolina, were very concerned with avoiding hypocrisy—"practicing what they preach"—in order to set a good example:

The message of Jesus is love. Wouldn't it be more appropriate for all of us to work more towards that ideal in our own lives before we start taking it out, you know? Shoving it down the throats doesn't do any good. We can graciously invite, but that's different.

Others, like one Congregational man from Massachusetts, made a theological distinction between the things of the church and the surrounding world, and noted the difference in moral expectations that this entails: "The church's responsibility is not to make society as Christian as possible, but to be the church, to be a witness, true to itself and obedient to God. The idea that we can just get as many Christian senators as possible and push issues that we consider Christian gives us a false sense that things are more Christian than they are." An Evangelical Free Church woman from Illinois agreed that Christian ethics are for Christians, and that others must voluntarily choose to join in the faith:

Some Christians are concerned with personal morality and traditional values and all that kind of stuff. We should be concerned about that in the church, but in a certain sense there's no spiritual value in it. I don't think the church should be out there trying to get people to live like Christians if they're not. The Bible does tell us to defend the oppressed and voiceless. And God's people should obey in things like love and compassion, and with matters of personal morality don't be a stumbling block to people. I don't think we should be bombastic, but just go ahead and live out the Christian faith, and those who will come, will come. I think I kind of take it all in stride.

Others, who held high views of individual spiritual autonomy and responsibility, were concerned that expending a lot of energy trying to Christianize America would distract believers from the important spiritual struggles in their own lives. One Minnesota woman who attends an Evangelical Covenant church said:

Someone is always going to try to control someone else. But I think that we need to be concerned with our walk with the Lord, because it isn't strong. We need to stamp it on our doorposts. We can burn TVs and bad books, but Satan can still have the power to get in there and do something else. We put a lot of energy into trying to control other people and blame external problems. We're always looking for the easy way to our salvation—saying things would be easier if kids didn't have to go to public schools, or could pray in schools, or that if we didn't have to listen to secular stuff, that we would be better Christians. I don't buy that. We're just looking for a scapegoat, saying we are the way we are because of all this stuff. But that's not right. We are the way we are because of *us*, because of me, myself—not because of you or anyone else, but because of me and my choices.

The concern of one nondenominational Michigan woman to preserve and bring light to the nation translated into attending to the spiritual needs of her family: "I would say that Christians can be 'salt' and 'light' in America. But to take the position that we want to have recited prayers in school by teachers is a wrong-headed approach. I think we need to look more at our lives and make sure that we're immersing our children in church and Sunday school."

The starting place of concern for most ordinary evangelicals is getting their own houses in order before trying to straighten out the world. Many evangelical leaders also encourage this. Consider a recent book by noted evangelical author Tony Evans, entitled *What a Way to Live! Running All of Life by the Kingdom Agenda*; its bold back-cover advertisement in *Christianity Today* announced that one gets a better world and a better nation by becoming a better person:

"If you want a better world composed of better nations inhabited by better states filled with better counties made up of better cities comprised of better neighborhoods illuminated by better churches populated by better families, then you have to start by becoming a better person."

Christians should always be loving and confident, not defensive or angry. We asked our interviewees how Christians should deal with the kinds of groups they often identified as problems, such as abortion-rights activists, homosexuals, feminists, the ACLU, the media, and new-age religionists. Their replies were almost always the same. "Christians should respond in love and understanding," said one Presbyterian woman from Maryland. "We need to share our faith very diligently, to show our care and concern," expressed a Baptist woman from Texas. An independent seeker-church woman from Georgia elaborated:

We're commanded to pray for and love our enemies, to have a relationship with them. We're not supposed to hate them. Gay-rights activists say, "Hate is not a family value," and they are right. That is a Christian principle. If you treat them respectfully and with a spirit of love, then maybe that will change them. It's hard because I don't like what they are feeding my children and the public at large. But as a Christian, I have to keep reminding myself that I can't combat hate with hate. It's not going to work.

Some, like one Congregational man from Massachusetts, stressed the importance of a nondefensive confidence when interacting with hostile forces:

The media in general looks down on Christianity. I think we should just try to articulate our position as clearly as possible without being defensive or getting too threatened. Just have a sort of confidence in our beliefs and what the truth is. Not be afraid to engage in genuine dialogue without getting hostile and defensive.

Certain evangelicals, like one Missionary church man from Michigan, relied on their own preconversion experiences to guide them in relating to non-Christians with love:

I don't feel hostile to militant Muslims and new-age and humanistic people. I am opposed to the philosophies that are behind them, but people are usually pawns of a philosophy. I know I lived the majority of my life believing in a system that was false. Until something happens to make them see it is false, it's foolish to be mad or angry or hostile. Personally, I believe very strongly in loving people and caring for people and, given the opportunities, making stands. Speak the truth in love. That is the challenge: really loving the person you speak truth to.

Love is not a passive response, according to one Presbyterian woman from North Carolina, but an active and disarming weapon: "We need to love and forgive groups that stand and speak against Christians. We have weapons of love and forgiveness, which work in the heart. It's a movement-by-movement response not to play the same games." Still, according to one nondenominational man from Illinois, who quoted two famous New Testament teachings on love and non-resistance, Christians should be willing to be mistreated in the process of loving their enemies:

We should respond with love. Love is patient, love is kind, is not angry. . . .
Does it let itself be walked over?
I think the expression "turn the other cheek" is true. You don't have to put up a big fight. I guess it depends on the issue. If you are being walked on, I think it's okay—you can accept that.

This applies, explained one Congregational man from Massachusetts, not just to nice outsiders, but to sinners as well: "We certainly shouldn't condemn them for their views. We shouldn't condemn them. You may condemn the sin, but, hey, you just love them like anybody else. And you try to share with them the good news that you understand, and to the best of your ability just try to love them."

Christians should show tolerance and respect. Sometimes this view was expressed as a liberal attitude of live-and-let-live. As one Covenant church woman from California said: "My response is tolerance of other people's views, as long as they don't interfere with our being able to express our views or live our lives." Other times tolerance was cast in more spiritual and theological language. In the words of one Congregational woman from California: "I used to feel hostile toward homosexuals. Then some godly people slowly opened my eyes to the fact that they are still human beings, they are alive, and Jesus died for them too. And many times the path to where they are is very understandable—one that, had I been in their shoes, I might have followed too." For some evangelicals, like a Christian and Missionary Alliance man from Georgia, respect and tolerance are important to retain minimal dignity as well as forward movement in conversations with outsiders:

> We do not agree with the homosexual lifestyle they have chosen. But to hate them, or to not be part of them, or to feel like they should all be thrown on an island—no. We will not allow ourselves to bring this down to a mud fight of "I don't like you and you don't like me." At that point, the battle is lost on both sides.

Certain evangelicals, such as one Nazarene man from Oregon, spoke of the need to be careful and work hard at respecting others while sharing one's Christian views: "To me, it's a real fine line between caring about people, and wanting to tell them the truth that I know without infringing on their space, being disrespectful, or whatever. The way to do that is to check your motives. If you are trying to convince someone to make yourself feel good, then that's a problem."

Christians should allow adversaries and antagonists to have and express their own opinions. Evangelicals are often seen as people who try to censor beliefs and views that they consider threatening. But in our interviews we continually heard evangelicals affirm everyone's freedom to think and speak as they believe. "Christians should have respect for other people—that all people have the right to have their opinions," said one Swedish Covenant woman from California. "Love them, and let them. Really, they have the right to their opinion," argued a Presbyterian woman from North Carolina. "It is really hard to get in a one-on-one discussion with somebody and say, 'Here is how I am, and you should be like me,'" observed one Evangelical Free man from Colorado, "I never get into those, because chances are pretty slim you are going to change somebody's mind." Some, such as a nondenominational Bible church woman from Illinois, framed the issue in terms of the justice implied by everyone playing by the same rules: "I think Christians can't demand all the rights and privileges. If we are not going to let homosexuals and gamblers and liquor vendors speak and do what they want to do, then we can't either. I feel if Christians want to keep their freedom to speak, to push our ideas, then everyone has to have the same freedoms in this country." Others, like one nondenominational woman from Ohio, again drew on their own preconversion experiences in thinking about treating non-Christians fairly:

> Christians should be loving, merciful, gracious, living their lives in a way that would honor God. What we shouldn't do is attack them. You can't shout on a street corner about going to hell. We need to love people into the kingdom. People against Christianity are entitled to their opinions too. You've just got to pray for them. I don't think you should be hostile or pushy with them. You have to understand because they have a right to what they feel—possibly things I felt before I was a Christian.

In their responses, these evangelicals exhibited the capacity to carry on with people with whom they fundamentally disagree. One Baptist man from Minnesota, for example, declared:

> In terms of their beliefs, certainly I don't agree with them. But I certainly will not deny them the right to speak their mind. I think that's part of our freedom we have in the United States. We need to be articulate in having a response, not to be condemning, but showing the Christian way. The idea of condemnation and criticism is always kind of hard to stomach. A person who is dying of AIDS—you can't point a finger and say they're a sinner. I mean the person has a human soul with human needs, and we need to be compassionate.

Christians should never force Christian beliefs on others.   The evangelicals we interviewed not only believe they should tolerate the views of others with whom they disagree; they also nearly unanimously repudiated trying to force their beliefs and values on non-Christians. This is completely in keeping with the basic evangelical belief that conversion to faith is a voluntary, individual matter. "You can't make people Christian by forcing it on them," contended one Baptist man from Oregon. "In fact, you would probably do more damage than good. Christianity is something that happens on the inside. Then, results are behavioral change on the outside." "I don't want to try to push anything over on anyone," related a Christian and Missionary Alliance man from Georgia. "I'm not here to ram my beliefs down your throat. Mainstream America views Christians as radicals, but they're wrong in that." And a New Jersey woman from a Baptist church remarked,

"You can't make people have a heart for God. You might be able to try to control their behavior, but you don't want a dictatorship that makes people go to church. It has to be an individual choice."

Many evangelicals were quite aware of how Christian domination can be abused. One Minnesota woman from an Evangelical Covenant church, for example, observed:

> I get real nervous with Christian beliefs as well as non-Christian beliefs, because we're always going to be living someone's idea of how we should live. And again, it's one sector or clique or one organization trying to control how everybody else should be and feel are the moral issues. I'm wary of that. A lot of things have happened in the name of Christianity that aren't good because of a person or organization's belief.

Most of our interviewees, like one man who attends an independent church in Ohio, were also keenly aware that many evangelical "tele-vangelists" and political activists are creating a bad reputation for Christians:

> A lot of people form their opinions from the psycho-fanatics that they see on TV. But to me it makes no difference, I'm going to be a Christian and stand up for what I believe is right. And if people like it and want to hear it, great. I'm not going to go and jam the Word down their throat, because God didn't do that to us. He gives us our own choice.

The refusal to force Christian beliefs on others applies to more than theological beliefs. As one Missouri Synod Lutheran woman from Michigan explained, it also applies to the issue of saving America from moral chaos and social breakdown by returning to its Christian heritage: "When you show someone what can happen to this country going downhill, tell them it's up to them. They have a choice. You can't force anybody."

Christians should avoid disruptive protests and hostile confrontations. Recent events surrounding abortion clinic protests seem to have made a deep impression on many ordinary evangelicals. They have never been advocates of demonstrations and civil disobedience. The abortion clinic protests, however, seem to have solidified a strong distaste for confrontational and violent strategies. Most ordinary evangelicals, like one pentecostal man from Ohio, are firm believers in using conventional channels and procedures of influence instead:

> You need to stand up for what you believe in, but there's a procedure that you go by. If you have an abortion clinic down the street, I'm not going to

be out there protesting, throwing—you know, walking up and down the street, jumping in front of cars, stopping people from coming into the parking lot. I would handle that altogether different. I may start with writing letters to my mayor, my congressman. There's ways to talk to people and get attention without being that radical.

The evangelicals we interviewed expressed more faith in the power of religious conversion than in organized demonstrations and protests. An Assemblies of God man from Wisconsin voiced this view:

> God has given me enough grace to see that they're blinded to the truth. I'm not one to go out and picket against that type of thing—abortions and things like that. I'm not one to picket. I just believe that Jesus Christ is the answer and that's what they need. I'm not one to form an organization to go against these people.

Many evangelicals were particularly repulsed by abortion clinic shootings in the name of pro-life activism and, like this pentecostal woman from Ohio, preferred to place their faith in God's work than in human confrontation:

> I definitely do not think any Christian should ever, ever, ever respond to antagonistic groups with violence, with demonstrations, even, that are not peaceful. I believe we need to do it on our knees in prayer. I would never demonstrate outside an abortion clinic; I don't think that's right to do if it's going to cause violence. They don't need to chain themselves to doors. There's abortions going on across town or the next town until God comes in and moves. I don't believe going in after individuals is the way to end it.

In contrast to the impassioned confrontations of the protests, most evangelicals, including this Colorado man attending an evangelical community church, expressed belief in patient discussion with individuals:

> I don't really have a big problem with other groups. I am not one of those types who is going to go out and picket in front of Planned Parenthood. That's not my personality. I am more inclined to see how I can make amends, or how we can work this out, instead of "my way is right, your way is wrong; believe my way." That is not the way to approach it. Screaming is not going to work. I need to spend time and communicate. That may take a year, but it's going to be more productive than trying to fight to convince anyone.

According to a Southern Baptist woman from Georgia, the responsibility to de-escalate the conflict lies with the Christian:

> Christians need to continue with their Christian beliefs. They need to speak to people who are against them if the situation arises. If it does become hos-

tile, then I think you need to back away. But I think you also need to be there to talk with them. Say, "Look, I would like to discuss this amiably." We can't be hostile or overbearing. That's where I would back away if something came to a situation like that.

And a Calvary church woman from California maintained, "It doesn't help to get angry and fight with them, because that's what they want. Somehow we have to respond with love, and not get mad." Evangelicals extend this attitude to their practice of evangelism, as the words of one pentecostal woman from Washington State illustrate:

> The Bible says to be humble. You just don't go out on a corner of the street and start yelling and screaming, "Repent your sins." Jesus never did that. People saw Jesus being himself, and they came to him. He never came to them. Try to live as Christ did. Don't go screaming Christianity all over, because it's going to turn people off. You need to live your life so people say, "Hey, there's something different about this person." And people ask, "Why are you smiling all the time?" They really do.

Christians should rely on the power of individual good examples and shared faith in personal relationships.   The core method employed by evangelicals to exert an evangelical influence in the world around them is what I call "strategic relationalism," or "personal influence strategy."[11] Their aim is not to gain control of the reins of politics, take over school boards, or hound those who differ from them in the public square. It is, rather, to build personal relationships with people, impress them with lives that are good examples, and share with them their own beliefs and concerns. This method is strategic in that it consciously attempts to influence others. It is relational in that it relies on interpersonal relationships as the primary medium of influence. Strategic relationalism mirrors evangelicalism's emphasis on a "personal relationship with God," personal conversion of the heart, and the centrality of family relationships for moral life and spiritual growth. According to one Baptist man from Oregon, this is the proper means to achieve a Christian America, if indeed that is the goal:

> The way you try to get Christianity into your country is by working with individual people. That is exactly what Christ did. If the numbers seem overwhelming—and they are—you don't really worry. That the country isn't Christian is not a worry to me.

A Christian and Missionary Alliance man from Georgia agreed that influence through relationships is key:

I am compassionate toward humanists, feminists, homosexuals, radical new-agers. I am not reactionary toward them at all. I would rather reach them and bring them over.

How would you do that?

One at a time, by relationships—if there is an opportunity to have a relationship, to have some influence that way.

Again, an Evangelical Covenant woman from Minnesota stressed living a good example as crucial in itself: "We should focus on helping other people, being there, being a friend, being able to love. It really comes to love, and not just saying the words but actions." A Church of God woman from Alabama concurred:

I don't see an open confrontation with people opposed to Christianity. I don't feel that way about it at all. I just feel like—and I have been confronted by a few—all we can do is answer their questions and show them that we are different by our manner, by our disposition, by the way we handle our answers to them. God will lead us.

We asked a Lutheran woman from Michigan what Christians should do to turn America back to its Christian heritage, which she seemed to think was a worthy endeavor. She began by talking about individuals selecting against certain consumer items, then changed to a strategic relationalist focus, and—when we probed about systemic change—concluded by emphasizing individual freedom to choose one's beliefs:

We can turn back to a Christian heritage by not supporting some of these TV programs—shutting off the TV, for one thing. Violence, murder, love stories, soap operas. Watching how we present ourselves. Saying no to drugs and alcohol. Not supporting the movie industry that is showing lots of junk. Trying to outdo one another in sharing with one another, really being a neighbor to someone.

So, these individual actions can turn America around?

I think so.

Are there any institutional or system-level changes you envision to get America back to its Christian heritage?

Allow each person to pray in their own denomination. Some try to lay guilt on others and shove religion down their throats. You can't do that.

This individualistic, relationalist, and voluntaristic mentality is not exactly the kind of approach that could sustain a mass-mobilized Christian Right movement to reclaim America for Christ by force.

To influence others, Christians should rely for influence on voluntary persuasion through positive dialogue and communication. The first seven beliefs taken together support the eighth: relying on voluntary persuasion, which seeks positive discussion and exchange, in order to influence others. A California man who attends a Congregational church, for example, noted:

> Some Christians tend to overreact. I think it's important to maintain a distinction between church and state. You can't go to extremes. There's certainly a middle ground there. And for people who are hostile, I think we should just understand their point of view. Dialogue is certainly key. Just ignoring them or blasting them won't help the dialogue.

Aware of the temptations inherent in power, and viewing Christian political mobilization as an attempt to seize power—and thus as undesirable—one Bible Fellowship man from Pennsylvania related:

> I know a man who goes out of his way to befriend leaders of other camps, and he says it makes a real difference when you show these people that you are a human being and not just an ideologue. I think some kind of loving attempt at communication gets a whole lot more mileage than sign carrying and ranting and raving in microphones. Rallies are great, but I prefer to stay positive. It is so easy for rallies to become directed at enemies. Even Hitler used mass hysteria in his quest for power.

Evangelicals appear to place great faith in patient, noncoercive persuasion, even with homosexuals—a population that they tend to view as hostile toward Christians. A Baptist man from Pennsylvania, for example, said:

> If you believe the scriptures, then a gay lifestyle is wrong. But that doesn't mean we are to be out there eradicating them. We are to try to persuade them that this is not God's design. They have always existed and will continue to. Our job is to be patient, to be concerned, and to let them know our viewpoint.

A Baptist woman from California also stressed the need to listen to cultural adversaries with love and with an open mind:

> People talk about extreme fundamentalists, but I see just as extreme the women's lib, the media, Hollywood.
> *How do you feel toward them?*
> I feel very sorry and I pray for them. I understand how people can get angry too, because they won't listen and they put you in a box. And that's exactly what I try not to do with each one of them as I meet them one by one. Just keep plugging away in love. If you fight it with anger and hostility, you're gonna get it back.

According to one Congregational man from Massachusetts, acting at the organizational level cannot compare to the value of sharing one's perspective, in the hopes that it will bear fruit in the future:

> It's the Christian's responsibility to just keep planting seeds. Anytime you can present a Christian viewpoint and why we believe it, down the road you never know. The more we can do the better. I don't know if there is anything organized we can do against people who are especially hostile toward Christians.

Similarly, a Pennsylvania woman who attends an independent church suggested, "I think we should be vocal, be ready to explain God's point of view as shown in the Bible. And then work individual by individual."

Summary.   Evangelicals are often stereotyped as imperious, intolerant, fanatical meddlers. Certainly there are some evangelicals who exemplify this stereotype. But the vast majority, when listened to on their own terms, prove to hold a civil, tolerant, and noncoercive view of the world around them. For some readers this may be unexpected, perhaps even unbelievable. We ourselves—presuming we would hear more echoes of Christian Right rhetoric in our interviews—were surprised by the pervasiveness of this outlook in evangelical talk. Yet pervasive it was.

The strategies for influence of evangelical political activists and those of ordinary evangelicals are obviously worlds apart. The former can be alarmist, pretentious, and exclusivist. The latter emphasize love, respect, mutual dialogue, taking responsibility for oneself, aversion to force and confrontation, voluntaristic ground rules of engagement, and tolerance for a diversity of views. Clearly, many of the evangelical political activists who are in the public spotlight do not accurately represent the views and intentions of their supposed constituency. (The fact that they are largely self-appointed, not elected, with little accountability to the grassroots majority may help to explain this.) Yet many outsiders make little distinction between the two, and the masses of ordinary evangelicals around the country remain misunderstood, their views thought of as no different from those of Randall Terry, James Kennedy, Pat Buchannan, and other evangelical leaders of similar persuasion.

Scholars talk of "culture wars" dividing America between traditionalists and progressives. But relatively few ordinary evangelicals, though they are clearly traditionalists, have any serious interest in culture wars—including ones fought for a Christian America. Even those evangelicals who wish for the recovery of a bygone Christian America largely lack the kind of strategic orientation required to reclaim it by force. In the end, most ordinary evangelicals believe and invest in building personal relationships, sharing their faith politely, setting good examples, and hoping the unbelieving world will see the truth and voluntarily respond with a changed heart.

FOUR REPRESENTATIVE CASES

This chapter has broken evangelical discourse into bits and pieces in order to categorize and highlight major analytical themes. It has also emphasized difference and variety in evangelical views of "Christian America." In the following pages, I put the pieces back together by presenting excerpts from our interviews with four evangelicals whose comments represent the central trend of evangelical thought and feeling on "Christian America." Even while accounting for the diversity and multiple meanings in evangelical views noted in this chapter, it is possible to distinguish a most common evangelical perspective on "Christian America." These four specific cases represent that most common view and exemplify many of the analytical points made above.

Karen Anderson is a fifty-four-year-old, middle-class, self-identified evangelical charismatic woman from a small town in Minnesota.[12] During our discussion about "Christian America" she said, "I think that most of the people when our country was formed were Christians, and they did have Christian laws that they established and followed. They came here for religious freedom," she added, "so to me they were obviously Christians." But Karen thinks that, as an influential element in the nation, Christians are "not as strong as we were at one time." Indeed, she sees elements in contemporary society that are opposed to America's Christian heritage, including "support for abortion rights and the ridicule of Christian organizations." Karen also views homosexuals, the National Organization of Women, and the media as hostile to Christianity. But in her own life, Karen finds no particular conflict: "I haven't had any problems. The people I work with and most of my neighbors know I'm a Christian, and I don't find it a problem." One time Karen did march with a placard outside an abortion clinic, but she says she has "mixed feelings" about the pro-life group Operation Rescue and all of the "name-calling" and "back-and-forth yelling thing" she associates with it. "That's why," she says, "I think one-on-one evangelism is so much better. If you can reach one and then they can reach one, you know that's far better than this group stuff where you're so militant and radical. I don't like that kind of thing."

Karen confesses to feeling embarrassed by the actions of some Christians, particularly violent pro-life activists, that she hears about on the news. We asked Karen how Christians should respond to those who are hostile to them. She replied:

> First, in love. You're never going to reach them if you're as militant as they are, you know, so I really frown on evangelicals that are kind of hostile themselves. You don't win people that way. You've got to love them first. We should just stand firm in our beliefs, of course, but try to reach them in a loving way, try to talk to them and befriend them, rather than go and just start yelling things back and forth. What does that accomplish?

Commenting on her own experience as a Christian, Karen observed:

> I always want the light of Jesus to shine out of me so that people are attracted to Christ in me. I don't believe in what you call "hard-sell" Christianity. I like to befriend people first and show them kindness and love. I don't believe in preaching at people. I invite them to Christian things, and if the conversation can be such that I can talk to them about Jesus, I do that. I never hit anyone over the head with the Bible—that turns them off quickly.

Keith Roberts is a thirty-eight-year-old evangelical from central Michigan who attends a Wesleyan church. He is married and has four children. "The Declaration of Independence was written in a Christian spirit," said Keith. "The way they governed the country in those days was Christian ethics. Nowadays in courts and government it is pretty hard to see any evidence of any Christianity. Decisions are made by economics, and which group has the most pressure on them." Keith is not sure when the decline of America's Christian ethics started, but he is pretty sure it is on the increase as technology develops. In any case, he asserted:

> America as a whole is not the country it was two hundred years ago. America was founded by Christian people and had Christian principles, and laws were derived from that. Today we've lost that connection. Each decade we lose more and more. We are becoming a pagan nation. I guess I would prefer to live in a Christian nation.

Asked whether there are any groups that are hostile to Christians today, he replied, "I am sure there are some, but I don't know personally what they are and what hostility has taken place. But there is no doubt in my mind that there are some groups that are hostile." Upon further probing, Keith offered, "Gays and lesbians—my feeling is that they are hostile." Does he feel hostile or opposed to them? "I would be opposed to what they do. Hostile, no, or opposed to them as human beings, no." So what, we asked, should Christians be doing about this decline of Christian principles in America? "Well, I guess most importantly for me is what can *I* do?" he said. "What is *my* role?" Answering his own question, he said, "I think most importantly is my family and what my kids grow up to believe, what their moral values are. Outside of the family, the church, I guess I'm not crystal clear on what we should do." Then he added, "I support organizations like Right to Life and things like that, but you can't do it all. I guess for me it is to make sure my family has a solid foundation and is really in the Word of God and has high moral standards."

Erma Williams is fifty-one, a wife, and the mother of two grown children. She belongs to an evangelical Congregational church in the Boston area. Erma quickly turned our discussion about America into a critique of the mass media, which she says is liberal and anti-Christian. The media, she says, tells people to "be your own person, you're your own god." Since the 1960s the media has become progressively more hostile toward Christians, and today is "mean-spirited and biased and hateful" toward them. We asked if she believed that some groups were trying to turn American away from its Christian heritage. "There's some truth in that. I think there's a certain segment that would like to see this country completely atheist." Erma specifically cited the media, "many political leaders," and "a myriad of special interest groups" as comprising this segment. She also identified pro-choice activists, homosexuals, the new-age movement, and environmentalists as hostile to Christianity.

Things have not always been this way, Erma observed: "America was founded by a group of people who were, for the most part, God-fearing people. Obviously, we got off on the wrong foot when we started selling slaves, but, yes, probably up until the end of the last century the country was a lot more God-fearing than it is now." At the same time, Erma thinks that Christians should own their share of the blame: "There are some Christians, or people who claim to be Christians, that behave as sinfully as some of the groups that call us evil." And how, we asked, should Christians respond to groups who are opposed to them? "Lovingly. In situations where I deal with individuals like that, I let people know what my beliefs are. But I don't let my beliefs hinder building a relationship with that person or extending myself to that person and being friends."

Nancy Erikson is a thirty-nine-year-old Christian and Missionary Alliance woman who lives near Youngstown, Ohio, with her husband

and two elementary-school-age children. Like Karen, Keith, and Erma, Nancy believes that America was Christian in the past but is no longer so: "That's what the founding fathers really had in mind. The Constitution and everything talks about, you know, 'In God We Trust,' and everything makes reference to God. It's really gotten away from that, but that's how they started it, how it was based." Nancy said many Americans think that "a lot of evangelicals are nuts," and that pro-choice activists and homosexuals "definitely seem like they're out to get Christians." She also thinks that the televangelist sex scandals of the 1980s and 90s have hurt Christians' reputations. And she denounced the anti-abortion shootings that she has seen in the news, insisting that Christians must always be peace-loving. They should "witness" to other people through the way they live their own lives:[13] "I think each individual Christian has such a witness just in their own community." Nancy thinks that homosexuality and abortion are morally wrong, but says, "I don't know if there's a lot I can do that's very big about either." Nancy recently discovered that one of her cousins is gay, which she says is difficult for her family. But, she remarks, "I'm not hostile, I just pray for them."

Nancy is also concerned about Hollywood movies, television commercials, secular music, and MTV—although she admits that when she was younger she watched MTV "for hours," and so can "see both sides now and understand how people feel." When we asked her at what point the old Christian America began to erode, Nancy replied, "I would say sometime in the 1960s, when prayer was taken out of schools. It seemed like the 'me' and 'self' stuff started back then. I think a lot of it was as soon as they took prayer out of schools." Then she quickly added:

> But I'm not an advocate for actual prayer in schools. I think there should be a silent time so that other people of faith aren't forced to pray. The Christian can pray, and if someone is not [Christian], they can just have a time of silence. Because I don't think it should be forced on anybody. I don't think the Lord wants that. I think he wants us to inform people, and it's up to them to make the choice to accept or not accept him. I have a lot of trouble being forceful with people, because I'm just not like that.

The responses of these four evangelicals represent the most frequently articulated perspective of ordinary evangelicals on the topic of "Christian America." This viewpoint can be summed up: Yes, America was once what we might call a Christian nation in some important ways. Much of that has eroded in the twentieth century. As a result,

America has lost its moral bearings, which in turn has produced significant, harmful social breakdown. There may even be some groups who are actively hostile to Christianity and who seek to secularize America. In response Christians should be loving and understanding of their adversaries, live rightly themselves in order to set a good example, pray, raise their own families well, speak up for what they believe in, and attempt to persuade others of the same. But they should never force Christian views on people who do not share them. This view is basically nonmilitant in outlook. It hardly represents an ideology capable of sustaining a forceful "reclaiming America for Christ."

ANOMALIES

As we conducted our interviews, we noted the fair number of evangelicals who expressed opinions contrary to the typical ones. There were counter-opinions for every conventional view. Some of these exceptions and anomalies are worth noting. For example, evangelicals are generally opposed to the gay and lesbian rights movements. Yet some interviewees took a different view. Some, like one Baptist man from New York, advocated a more live-and-let-live attitude: "The issue of homosexuality—I admit there needs to be a certain amount of tolerance." But others, like one pentecostal woman from Oregon, expressed a more accepting approach:

> Well, the OCA [Oregon Citizens Alliance, a conservative political group that sponsors anti-gay legislation]—maybe I don't know it well enough, but the parts that I heard I didn't like, about homosexuals trying to ruin. . . . I don't believe it is right or wrong to be homosexual. I don't think it is my place to judge a person. I have met many homosexual people before, and they are not out to convert everybody, which is a lot of what I hear coming from the OCA.

Some evangelicals who do believe homosexuality is morally wrong also believe, nonetheless, in granting homosexuals civil rights. One Presbyterian woman from Pennsylvania, for example, argued, "I think this bit about [denying homosexuals] health benefits is ludicrous. I mean, as human beings they should be allowed to have health benefits just like anybody." And a nondenominational woman from Indiana remarked, "I don't agree with homosexual marriage. I think it's really sick and twisted. But you know, if they want to, I guess it's fine. They've got to answer to God, and I'm not responsible for them. I don't think it is right, but I wouldn't try to get a law against them."[14]

American evangelicals are also notorious for their strong pro-life views on abortion. Yet there are contrary voices among evangelicals on this issue as well. One nondenominational woman from Indiana, for example, redefined child protection, using a utilitarian calculus of suffering, in order to justify some abortions:

> I think abortion should be the choice of the person. If I am a Christian, it would be wrong for me to abort the child. Where I have a problem is people who are Christians trying to make laws that affect other people. If people don't want to be Christians, I don't think you should ram it down their throat. If the child is going to be abused or hated or born into poverty and the parent doesn't want them, to abort the child would be protecting them. The world is such a miserable place, to protect them they'd be better off not being born.

Most of the pro-choice evangelical minority, however, cited the belief in individual freedom to make moral choices and the futility of forcing morality on dissenting others to support the pro-choice view. One independent church man from California, for example, argued:

> Abortion should never have been a government consideration. Abortion is a religious decision. It's a decision that a person makes which is really no one else's business. And if they decide that in the eyes of God that what they're doing is right for them, or that God will forgive them if it's wrong, then they should have the prerogative to make that decision.

Likewise, a Methodist woman from Illinois interestingly combined concern about individual responsibility before God on Judgment Day with defense of autonomy over one's body more typical of a politically liberal viewpoint:

> That's where I really get into it on abortion. I still say it's between the woman and God.
> *So politicians shouldn't be trying to . . . ?*
> No, every time I hear it I think, "You people are not gonna have to answer to God for her decision! It's none of your business; don't try to get in between there!" She's making the decision, right or wrong, but she's making it. It's her body, it's her life, and she'll have to answer for it. God'll judge how He thinks that she made that decision, and that's nobody else's decision.

Similarly, a pentecostal woman from Washington State added to her mix of reasons the widespread evangelical discomfort with abortion clinic demonstrations and protests:

> I don't approve of Christians going down to abortion clinics and standing there and acting like a bunch of idiots. To me that is what they are. People

have that right. No, I don't believe in abortions. I would never have an abortion. [But] I can't tell somebody how to run their own life. There is going to be a Judgment Day one day: those people are going to have to stand up before God just like I will have to. I can't go and tell somebody how to run their life.

We came across other instances of evangelicals voicing atypical perspectives. Most evangelicals, for example, believe that Christians possess unique answers for the problems of this world. But not all do. A Congregational man from Massachusetts, for instance, answered our question on whether Christians have solutions for the world's problems this way: "I don't necessarily think Christians are any better than some leading moral sociologists or whatever, or someone who studied long and hard. I don't think that just because we are Christian we have an instant answer." Most evangelicals are also suspicious of secular humanists. But some, including one Evangelical Free man from Minnesota, are not: "My wife's brother, they're just dyed-in-the-wool humanists. They're just really the nicest people on the face of the earth."

Again, most evangelicals fall on the conservative side of the political spectrum and support the Republican party. But not all do. A nondenominational woman from Massachusetts, for example, comes from a different political background: "When I lived in Chicago, I was part of a church group of leftists who really were very tied to religion and felt that spirituality was missing from what we call the revolution. And we would go to annual church conventions to try to get church functionaries to address social and political issues, like American investments in Africa."

Evangelicals also tend to think that liberals and secularists are the people most opposed to Christians, and most evangelicals readily endorse American capitalism. But some agree with the Missionary church man from Michigan who stated, in a discussion about anti-Christian forces in society, that the upper management of the business class contribute the most to the erosion of Judeo-Christian values:

Well, a lot of the upper-end business people are greed-motivated, selfish. They don't want a conscience. It is hard to downsize a thousand employees and families for a one-point margin of profit this year, knowing that it is not going to last. I see a lot of business in our country taking advantage of people and reducing them to statistics, causing a lot of instability with people. A lot of those are not pro-ethics, pro-Christianity. Really, it comes down to a bunch of morals, back to your Judeo-Christian values are under attack a lot. Relativism is trying on several levels, from the media to business.

These voices are nowhere close to those typical of most evangelicals. They exist as minority perspectives within evangelicalism, underscoring the fact that evangelicals do not espouse a single, unified perspective on social and political issues. Within the evangelical religious subculture, it is possible to generate and embrace alternative views.

EXPLAINING EVANGELICAL CIVILITY AND TOLERANCE

Given conventional wisdom to the contrary, why do most evangelicals practice civility and tolerance when it comes to the perceived loss of a Christian nation, and why are most evangelicals decidedly nonmilitant about reclaiming a Christian America? Has the evangelical subculture become so secularized internally that evangelicals cannot formulate a distinctive and resolute response to this perceived loss?[15] Or is there another explanation?

Part of the answer certainly is that evangelicals have simply absorbed a fair amount of liberal American tolerance. American evangelicals have made common cause with elements of the secular Enlightenment since the eighteenth century.[16] And as children of their own time and place, contemporary evangelicals embrace and readily express many central features of the dominant American political culture, including respect for individual autonomy and tolerance of difference—even as they criticize and resist these traits in other ways. Certain more self-critical evangelicals—typically on the margins of evangelicalism—have observed this tendency toward political acculturation in evangelicalism for a long time.[17]

Part of the answer, too, is that much of what appears as denunciation of non-Christian influences in America and movement to reclaim a lost era of Christian America, perhaps by force, is simply talk to construct and maintain collective identity.[18] This evangelical rhetoric is functioning not so much to actually get the troops ready to re-Christianize America as to express and reinforce a distinctive identity for its adherents. What many outsiders mistake for evangelical "report talk" (talk about real intentions, expectations, and actions) is mostly "rapport talk" (talk about establishing relational connections and meaningful identities), to use Tannen's apt terms.[19] Few evangelicals have any intention of literally reestablishing Christian dominance in politics and society. But reflecting on and proclaiming the godliness of America's founding fathers, Christian "principles and values," the decline of Christian influence in the culture, the breakdown of morality, and Christ as the nation's only hope serve to evoke and reaffirm a distinctive evangelical identity. This kind of talk is a way of reciting a particular narrative that functions to constitute and sustain a particular community, tradition, and subculture.[20]

But even these two explanations together do not give adequate reason for evangelicals' relative civility and tolerance. Yet another factor is the anti-establishment, decentralized, voluntaristic, fragmented, and individualistic culture that has permeated most sectors of the broad American evangelical church tradition for nearly two centuries.[21] The established church heritage of Roman Catholicism and Anglicanism is foreign to American evangelicalism. Most contemporary evangelicals are heirs of denominational and nondenominational traditions that grew as upstarts outside of the religio-political establishment in America. Most evangelicals are Baptists, Methodists, pentecostals, Restorationists, Holiness Christians, Free Church believers, and members of smaller Presbyterian and Lutheran denominations. A large proportion of contemporary evangelicals attend independent and nondenominational churches. We know that organizational structures and practices shape group consciousness and culture. We also know that the long American evangelical church tradition provides few cultural tools to help mobilize or legitimate any kind of centralized, unified, or cooperative action. The organizational ontology that comes most naturally to most evangelicals is a decentralized, voluntary association situated on a fragmented field of church groups and para-church organizations. A unified, widespread conservative Christian campaign to "reclaim the nation for Christ," therefore, is simply not in evangelicalism's organizational "cards" or its cultural "DNA."

But another important factor explaining evangelical civility and tolerance may still be overlooked: the moral and theological teachings inherent in the Christian tradition itself about how believers should relate to the unbelieving world. Although perhaps not deducible from aspects of the Christian Right agenda or from certain Christians' behavior, in fact the Christian scriptures and moral tradition are full of ethical instructions which naturally lend themselves to civility and tolerance. Christians do not have to imbibe secular Enlightenment liberalism in order to act civilly, openly, and charitably. Their own faith's inheritance abounds with the resources to maintain this orientation.

Consider Gospel teachings, for example.[22] Jesus taught his disciples not to judge others, not to take revenge, but to give generously and forgive indefinitely (Luke 6:30, 37; Matt 5:38–42, 18:21–22). God, Jesus said, sends the rain on the just and the unjust, and so God's children should love everyone equally, without discrimination (Matt 5:43–48). In the Gospel narratives, Jesus never forced anyone to follow him. Rather, Jesus stood at the door, waiting for anyone to knock, to ask, to seek (Matt 7:7; Rev 3:20). Jesus was comfortable associating with tax collectors, prostitutes, and sinners (Matt 9:10–13). His actions violated deep cultural norms that divided Jews from Samaritans, men from women, the clean from the unclean (John 4:7–26; Matt 15:1–12). Jesus healed, fed, and taught the multitudes who may or may not have declared by then their allegiance to his movement (Luke 9:10–17). Jesus taught peacemaking and love for enemies (Matt 5:9, 43–48). Do not resist an evil person, he commanded (Matt 5:39). Do not try to take a speck out of your neighbor's eye when you have a log in your own, he instructed (Matt 7:3–5). Jesus' ethic required his followers to treat others as they themselves wish to be treated (Luke 6:31). In general, Jesus' teachings assumed that his followers would always be a minority surrounded by a plurality of nonbelievers, whom they should not try to dominate, but should love and serve for God's sake. In the parable of the wheat and the weeds, Jesus taught his disciples not to try to weed out the unsaved from the saved, but to leave that task up to God for another day (Matt 13:24–30, 36–43). In the parable of the prodigal son, the loving father allows his foolish son to choose a wayward life, and only rejoices without recrimination when the son voluntarily repents and returns home (Luke 15:11–31). Throughout his ministry, Jesus declined the political power of the sword and of the crowd (Matt 26:51–52; John 6:14–15). In his wilderness temptations, Jesus rejected all paths to glory except that of the suffering servant (Matt 4:1–11).[23] And Jesus loved and forgave even his executioners (Luke 23:34).

Consider also the teachings of the apostle Paul. Christians should make no effort to separate themselves from nonbelievers, he wrote, even though they may be very immoral (1 Cor 5:9–10). As far as it depends on Christians, they should make every effort to live at peace with all people (Rom 12:18, 14:18). It is not the business of Christians to judge non-Christians in this world; they should rather judge only those within the church (1 Cor 5:12–13). Christians should use all opportunities to do good to all people, not just to other Christians (Gal 6:10). Salvation is entirely a gift of grace from God, so that no Christian has any right to boast in their own superiority over anyone else (Eph 2:9; Rom 3:27). Christians should not judge anything or anybody, but should leave that up to God on the day of judgment (1 Cor 4:3–5).

Christians should happily eat meals when invited into the homes of unbelievers, and not raise purity questions about whether the food prepared had been sacrificed in pagan worship to idols (1 Cor 10:25–27).
Because Christians will stand before God's judgment seat and give an
account of themselves to God, Christians ought to suspend their judg-
ments of others and concern themselves with the righteousness of their
own lives (Rom 14:10–13). Married Christians with unbelieving
spouses should feel no need to leave or divorce their spouses, but
should live together with them in peace (1 Cor 7:12–16). And Christians' lives should be distinguished by love, peace, patience, kindness,
gentleness, humility, service (Gal 5:22; Col 3:12).

Consider too the teachings of the other Christian apostles and New
Testament writers. God is the only lawgiver and judge, claimed the
apostle James, so it is not the job of Christians to judge their neighbors
(Jam 4:12). Christians should make every effort to live at peace with
all people, writes the author of the book of Hebrews (Heb 12:14). The
apostle Peter taught that Christians should win over their pagan neighbors not through force but through the example of the good lives they
live (1 Pet 2:12); that Christians ought to show proper respect to everyone (1 Pet 2:17); and that Christians should expect and endure suffering in the world without retaliation because of their faith (1 Pet
4:12–19). The apostle John taught that the chief Christian virtue is love
for others (1 John 3:11–20, 4:7–21). And the author of the book of
Revelation wrote that the calling of Christians in the face of mistreat-
ment and persecution is patient endurance and faithfulness (Rev
13:5–10). It is only the blood of the Lamb (and the martyrdom of believers), and not any earthly power or influence of Christians, that con-
quers evil (Rev 5:9–10, 12:10–11, 19:11–13).[24]

The Christian theological and moral tradition, like all rich traditions, is multivocal.[25] It can be read in a variety of directions, including
in coercive ways. But it clearly comprises a host of ethical teachings
that together can form in Christians a posture of charity, peace, for-
bearance, and respect toward non-Christians in a pluralistic environment.[26] That American evangelicals have proven in this analysis to be
more civil and tolerant than their popular image would suggest is, in
part, because they have somewhat internalized this body of teachings
and exhibit them in their daily lives. This, together with their decentralized and voluntaristic organizational heritage, and the influence of
the dominant American political culture of liberal tolerance, helps to
explain their surprising civility and tolerance.

CONCLUSION

Examining the views of ordinary evangelicals (as opposed to a handful of outspoken evangelical elites) in all of their depth and subtlety (instead of compressed and oversimplified in rudimentary answer categories on surveys) reveals a diversity and complexity that contradicts conventional wisdom about evangelicals. Most evangelicals in fact do not long with obsessive nostalgia for a Christian past that they hope to restore. They have no intention of rolling back America's cultural and religious pluralism through the reestablishment of Christianity. Few think that exerting pressure of any kind—much less political coercion—is an appropriate way to put forth a Christian influence on society. Most evangelicals believe instead in the influence of a good example, loving interpersonal relationships, persuasion, and prayer.

American evangelicals are disturbed by social and moral ills and issues, as are the majority of other Americans. When evangelicals employ their own cultural language—their subcultural tools—to express their concerns, it sometimes does sound exclusivist and imperious to outsiders. But in fact few ordinary evangelicals actually subscribe to James Kennedy's program of "reclaiming America for Christ" in the way their opponents fear.

When vocal evangelical political activists stand up and preach about the loss of or need for a "Christian America," they often do strike a chord in many ordinary evangelicals. But it is not a chord that sustains for long or sets the dominant key of the evangelical cultural repertoire. And the chord that this rhetoric does strike with ordinary evangelicals is not necessarily the same chord that the political activists intend to strike. The activists are thinking about sustained Christian political mobilization. But most evangelicals are thinking about basic morality and faithful witness in their personal lives. The activists are usually able to generate some political mobilization of the evangelicals most sympathetic to their vision—like the 1,400 participants at James Kennedy's conference. But the mobilization is usually short-lived and often lacks a clear program for political transformation. (The reported strategies for action suggested by participants at Kennedy's conference, for example, ranged "from 'Impeach the Supreme Court' to running commercials for Christ during the Super Bowl.")[27] In the end, while "Christian America" does strike a certain warm chord for some evangelicals, it simply will not serve as a deep cultural wellspring sustaining a major Christian political movement that will somehow "re-Christianize" America.

CHAPTER TWO

The Problem of Pluralism

SUPPOSE WE GRANT THAT most ordinary evangelicals are not out to re-Christianize America through political power or other coercive means; this alone does not answer the questions with which we began this book. Evangelicals could still very well be exclusivist, intolerant people who obstruct civil American pluralism. In fact, one might suppose that, having lost the battle for a Christian America, disgruntled evangelicals might be even *more* likely to foster hostility and prejudice toward others. Perhaps, unable to control the culture, evangelicals are taking an antagonistic stance instead, and make a lot of trouble in the process.

To assess these possibilities, the present chapter explores the issue of evangelicals' approaches to social and cultural pluralism in a broad manner. Beyond the question of whether evangelicals want a Christian America and what they might do to get it lies the more general issue of how they relate to other Americans. How do evangelicals assess cultural and religious differences in America? Can they live with and in a society that lacks consensus on some important normative matters? Do evangelicals really want cultural uniformity grounded in their own worldview?

A DIVERSITY OF VIEWS

We asked all of the evangelicals we interviewed, "How do you feel about the fact that America is a pluralistic nation—that there are many

different kinds of people and religions and lifestyles in this country?"
And we probed further with questions like: "How do you think Christians should relate to others in society who don't accept Christian beliefs and morals?" and "What do you say to people who say that
America is a pluralistic nation and that Christians shouldn't impose
their beliefs and morality on everyone else?"[1] Similar to what we found
on the topic of "Christian America," our interviews revealed a great diversity of views about pluralism.

Opposition.   Some evangelicals said flatly that they did not like pluralism, they wished America was more homogenous, and they thought
America's growing cultural and ethnic diversity was hurting the nation.
They tended to be female (about 80 percent), were often older people,
and as a group resided disproportionately in California—a state where
immigration issues are very visible politically—and the Midwest.

Most often, what concerned these people was not broad religious
and moral pluralism, but the more narrowly perceived problem of immigration, social integration, and national identity. Many spoke of the
need for all immigrants to learn English. For example, a seventy-
one-year-old independent charismatic woman from California said,
"Before illegals were allowed in by the millions, I liked it. The different nationalities came in and became Americans; you didn't have
English-Americans and French-Americans and Italian-Americans and
Mexican-Americans. Everybody melted into Americans and it become
the greatest nation on earth." And a seventy-five-year-old Baptist
woman from Missouri remarked, "It's detrimental to our country, very
much so. I think people should try to maintain their heritage, to an extent, but not try to take over this country with their religion. An influx
of people has come here because they think we have the better life here,
but then once they're here, and there's groups of them, we're not going
to keep going."

A somewhat smaller group cast their answers in terms of religious
and moral diversity, whether or not it resulted from immigration. One
Baptist woman from Minnesota, commented, "Well it bothers me that
we can't come together on one word or one lifestyle that we're supposed to live—one religion. So it does bother me that we have all these
different lifestyles, different religions." A Baptist woman from California said:

> Now that's where I'm very narrow. I don't think a lot of these religions
> should even be in this country. Because I'm eighty years old, so I'm think-

ing back in the good old days, I guess, but it just irks me so much to see all these cults and shady religions. I don't think the people should be here in the first place. There should have been laws against their coming in and just nipped it in the bud.

A few, such as one woman from Minnesota attending an Evangelical Free church, connected their concerns to the "Christian America" issue:

> You have to go back to how this country was founded, not to be a Muslim country—and there are Muslim countries. We are founded on the Bible, and as a Christian nation we are to honor God and the Lord Jesus Christ. Just rolling back the things that they've done to take God out of the country. Our country did very well back then, with God in everything. I just don't like what they've done to take God out of things. I think it just worsens society.

Occasionally, people expressed a sense of desperation about the loss of moral standards. An independent charismatic woman from Oregon said, "I feel like we're trying to hold the line. I do get that sense—that there is sort of an erosion, erosion, erosion down, almost like an avalanche. It's sort of situational stuff where, you know, 'it's okay, it's not hurting anybody, doing this isn't gonna hurt you if you don't hurt me,' or whatever."

Ambivalence.   In addition to those evangelicals who clearly disapproved of pluralism was a cluster of about the same number whose response to the topic was real ambivalence. A man in Georgia who attends an independent church reflected: "I don't know. I've never thought of myself as a prejudiced person, and I know that our country was founded on the basis of people being able to come here from all over and have that freedom, but I don't know what I feel. I'm not sure maintaining diversity is a good idea. I guess I have a tendency to think, when you come here you become an American." And an Evangelical Free man from Minnesota commented:

> Well, I feel good about pluralism. But I do have a concern with people from Eastern countries, that their value system is very different; it doesn't seem to fit in with what our country is founded on—European Judeo-Christian beliefs. I kind of believe that if somebody comes to this country, they ought to learn the English language. They may want to persevere and practice their own cultural things, but I don't believe we ought to teach school in Spanish. I guess I believe our society is pluralistic. You hear a lot about immigration and different cultures. It's just the way it is, and we have to be

tolerant. But on the other hand, I'd like to see us keep our Judeo-Christian belief system, so I hope that we don't blend too much.

Realist Acceptance.   A larger group of evangelicals than those who held either oppositional or ambivalent views took a realist position, accepting pluralism in America as a fact of life. For them, pluralism simply *is*, and there is not much value in fussing about it. A Congregational man in Massachusetts, for instance, answered, "It's gonna be what it's gonna be. I mean, there's no right or wrong about it." A pentecostal woman from Ohio said, "I just believe it's a fact. I don't have any feelings on it. It's a fact of life—the way we were before and probably will be till the Lord comes back." One Presbyterian woman from North Carolina observed, "I don't think it could be any other way. That's what happens when people are searching. It makes for a diverse culture, but people are also open to a lot of gunk." A California man attending a Nazarene church remarked, "I think it's a reality. I mean, obviously we're living in a global society, a global economy, and it's gonna be that way until Christ comes back, as far as I can see." And one Assemblies of God woman from Minnesota stated, "Well I wouldn't mind changing some of those groups that are out there, but I know the fact is that it's probably always gonna be there. And maybe their actions bother me, but you know, basically it's around, you grow up with it, so it's not like it's anything new to get used to."[2]

TOLERANCE AND ENTHUSIASM

But the voices of opposition, ambivalence, and realist acceptance were in the minority. For every one evangelical opposed to pluralism, there were about *five* other evangelicals who voiced a strong commitment to freedom of choice and toleration of diversity. A Wesleyan woman from Michigan, for example, said, "To each his own, I guess. I don't know that pluralism bothers me." In fact, twice as many evangelicals as those who opposed pluralism voiced not only tolerance but unqualified enthusiasm for pluralism in America. These open-minded and approving voices were in fact the dominant viewpoint on the matter.

Some, such as one Baptist woman from Michigan, cast their views in the language of rights and voluntary choice: "I think that is fine. Christians should relate to others who don't accept Christian beliefs and values, I guess I would say tolerantly. I don't see anything wrong with people doing their own thing, as long as it doesn't infringe on me doing mine." A Congregational man from Massachusetts stated, "I come back to that 'terrible' word, 'tolerance.' Christians would jump on me, but there is a sense of fairness, you know, realizing that we don't live in a Christian nation. That we can't enforce." And a Illinois woman attending a Methodist church observed, "Well, it goes back again to: this is what our country is all about—freedom. That's why a lot of people like to come here. People can come practice their religion, do whatever you want, but don't try to shove it down anybody else's throats."

Others, such as one Lutheran woman from California, spoke more in terms of the value of reciprocal respect and the marketplace of ideas:

> I believe that my religion is the right religion, but they believe their religion is right. As long as it doesn't hurt anybody else, and they're willing to let everybody else believe in their own rights. I mean, you have the freedom to talk about yours, and if you want, to try and convert them, or they may want to try and convert you. I think everybody has their own right to believe in their own thing, as long as I have the right to believe the way I want to.

Similarly, a Baptist woman from North Carolina claimed:

> I would respect them for their beliefs, just because I want them to respect mine. And I feel like they need to worship, if that's what gets them into their way of feeling good about what they are doing. I'm not going to insist that they come over to my way as long as they have their religion. It's not right. We are made up of different personalities, different ways, different beliefs. But if we can know in society how to blend, not saying everybody has got to believe like I do. We can't live like that. Respect each other. Live and let live.

A man from Illinois who attends a nondenominational Bible church spoke in more abstract terms about the impartial character of a just social order: "If you're talking about legislating Christianity, I guess I would agree that Christians should not try to impose their views. If I were a legislator, I should not be imposing Christianity on everyone else. I would try to support an environment where people could choose without being persecuted anymore than anyone else having other beliefs." A Missionary church man from Michigan emphasized the negative impact on the church of trying to Christianize society:

> Well I think that is the way it should be. I don't hold to a philosophy of life that we are ever going to become a Christian world. I think the best we can do is to have a pluralistic society. I don't think it will ever suit us to force Christianity upon the world. In fact history shows us that this was the

singular worst move that the church ever made. [The Roman Emperor] Constantine declared Christianity the empire's religion, and it became the most pagan organization that ever existed. And so whenever we try to legislate conversion or spirituality, we lose a lot. So I think pluralistic society ends up functioning more realistically.

Other evangelicals, by contrast, framed their accounts of tolerance and voluntary choice in more biblical language. A Baptist woman from Illinois, for example, spoke of Jesus' teaching not to judge others:

> If we try to force our views on others, then we're becoming the judges. Judge not lest you be judged yourself. I would not judge another person's choice because the sin or lack of sin is on them, not on me. I mean, if they asked my opinion I would say no [it's wrong], but I wouldn't tell them if they didn't ask me.

An Evangelical Free man from Colorado focused on Jesus' teachings on love: "I think you still have to be nice to those people. Part of the whole Christian thread is love your neighbor. That is the hardest thing for a Christian to do, to have unconditional love for your fellow human being, but you have to accept other beliefs."[3] A Baptist man from Oregon derived his reasoning from Saint Paul's teaching to be at peace with all people:

> Live and let live. In terms of religious systems and beliefs, the Christian's responsibility is to be at peace with all men. So, if I am able to talk with some individual and they don't believe the way that I do, I also don't believe the way others believe. I still believe I can be at peace with that person. I don't have to be enemies with them because they don't believe just like I believe. That would not be in line with Christian principles.

Yet others, such as a Colorado man who attends a community church, linked their explanations to the example of Christ:

> Big on acceptance, you know. Yeah, we disagree with what their beliefs are. Doesn't mean we don't accept them. You look at Christ's lifestyle, one that people would spit on and curse, and he still loved those people. Jesus realized they weren't going to accept him, so he moved on. He said he wanted to love and serve them, and they said no. So he moved on. I think for us, really, an attitude of service and acceptance is really big for me.

Similarly, a Baptist woman from Texas argued: "I think we should be very accepting and we should love them. Jesus didn't cast out the sinner; he loved them wherever they were."

Evangelicals of this majority perspective certainly do not abandon their commitment to exert a religious and moral influence on non-

Christians around them. But in this general context of tolerance and choice, the use of control or force is renounced. Instead, most evangelicals believe in the strategy we have already seen in the previous chapter: strategic relationalism—that is, influence through setting a good example and through persuasion in the context of interpersonal relationships. A Nazarene man from California, for example, began his response by expressing a realist acceptance of pluralism: "I just think that's the way it is. I mean, our government is set up with freedom of speech and religion, and how would you ever do it otherwise? It goes against the basic tenants of how our nation was set up." Then he clarified the ways a Christian may and may not still work to change others in this situation: "We believe in the freedom of all peoples to come here and worship, however they worship. I just don't see how they're going to change, other than person-to-person influence, caring about them, having them see another way. I don't think they get convinced by forcing one religion on them, or 'this is our religion and you're here now so you've gotta do it our way.' I don't think it comes that way." He gave an example: "I think, say, someone moves in on your block and they're Buddhists, but you take them a housewarming gift, you pay attention to them, you learn their names, you say 'hi' when you walk back, nice gestures, get to know them. I mean, it comes out of relationships. And if the relationship's there, over time you earn the right to sneak into their life because of the acts of kindness, and now they're asking questions—I think that's how it happens."

A Congregational man from California also expressed the importance of setting a good example:

> We are a melting pot physically and culturally. I think it's difficult to see a point of view beyond our own. It's good to have diversity in the Body [of Christ], as well as in society as a whole. I think we tend to look at our point of view as *the* point of view, when in reality it's only one of many. But it's important for us to keep our point of view for ourselves, for obvious reasons. I do support the idea of a society that is pluralistic and has many facets. It's healthy certainly to a point. We are a nation of tolerance with religion, politically and culturally. I support anybody who wants to follow whatever they want. I'll keep trying to walk out my faith in real life. But if you want to practice anything or nothing at all, that's certainly your prerogative. It's important to have our voice be heard. Living out an example, a proper lifestyle that would encourage others to follow that direction would certainly be a good idea.

And in explaining the significance of setting a good example, many interviewees were concerned to mention the need for relational respect and diplomacy, if for no other reason than pragmatic tactical effectiveness. For example, a Christian and Missionary Alliance woman from Ohio said:

> I think Christians should definitely be friends and work and talk with these people, and just show them, you know, the Christian life, instead of what they're doing. But you have to do it in such a way that you don't put down what they believe in. My husband is good at this, showing the differences between the two. You can't just go say, "No, you shouldn't believe this and this is wrong." Because people, even somebody like me, will go, "Wait a minute, whoa." I just think the way you do things and how you react to things can change a person, I really do.

All of these evangelicals expressed one way or another the need for Christians to accept the plurality of America's different peoples, lifestyles, and religions. But another group of evangelicals went even further, positively declaring their enthusiasm for American pluralism. One Illinois woman who attends an Evangelical Free church, for example, remarked, "It's fine with me, I kind of like it that way." These people were not merely willing to abide America's great diversity; they were emphatically approving of it. "Different religions, lifestyles, ethnic groups I think are good," said one Evangelical Free from Illinois, "and Christians should treat everyone just the same. Why should they be treated any different?"

Some evangelicals, such as one nondenominational woman from Oregon, value pluralism because of its respect for individual freedom of choice: "I feel great about it! You know, it's wonderful to live in a country where we have this freedom. It should be that way. It's up to each person to decide what to believe. I don't think there should be any kind of regimented culture or structure to make people believe a certain way. It's great." Even knowing that many people will choose what in her view is wrong, she still affirmed the freedom of choice that pluralism affords: "It is unfortunate in a lot of people's cases, but then again, it is their decision. That is the way Christ was. He didn't say, 'Okay, you are going to be a Christian.' He let us make that choice."

Other evangelicals viewed pluralism as good because of the positive impact they think it has on the nation. One Baptist man from New York observed, "I have no problem with pluralism. It's always been, as far as I can see. We started out with the English, and [increasing diversification] ran down the line, and I think it's been good for the nation." A Covenant church woman from California said, "Pluralism is a good sign that society is not in a state of war. Christians should respect people with other views—not just turn them off, like, 'I don't want to talk to you,' but have a dialogue." And a Presbyterian woman from North Carolina stated, "Well that is what brought us into being, people coming from all over. I think in a lot of respects it makes us very unique, because we draw from a lot of the good things in a lot of societies."

Many evangelicals emphasized how personally enriching and stimulating American pluralism is. One Baptist man from Minnesota, for example, declared, "I love it! Yes, I think it makes it very exciting. I'm the type of person who likes to go to new places, discover things, to get outside my comfort zone, and that's what I like to encourage people to do—get out of their comfort zone." A Christian Reformed man from Michigan said, "Oh, I think it is great. Being exposed to other people and other ideas and philosophies, it just broadens your horizons. You can't close people out that way." Similarly, a Congregational man from Massachusetts remarked:

> I like it. I think that's one thing I enjoy very much. It's a little bit of heaven here on earth still. I don't think we integrate enough. When you go to Germany you meet mostly Germans. So it's sort of fun to live in America. I like different cultures.

And a Church of God woman from Alabama observed:

> How do I feel? You know, at one time America took everybody, but recently they have curtailed that. I don't have any trouble with other nationalities living around me. As a matter of fact, I think they are interesting. I am always attracted to other nationalities.

Some, including one Georgia woman who attends a Presbyterian church, stressed the importance of not only enjoying but also learning from different people and cultures:

> I think it is good. We struggle with diversity because we are afraid of or adverse to things we don't understand. But to me a person who is a refugee living here is maybe as different to me as I might be to a person who is not a Christian. We are coming from different backgrounds, but I think we can all learn from each other. Everyone has something valuable to share. If we could only get over our prejudices, it would be great if we could learn from each other. Christians can be such a subculture that we don't understand sometimes what is going on in the world. I think if you are confident in your faith, then you can have free discussions with people and maybe gain some insight into society that you would never get with just Christians. So there is a lot we can learn from them.

One Baptist woman from California even went so far as to suggest that making pluralism work was a task that Jesus Christ himself was interested in: "I think it makes this country more complex, complicated, and wonderful, because you have all the different cultures. It's very difficult to blend so many different beliefs together, living in one place, but that's a challenge that the Lord is up for."

One struggles to imagine how a religious tradition dominated by this attitude with respect to social and cultural pluralism could serve as the constituency for a movement for Christian social control and cultural domination. The common sentiment here is simply contrary to that outlook and those goals.

LITTLE PERSONALLY EXPERIENCED HOSTILITY

One wrinkle worth observing at this stage of our discussion is that almost all of the evangelicals we interviewed said they do not personally experience the hostility and discrimination against Christians that they nevertheless identified as a big problem in America today. Most of the evangelicals we interviewed maintained that American Christians face widespread opposition and prejudice from the secular world. And in our telephone survey, 92 percent of self-identified evangelicals agreed that "Christian values are under serious attack in the United States today." But time and again, when we asked evangelicals whether they *personally* suffered any of this intolerance, they said no. Non-Christian friends, neighbors, and colleagues, they reported, generally treat them with respect and goodwill, and even if they disagreed about religious views, they managed to carry on considerate and friendly relationships with them.

Examples are numerous. One Baptist man from South Carolina reported, "I don't see Christians being persecuted or ridiculed, I really don't. I'm sure there are individual circumstances, but for the most part I don't." Likewise, a self-described "born-again" man from Ohio said about people hostile to Christians, "I don't have any exposure. There probably are some, but I haven't had any exposure to that kind of element." One Presbyterian man from Pennsylvania commented: "It is generally acceptable to be a Christian. Very rarely from my experience or knowledge does anyone reject you based on it." A Lutheran woman from California observed, "We haven't ever been in an area or situation where there's been a problem or a confrontation, so I have no experience in that. So you kind of look on the rosy side of life." And a

Baptist woman from Massachusetts noted, "I don't think that people object to Christianity. People say, if you want to believe it go ahead, and leave me alone."

Evangelicals know what kind of behaviors *might* elicit animosity from unbelievers, as this evangelical Moravian woman in North Carolina implied: "I haven't personally felt a backlash, but then again, I'm not standing on the street with a megaphone, so. . . ." Yet even in cases where one might expect antagonism, evangelicals still reported friendly relations. One pentecostal woman from North Carolina, for example, who was quite forthright about her belief in Satan, demon possession, exorcism, hell, prayer healing, and miraculous recoveries from the dead, had only this to say on the matter: "Well, everyone's always been okay with me."

Some evangelicals explicitly recognize that their personal experiences differ from what they hear or read about, most often in the Christian media. A Baptist woman from South Carolina, for instance, answered, "According to what I read, yes, but I have not seen persecution in America. Maybe I'm not as sensitive as some people—some say I'm laughed at, others not. I think there are people who disagree with me, but they haven't made me feel like I'm wrong." And a woman from California who attends a Wesleyan church likewise reported, "I hear these negative things from the media, but when it comes to face-to-face with people myself, I think we're not rejected or anything like that."

Indeed, some evangelicals offered examples from their own experiences of amicable disagreements with colleagues and friends. "Take my office manager," said one woman from Oregon who attends a charismatic church. "We get along so great together. We are really close friends—until it comes to religious views. She hates Christianity. She likes *me* just fine, but she hates Christianity per se." And a Presbyterian woman from Maryland recalled, "When I was working, people would ask for my opinion, but were not hostile. One of my friends asked my opinion about living with her boyfriend, and she knew I didn't agree, but she didn't take offense."

Occasionally, our interviewees even self-critically conceded that evangelical perceptions of hostility may involve some degree of paranoia about a largely nonexistent conspiracy against Christians. A Baptist man from Pennsylvania, for example, noted:

> I think there is a tendency among ourselves to think we are the objects of some design. I have not seen enough convincing evidence to really persuade

me that this is true. There are elements of it. I think there have always been
elements of it and will continue to be. I personally don't feel under any real
persecution.

Practical consequences must certainly flow from the fact that most
evangelicals' friends, neighbors, and colleagues seemed to treat them
generally with respect and goodwill, and that evangelicals manage to
carry on friendly relationships with them even when they disagree
about religious matters. Religious ideologies certainly have power to
shape people's consciousness and experiences. But people's everyday
experiences also help to interpret, redefine, and possibly moderate the
influence of ideologies. Ordinary evangelicals apparently get along
with the non-Christians they live with, without hostility or struggle.
And this must help to neutralize the possible belief that outsiders are
malevolent threats who need to be combated. Evangelical activist leaders who might wish to mobilize the mass of evangelicals by inciting fear
or antagonism regarding outsiders will inevitably come up against the
fact that this approach contradicts ordinary evangelicals' everyday experience. Their message simply will not resonate with most of the millions of ordinary evangelicals.[4]

VIEWS ON OTHER RELIGIONS

It may be one thing for evangelicals to speak positively about American pluralism and get along with their neighbors and colleagues, but
quite another when the discussion focuses on a matter closer to home:
the acceptability of competing religious faiths. How did the evangelicals we interviewed evaluate other religions in America? We asked
them specifically about their views on other religions, and whether
those religions presented any difficulties for their own faith.

It would be hard to conceive of evangelicals giving unequivocal endorsements of other religious faiths. "Evangelical" itself (from the
Greek word *evangelion*) means the kind of "very good news" one
wants to tell those who have not yet heard it. Corollary to this idea is
the reality that some people may not want to hear or to believe the
good news, and this creates a division between Christians and non-
Christians. Many critics of evangelicalism decry the evangelical worldview as arrogant, exclusivist, and promoting contempt and bigotry toward other religions. Did our interviews with ordinary evangelicals
verify this appraisal?

In keeping with what we have seen so far regarding the topics of

"Christian America" and cultural pluralism, ordinary evangelicals exhibit a broad diversity of viewpoints when it comes to the issue of evaluating other religions. Some evangelicals are hard-line exclusivists, and others are virtual universalists. Most fall somewhere in the middle, working to retain both their belief that Christianity is the true religion and their belief in mutual respect and religious freedom of choice.

That some evangelicals condemn other religions is clear. One independent charismatic man from North Carolina, for example, stated flatly that "Jesus is the only one that ever came back from the dead, who overcame the grave, and the only one who can give us hope. All the others are serving a dead god." A Church of God woman from Alabama echoed the same theme:

> The scripture says that if any man tries to come except through the saving blood of Jesus Christ, he is a thief and a robber. There is no other way he can get to heaven except through Jesus Christ. It is that simple. Muhammad is dead, Buddha is dead, Confucius is dead. They are dead. Jesus Christ rose again.

Some, such as one charismatic woman from Indiana, tempered their judgment a bit with an attempted sympathetic understanding of how people could be wrong in their faith:

> I think they're wrong. Jesus said, "I'm the way, the truth and the life, no one comes to the Father but by me." So, yes, I think they're wrong, they're deluded. They can have all the right intentions. I'm not saying they're bad, just wrong. I mean, I was wrong for years, too. I was following something that was getting me absolutely nowhere. I was truly sincere in what I was doing and was a pretty good person in the eyes of most. But it's the difference between night and day, darkness and light, between those beliefs and where I am now. So, yeah, they're wrong. I'm sorry that they're wrong, and our job is to do something about the fact that they're wrong.

A very few evangelicals, like one pentecostal woman from Pennsylvania, even advocated the active deterrence of other faiths in America: "Christianity should be our religion because this is what America was founded on. I can tolerate other religions, but I don't think they should come in here to our country and just overflow America. Muslims should be discouraged. We should Christianize them—they are in America." But these voices were very few and far between.

More typically, the evangelicals we interviewed were interested in softening such judgmental exclusivism. One Presbyterian woman from Georgia, for instance, said, "Well I think other religions are on a journey but they have ended up at the wrong place." A Congregational

man from California partially reserved his judgment and said he found
other religions interesting, even though he thinks they are essentially
misguided: "I think from our point of view they're wrong. I can't condemn those who believe in them. I condemn what they believe, but I
don't condemn them personally. I find them at times interesting, but
certainly would not grasp them as reality." Likewise, a Christian and
Missionary Alliance man from Georgia expressed an interest in understanding other religions better, and an incipient self-reflexive awareness
that Christianity also probably looks strange to outsiders:

> I think it's real sad that people have embraced things that aren't true. I
> would love to understand better how other beliefs got started and spread.
> It's intriguing, especially when you read about some of their strange doc-
> trines. Why does a thinking person believe this? But then you know, I read
> the book of Revelation, and [if] you take the view of an outsider, there is
> some pretty bizarre stuff [there]. So I guess people could say the same thing
> about Christianity.

Some, like this North Carolina man who attends a Baptist church, emphasized the commonalities between religions:

> Many of those faiths have many elements of the Christian faith. Many of
> the things they hold, we hold too. There are a few fundamental things they
> have steered differently. And but for those few things they would be at the
> same church I am at. So that doesn't challenge my faith except to help them
> see where they made the wrong detour.

Others, such as one Assembly of God woman from Texas, stressed mutual respect between religions: "Muslims do believe in a different God,
but I see them as respecting Christian beliefs. I respect other religions,
even though I disagree with them. I don't feel hostile toward them, and
I guess I don't see that they are hostile or antagonistic toward Christians."[5] A Presbyterian woman from Pennsylvania advocated Christians learning acceptance from other religions: "In some ways, we can
learn from them and it's good. We can learn to appreciate other people
for who they are. And it also gives Christians an opportunity to share
the gospel." One woman from North Carolina who attends an independent charismatic seeker-church suggested that in the end all people,
even if they have been misguided by their religion, have a chance to accept or reject the truth: "I honestly believe that every person at some
point in their experience, even if it's after death, has an opportunity to
be presented [with the gospel], to have a sense of this being the truth
and having to accept it or reject it." But others simply declined to offer

any evaluation when we asked what they thought of other religions. As one Christian Reformed man from Michigan said, "I don't know enough about them to judge them."

And then there were other evangelicals who pushed the boundaries further, suggesting the partial validity or acceptability of other religions. One charismatic man from North Carolina, for example, reflected:

> Do they have the truth? I'm not supposed to judge other people, you know. Someone's of a different religion, maybe Jewish, and they don't believe that Jesus is their savior. I don't know. Maybe they won't go to hell.

Similarly, one nondenominational woman from Georgia suggested that people from other religions might be saved: "Each person has to decide for themself. I believe that 100 percent. Whether they want to serve Buddha or Confucius or Muhammad or whoever. 'Cause you know, there are still people saved in all those different denominations, right? I believe that." When we asked her whether she was really saying that Muslims are "saved," she wavered: "There might be some sincere people in that. They can be sincerely wrong, now. But God doesn't hold us accountable for ignorance." It is not easy for evangelicals to declare that Muslims are saved.

One variant of this, illustrated by a Presbyterian woman from Indiana, was the claim that other religions unwittingly worship the true God: "I believe that it's still my God that loves them. And however they choose to worship, whatever they call it, I still think it's the same one, really. I don't know, but that's what I think." We probed: So, Hinduism and Buddhism and Islam are really trying to worship the same God? "I think so," she replied, "that's how I see it." We probed further: So what is the difference between Christianity and Islam or Hinduism? "Well," she said, "they dress differently. They have a lot of rules and I think they meditate pretty differently." Then we asked whether she thought that Christianity is better or just a different way to get to God. "I just really don't know," she answered, "but I try not to judge them. I think there's more damage in trying to judge them, because I don't know what's in their heart and I don't know their God. I don't think it's a better way, it's just the way I've been brought up, and I choose to continue to believe that."[6]

A somewhat different approach, taken for instance by a nondenominational man from Georgia, was to say that God put other religions on earth to supplement Christianity in some way:

I don't see my Christian faith as having boundaries where I don't communicate with other people or can't augment. God put all these people on earth with other faiths, and there are truths in other faiths that are very profound, that really supplement the Christian faith. I think Jesus would have had a rip-roaring discussion with some of these patriarchs of other faiths. It would be nice to get them all in a room and discuss differences.

Yet others, such as one woman from Washington State who attends a pentecostal church, downplayed religious labels and emphasized Christian living as the central issue:

Christianity is a very generic term. Anybody can call themself a Christian. Buddhists, Mormons, and everybody can call themselves Christians. It depends on what's in your heart.
So what is distinctive about being Christian?
I think it is how they live their lives—do they go by what the Bible says?

The sometimes artful capacity of some evangelicals to sustain belief in Christianity's superiority while considering the possibility of the validity of other religions is well illustrated by the reply of one Baptist man from Pennsylvania. This man is someone who is engaged in culture war issues, who regularly gives money to Christian Right political organizations, and who even sends his children to James Dobson's leadership training summer camps. Yet when it came to the issue of other religions, he delicately weaved back and forth between the two positions. Notice the A→B→A→B pattern of thought:

Obviously there are people who seek God in different ways and different religions [A]. But I just have to go back to the scriptures and say that I believe these are inspired and from God [B]. And if there are other religions that God has revealed himself in, then He will honor them too [A]. But I believe definitely that he has revealed himself through the person of Jesus Christ and through the scriptures that have been given [B].

At the farthest end of the spectrum were evangelicals—a small minority, like the hard-line exclusivists at the opposite end—who essentially admitted there is nothing wrong with other religions. A Presbyterian woman from Ohio, for example, simply said, "I don't think other religions are wrong." And a Lutheran woman from Michigan maintained that all religious people wind up in heaven in the end:

I think everyone should have religion. If it is not my religion, at least have their religion. There is only one God. We all combine when we go up there, all the other religions. They are not wrong, just different. As long as they believe in God, sooner or later they will meet their maker.

But simply observing that evangelicals hold a diversity of views on other religions does not adequately plumb the complexity of this matter. For crosscutting this diversity of views are a set of intellectual, experiential, and emotional tensions that generate noteworthy ambivalence on the question of other religions.

The first of these is that while strains of religious exclusivism run deep in evangelical thinking, at another level, evangelicals appreciate certain commonalities they find with other people and traditions of faith. Compared to their feelings about secularists, especially, evangelicals can feel quite warmhearted toward other believers. Other religions may not be on the same team, so to speak, but at least they are playing the same sport. This sense helps to generate a level of acceptance one would not expect from the more exclusivist line of evangelical thought. One Presbyterian man from North Carolina, for example, who struck us as rather strict in his notions of Christian truth still felt a commonality with other religions because of his perception of a shared commitment to a basic morality:

> I don't have a problem with us being a country that tolerates all religions. In general, the major religions of the world are in agreement about a lot of moral issues. Maybe not for all the same reasons, but in general. That's why I have said that I think freedom of religion is good. If there were a large population of Muslims in a country and the government was threatening to close down mosques or something, that is not what this country is founded on.

A man from North Carolina who attends a Pietist church took the same approach with regard to accounts of creation: "Most of the religions of the world, you know, have a creation belief. So I think it's fine to teach that." A Swedish Covenant woman from California reflected more generally: "I think Jesus is the only way, so then I must think they are wrong. But not everything in these religions is wrong. Maybe some things are good." Similarly, an evangelical Moravian woman from North Carolina contrasted other religious believers with the nonreligious:

> All religions have themes of peace at their center. Living around people of different religions wouldn't bother me if people had some kind of morality about them. So I wouldn't mind living in a town full of Muslims, you know, because we are all peace-loving people. It wouldn't bother me at all. But the people that don't have any faith in anything don't care about who they hurt, who they have to walk on to get where they want to go. They don't care about selling drugs to kids.

Even so, in the same discussion, this same woman also said of other religions, "Well, none of them have what I have. You know, none of them have a God who knows me by name, and who I can personally talk with anytime, anywhere. None of them have that." So the tension is sustained.

A second tension evangelicals exhibit on the question of other religions lies between what certain theoretical ideals may tell them and what they learn from their own experiences with people of other faiths. A Presbyterian man from Pennsylvania, for instance, recounted:

> I know these dedicated Muslims who are more dedicated to their faith than I am. They do their prayers three times a day. We can work all day together and they will say, "You take the shower first, I have to say my prayers." They aren't saying that in a self-righteous way, but they live righteous, so to speak, and seem to be blessed by doing it. So sometimes I get thoughts like "well, basically as long as you believe in something outside yourself." But then I take the good from him, and ask God to put more of that in me.

Similarly, a man from California who attends a Nazarene church observed:

> For us to say, "Okay, you're here now, so you can't be a Buddhist"—I don't think it happens that way. Culturally, within their religion, that's a part of who they are, and it goes way further back generationally than most of ours do. And for the most part, in my experiences, they are more devout in their beliefs and lifestyles than many, especially Western, Christians are. And they pay a price and live their beliefs more than we do. And I think that's a challenge.

The third source of ambivalence about other religions is one we have already encountered in chapter 1. This is the tension between, on the one hand, the implications of an exclusive claim to religious truth (and perhaps a lingering desire for a Christian America) and a resolute commitment to religious voluntarism, liberty, and freedom of choice. The words of one Baptist woman from North Carolina clearly illustrate this tension:

> Other religions are allowed to live here and be, you know, that's fine. I think we have to have a choice. I don't think we should be made to believe something or follow a certain creed or whatever. But as far as our nation is concerned—and that's pretty much what I have a struggle with—we were founded on biblical principles. I think we should do all that we can to maintain that as a nation.

Likewise, a Congregational man from Massachusetts commented: "I believe what I believe about Christianity because I think it's the truth, so I don't have a view that all religions are on the same footing. But at the same time I don't think you can legislate or dictate what other people are going to do with their own beliefs." A Presbyterian woman from North Carolina also reflected this tension in her thinking: "I think other religions have been deluded. The evil one, Satan, deludes us into thinking that what we think is okay. I think it is culture, a lot of family upbringing. But in my opinion, there is only one way to God and that is through Jesus Christ." But when we mentioned the problem of requiring a Christian morality in a pluralistic society, she confessed, "I have really struggled with that, because to me God's way is the right way. But at the same time I wouldn't want, say, a Buddhist to insist that I take on their standards. God is big enough to deal with both of us. I don't know if that answers it or not."

Finally, there is another somewhat related though distinct tension concerning other religions that we have also already encountered in chapter 1. This is the tension between evangelicals' capacity—and for some, a strong inclination—to judge other religions as false and idolatrous, and their belief in holding a loving, nonjudgmental attitude toward outsiders. For example, when we asked a Bible Fellowship woman from Pennsylvania (who happened to be selling her house to become a foreign missionary) whether the existence of other religions ever caused her to doubt her own faith, she said, "No, they are phonies. They are imitations and they have problems. They don't answer everything the way Christianity does." But, incongruously, in the same conversation her response to the question of cultural and religious pluralism was:

> Well, I think that's the way it is. You have to take it on one individual at a time, trying to be there and doing good, being responsible, being a model and being open to people. We are just not allowed to reject people. Christ doesn't call us to reject people because they are unbelievers. I mean it is wrong. And there *is* this feeling of rejection from Christians sometimes that comes across harsh. Some Christians can be very hard in their self-confidence. And that rules [out] somebody else's ability to say, "Gee, I wanted to know about what you were thinking, but now that you appear so dogmatic, I can't even approach you."

We see, then, that on the question of how evangelicals relate to other religions, evangelicalism both encompasses a broad range of views and grapples with a variety of ideological and experiential tensions that are the source of more than a little ambivalence. The evangelical perspective on other religions is not the straightforward matter that some observers think it is. Still, if a most consistent theme among evangelicals on the question of other religions can be identified, it is the imperative of religious freedom and toleration. For most evangelicals we interviewed, when all was said and done, religious liberty was the touchstone of their thinking on the matter. For this reason, few of them sounded like intolerant bigots, though critics sometimes describe them that way.

Consider these representative voices. One Christian and Missionary Alliance man from Georgia said, "We truly have to accommodate the masses that are coming to this country with other religions. The whole idea of freedom of religion is to allow all these people the freedom to worship as they believe, and they truly can, as long as they're not immoral." A pentecostal woman from Oregon maintained:

> I don't think we should force Jesus down people's throats. If I had a Buddhist in my classroom, I don't feel I would have the right to tell them that Buddha was just a man: He was a wonderful man and did wonderful things, but he was not God. That is not fair to that child, especially in public school.

A California woman from a Wesleyan church observed, "Everybody has the right to practice their religion legally. I believe fully in that respect, although we don't need to stop sharing with them or coming alongside them." A Congregational woman from Massachusetts maintained:

> I guess I think that you should respect everyone's faith if it's sincere, and try to get along. If by your living and standards you can cause them to see your way, the Christian life, then good. If they have their own faith, I think we should live with them. I think people should be legally allowed to practice those religions in our society. They should have the privilege of maintaining that faith. And if we can convince them otherwise, fine.

Even some of the most judgmental evangelicals emerged on the side of religious freedom and toleration in the final analysis. A woman from North Carolina attending a pentecostal church, for example, told us what she thought of other religions: "I don't like [them]. That's false religion. Idols. Our God is alive. Their's are gods of clay, or wood, or whatever." But when we asked her what should be done about non-Christians, she replied:

> Well, there's not much our society can say about atheists and new-agers if a person really believes that way, other than pray for them. You know, they'll come around. I don't see that we have any other choice than to co-

exist in society with those people. I don't think you should try and push the gospel down anybody's throat. That is an individual decision. God gives them that choice. Either you do or you don't [believe].

HELL AS GROUNDS FOR CIVILITY

Conventional wisdom about hell among critics of evangelicalism—and, more broadly, of Christianity—is that it naturally disposes those who believe in it to be crusading and coercive. Hell, the logic runs, is such an ultimate threat, that anyone who seriously believes in it must and will be prepared to do *whatever* it takes to prevent others from suffering eternal damnation. No competing value or responsibility could possibly trump this imperative, since hell is believed to be excruciating and everlasting. Stated in such elementary terms, this logic makes sense. And there are certainly manifold cases in Christian history, and not a few cases in contemporary evangelicalism, that instantiate this reasoning. Doesn't belief in hell invariably compel evangelicals—all talk of toleration notwithstanding—to act in ways that violate respect for diversity and civil pluralism? Doesn't the dogma of hell produce beleaguering proselytization, zealous arm-twisting, and all manner of other coercive evangelism?

In fact, for most ordinary evangelicals belief in hell does not produce these results. Ironically, belief in hell tends to cultivate civility in evangelicals. It is often a strategic civility, to be sure, but it is real civility nonetheless. We have already encountered some clues as to why this might be so. But there is more to say on the matter.

Most evangelicals do believe in a real hell where people who do not or will not believe in Jesus Christ will go and suffer. (What most evangelicals mean by "hell" is a spiritual "separation from God," not necessarily a place of fire and pitchfork-wielding devils.) And this belief does indeed affect many evangelicals in a variety of ways. One nondenominational woman from Michigan, for example, told us, "I think of my family more than my neighbors [when I think about hell]. I know I can't feel responsible for others, and yet I have this overwhelming desire to get to each and every one of them. I am preoccupied with the thought of how to plant seeds with each of them. I think about it all the time." A Southern Baptist woman from Virginia related:

> I guess it makes you more aware that you need to get on with the job fast. You never know how long you or they are going to live, so why should I put that off? I did a poster one time and it said 'How lost is lost?' 'Cause

lost is lost all the way. And I don't want anybody to be lost, so therefore I think I need to do something about it.

"Doing something" typically means sharing one's faith with family and friends, as one pentecostal man from Georgia said: "It makes you want to witness to them more and try to bring them in. Because I believe there is a literal hell, I'm gonna work real hard to try to keep them from going." A few evangelicals, like one Baptist woman from South Carolina, conveyed a sense of desperation about the matter: "It makes me feel sorry for some of them, and you want to just take them up and shake them and say, 'You can't do this, you got to stop, you got to go this direction, 'cause if you don't you're going to end up here.' That's what worries me so bad about my dad." At the same time, many evangelicals, like one Presbyterian woman from North Carolina, emphasized the contrary—that their own evangelism derives more from an enthusiasm about life in God than a fear of hell: "I think I'm much more evangelistic now than ever before. But I don't live out of fear. When I share with someone else it is almost always out of the fact that I am so excited."

Belief in hell sometimes troubles evangelicals, as an evangelical Moravian man from North Carolina explained: "You have to be honest: sometimes that stuff really bothers you at an emotional level. All of these people are going to die and go to hell—how can God be a loving God?—and that sort of thing. Sometimes that really bothers you." Often, as an evangelical Episcopalian woman from Ohio disclosed, the most troubling are thoughts of family members going to hell: "It bothers me probably, not as much with neighbors and colleagues as it does with family. It hits home, more at home, with family." But almost all evangelicals, like this Baptist woman from New Jersey, ultimately trust that God is just in the matter:

> I know God is perfectly right. He's just and whatever He does is right. [But] in my lack of understanding I question Him sometimes. I fall back on: He's holy and just and if I know who He is, then I know He's got it all figured out. And if there's some way—whether it's through His creation that He gives them a true desire to know Him—He will show Himself to them and you know they will be saved.

At the same time, however, many evangelicals—perhaps up to 50 percent—confessed that they did not really think much about hell, and concern that nonbelievers will go to hell did not affect their relationships with other people very much. When asked whether they thought about hell and whether it shaped their relationships at all, many said simply, "No, I would say not," or "Probably not." A Michigan woman from a Baptist church explained, "Probably not as much as it should. I guess if one had the realization and the total impact of that, one would live a little different. But one tends to forget, or not think." Evangelicals sometimes seemed to feel guilty about this, or at least, like one Presbyterian woman from Maryland, *thought* they should feel guilty: "It should more, but it often doesn't. This is really bad, but my heart doesn't break for the unsaved, and I know it should but it doesn't." Sometimes it seemed that evangelicals had to work hard to convince themselves of the importance of hell. One independent church woman from Georgia, for instance, said:

> I don't think that it affects me enough. If I really believe in hell, why am I so content to not try to affect people's lives for Jesus? I'm not one of those "scare them into the kingdom" people. But I think we do have to realize it is very real. Jesus had more to say about hell than he did about heaven.

In this sense, some evangelicals, like one Presbyterian man from South Carolina, seemed uncomfortable with their own attitudes about hell:

> I'm afraid that we don't think about it often enough, because if we did we would have more zeal, we would be more concerned. It should make us try harder to reach them, and be more encouraged to pray for them. I do feel sorry for them because they don't share a view of right and wrong, but I don't relate it to hell so much. Which probably is a mistake on my part.

Certain evangelicals, like one Georgia woman who attends a Christian and Missionary Alliance church, had difficulty generating the evangelism that they thought their belief in hell should kindle:

> No, in all honesty I don't feel it as keenly as I wish I did. A friend of mine doesn't have the saving knowledge of Jesus Christ, yet I'm not at the point where my heart aches enough to risk the friendship, to be the witness to her that I need to be, and that a true evangelical would be. But yet there is a hell.

The majority of evangelicals, however, were able to give reasoned accounts of why their belief in hell did not compel them into aggressive proselytizing. These generally centered around two themes. The first was the widespread conviction that *fear of hell is pragmatically ineffective*, if not morally inappropriate, as an entry point into evangelism. And since evangelicals are more interested in saving people for heaven than in haranguing them about hell, they are keenly aware of the need for an evangelistic strategy whose effectiveness does not depend on the fear of hell. One Baptist man from Pennsylvania, for instance, observed:

> I just feel that is ineffective. It may persuade some, but with the vast majority of people it's not going to be a persuasive argument. They either think I am a jerk, or don't know what I am talking about, or just simply reject the whole concept. It's a meaningless term.

Similarly, a North Carolina man who attends an independent charismatic church related:

> I don't go home and talk to my brother: "Look you've got to become a Christian or you're going to go to hell for eternity." There's a clash of what's right and what will be effective. It might not be the best thing for me to go to my brother and say, "Look, you better be a Christian or. . . ." I think if that was real for me I would be compelled to do that. But I don't think that's what's going to do it for him, you know?[7]

The second theme was the widespread belief that *salvation is an individual choice* that each person must make for him or herself and take final responsibility for. This view shifts the burden of accountability for salvation away from the evangelizing believer to the evangelized nonbeliever. All the evangelical can do is share the gospel in word and deed. After that, the matter becomes the nonbeliever's (and, in the eyes of some, also God's) responsibility. This theme was pervasive in our discussions. One pentecostal man from North Carolina claimed: "I see it that the same opportunity I have, they have. It's going to be a faultless thing, a blameless thing, because everyone has the same right. They have the same opportunity, and then it's up to them to believe, to put things into action." One woman from Georgia who attends a seeker-oriented mega-church agreed: "I think it is their choice, and as long as I've done what I'm supposed to do, I'm not responsible for how they act on it. I feel sad, you know. You feel the burden of responsibility for it. But I feel like it is somewhat their choice, if they have heard and made their choice." A charismatic man from Maryland explained the evangelistic "division of labor" in a way that placed more responsibility on God: "It's our responsibility to go and tell, and it is God's responsibility and the Holy Spirit to put that person under conviction."

In the responses of many evangelicals, this individualistic and voluntaristic approach to salvation seemed to help relieve the psychological and emotional pressure of belief in hell. One Presbyterian woman from Michigan, for example, said, "It's on my mind. I worry about other people who are not Christians and the fact of what eternity is going to be for them. I don't know. I don't think about it. It's their choice." And an Ohio man who attends an independent church related, "I don't think it affects my relationships too much. Again, you got to love your brother as yourself, you got to live that life. It's a daily life. It hurts, it hurts. But it's their choice." The main outcome of this view is that few evangelicals use hell as a fulcrum to try to leverage force in their evangelism. As a Baptist man from Pennsylvania reported:

> I am also not trying to proselytize everybody I come into contact with, knowing they are going to be in hell. I can't deal with that pressure. I would cease to function. The burden would be too great. That does not mean I have no responsibility to make it clear to them that in my view of life there is going to be that clear-cut division. But I don't go up to people and say they are going to hell.

Not all evangelicals, it is worth noting, hold a traditional view of hell. Some draw on various biblical and theological themes to develop somewhat alternative views. One Bible church woman from Illinois, for example, emphasized responsibility in proportion to knowledge:

> Hell hasn't sent me on a fiery crusade. Romans 5 talks about people being responsible for what life they have been given. Everybody doesn't have to come to God through Jesus if he has never heard his name. God holds you responsible for what you did with what light you had. Whatever light God gave you, [what matters is] what you did with that light.

One nondenominational man from Ohio at first laid out a very conventional view of who is going to hell: "If they have not given their heart to the Lord, very simply not professed the Lord as their Savior and received him into their heart and their name is not written in that Lamb's book of life, they're not going to heaven." But when we asked about Jews who are moral, God-fearing people but don't believe in Jesus Christ, he replied, "I believe that there is going to be a revelation to Jews because they're of Jesus, they're his blood, he was born to a Jew. So I believe that there is going to be a revelation to Jews that has not yet been seen." And a Congregational man from Michigan explained a view of hell somewhat reminiscent of that of the evangelical luminary, C. S. Lewis:[8]

> I have a very narrow view of hell. You are going to think I am crazy, but I do not find anywhere in the Bible where it says that if you don't accept Jesus Christ as your Savior while you are physically on this earth that you will go to hell forever. My belief is that at any point in eternity where a person says that they accept Jesus Christ and repent of their sins, that they will then spend eternity in heaven. So I can't imagine that there are very many people

that suffer eternal damnation. That is not logical to me. So, yes, I think people can go to hell, that there are a lot of people that go to hell. [But] we Christians tend to build a great big wall in death. I just don't see the presence of that wall.[9]

Of all the evangelical views concerning hell, however, the one most consistently expressed was that belief in hell most appropriately prompts one to pray for nonbelievers, live one's own life as a good Christian example, and occasionally try to slip in a word of encouragement to nonbelievers to consider faith in Christ. One Baptist man from South Carolina, for instance, said, "It goes back to trying to be a model before them. I'm probably not—well I know I'm not—as active in trying to quote scripture and convince them of their sin as I ought to be. But my way is trying to hopefully let them see a little bit of Jesus in me." A Bible Fellowship woman from Pennsylvania suggested, "I think about it sometimes, and I think it affects my prayers most of all. It pushes me to say to one of the other teachers or neighbors, 'Well, that is because what Christ has done in my life,' or some kind of testimony." An Assemblies of God man from Ohio explained, "Well, you just pray for them. I mean, the Lord can change them in the twinkling of an eye. And they have to look at your walk. You can't beat this over anybody's head." And a Presbyterian woman from Indiana reported:

> Well, it kind of breaks my heart. But I feel it's my responsibility to display Christ-like characteristics whenever I'm around them. So if I'm doing that and the door is open for me to share with them, then I will do that. I've never been very pushy, and there's always that thought in the back of my mind that maybe they're lost. But, I believe it's an individual thing. I try really hard not to judge people. I just want whatever contact I have with them to be the right Christ-like thing, and then plant a seed or live an example.

Again, personal relationships and gentle, well-timed nudgings are central to this process of gentle evangelism, as one independent woman from Georgia made clear: "You don't go up to your friends and say 'you're going to hell.' But I think when you are establishing a relationship with someone you want to bring to Christ, then that has to come into it at some point in the relationship. Not in the front maybe, but at some point, you know. 'God wants you with Him in heaven'—that's your emphasis."

Many of these themes and beliefs came together in the responses of single interviewees. One woman in South Carolina who attends a Southern Baptist church, for example, explained:

I think sometimes I might forget that they might be going to hell. I believe in it, but I'm afraid I'm not as aware sometimes of making sure they know. *So it doesn't change how you relate to others?* No. I try to make sure that I am doing everything when I am in their presence that would give a positive witness. I'm trying to make sure of that—as I have opportunity to discuss things without just bringing it up. I don't think you do any good just hammering and preaching all the time. It's got to be lived in front of them. And just as opportunities come up, making them aware that there is a hell and that we're responsible—that God doesn't send us to hell, we send ourselves.[10]

The idea, then, that a sincere belief in hell inevitably propels evangelicals into proselytizing crusades is based on abstract projection, not reality. American evangelicals are clearly not liberal universalists who affirm all people in their beliefs and lifestyles, but most of them are also not particularly aggressive and triumphantist about their belief in hell. If anything, the evangelistic impulse within evangelicalism tends to cultivate a particular version of civility—a strategic civility that tries to reach people on their own terms. Most evangelicals believe that those who have not accepted Christ are bound for hell and are therefore in need of salvation. But knowing that, pragmatically, hell is a counterproductive evangelistic hook, and recognizing each person's right to reject Christ, most evangelicals believe that their responsibility is to pray for others, to provide a good "witness" by their own lives, and to speak an appropriate word when the opportunity presents itself. In the meantime, they can work on building strong relationships with others in the hope that in the future they may be able to influence their friends, colleagues, and relatives. Beyond that, the responsibility for people's eternal destinies rests not on evangelicals, but with God and with each freely choosing person him or herself.

EVANGELICALS SELF-AWARE AND SELF-CRITICAL

One final observation about the situation of American evangelicals in a pluralistic society adds an interesting twist to all we have observed so far. The majority of evangelicals are very conscious of the culpability of the evangelical community itself in creating a negative impression of Christianity. They know that many of their own people have acted offensively, and that this has brought deserved criticisms of evangelicalism as a whole. They are well aware that outsiders often view evangelicals as radically intolerant. And they are both prepared to take a certain amount of responsibility for that reputation, and concerned to remedy the situation. This attitude makes sense for a tradition that is more interested in engaging the culture with a relevant witness to truth, than in separating from the culture to maintain spiritual purity (which is the fundamentalist attitude). And this self-awareness and self-criticism has significant consequences for the way these evangelicals relate to their pluralistic surroundings: for many it generates a certain degree of humility and caution in their words and actions.

Some interviewees, like one Presbyterian woman from North Carolina, recognized that some evangelicals have alienated outsiders through their judgmental attitude: "I think mainstream society on the whole has been wounded by a group of Christians, and they carry those wounds." When we asked which groups, she answered, "Fundamentalists, and some evangelicals who are not willing to love them, who are judgmental." An independent church woman from Massachusetts commented on the harmful effects of Christian legalism:

> Because we are in various stages in our Christian growth, sometimes we come across as phonies or do-gooders or radicals. We're a mixed bag that they can't understand. In the 1960s, the young people were fed up with the church because they saw it as rules, regulations, and trying to manipulate and dominate people's lives and restrict them. They saw it without love and turned away from it. I think sometimes the churches have a tendency to have rules and regulations and obey the letter of the law, but the love of Christ is overlooked.

One California man who attends a Nazarene church thought the church has far too often rejected people who are different:

> The church has erred tremendously in being so judgmental and exclusive to say 'oh, bad people,' and almost shun them or label them and cast them aside like lepers. It's terrible. They ought to be embraced like anyone else who's hurting and lost. That's the way Christ would treat them. You put whatever labels on them, but just because they're different they need to be cared for, they need to be shown kindness and affection like anyone else. They still have all the same mechanisms and needs within them.

Some, like this Baptist man from Minnesota, were critical of factionalism within Christian groups:

> [Christians' problems are] internal, more than non-Christian groups trying to turn Christians away. There are so many breaks and divisions now, I think we're killing ourselves as Christians. Everyone wants to break off and start their own different group. Christians are going to commit suicide. They're letting us kill ourselves because they see we're doing such a good job of it ourselves. There are so many groups breaking off—more conflict, internal problems, internal struggles.

Others, such as one Congregational woman from California, criticized the church's historical isolationism:

> Christians for the most part have pretty much been treated the way they probably deserve. Christianity in the twentieth century became isolationist, tending to focus only on religious beliefs and relationship with God, so became very isolated from the mainstream of society. They stayed in their little churches without going out to really affect society. And because of that, society tended to feel, especially by the 1960s, that church was irrelevant. I think, by and large, the world has become antagonistic because of things we've done to deserve the antagonism.

One Congregational man from Michigan said Christians were wrong to think the world is always against them: "I think it is very presumptuous of Christians to think that they are being picked on. That is paranoia." An Evangelical Free man from Minnesota spoke of how some Christians think and talk in embarrassingly foolish ways:

> In general the world views us as nuts. Just last week in Sunday School, a man who did a talk show where Christians were calling in and asking questions said he was very embarrassed by some of the idiotic things people said in the name of Christianity, you know, totally off the wall and unbiblical. People in the media, that's all they know. To them, that's Christianity. Some Christians just say, "This is what I believe and everybody else that doesn't believe it is wrong or stupid."

And a Michigan man who attends a Missionary church criticized Christians for resisting creativity and innovation: "Hollywood and television have predominantly been negative towards Christianity and anything that holds a moral absolute. Unfortunately, I think a lot of times the church has been guilty of pushing creative, artistic type people away from the church by not allowing innovation and change to be something that is acceptable within the church." One independent church woman from Georgia related a telling story about evangelical insensitivity:

> Just the other day in the bank there was a Christian lady talking to one of the tellers about a Bible study. So I tuned into what she was saying—about a Catholic friend with whom she was trying to share the gospel. All those tellers heard was "because she is Catholic, she can't be a Christian, so I went after her." Her teller very sweetly said that she viewed things a little differently. And when the lady left, they just went to pieces: "I'm so sick of these good for nothing. . . ." That is their view of an evangelical: judgmental and critical. This lady approached the whole thing the wrong way, trying to witness to these ladies, but she put a wall up before she even got started.

Other evangelicals noted the hypocrisy that can rightly give Christians a bad name. One man from Massachusetts attending a Congregational church observed, "Just about everyone you talk to has seen some kind of hypocrisy or had some negative experience with someone who they associate with Christianity." A Baptist woman from Minnesota maintained that "Christians can do a lot more damage as Christians because they're not consistent. They may sit in the front row of church every Sunday, may be big givers, but they're not living it. And I think a lot of times it's the Christian that does damage." And a Southern Baptist woman from South Carolina suggested, "If you're on the fence and not really sure if you're a Christian and you read all about Jim Bakker or Jimmy Swaggart or David Koresh, why would you want to be one, after taking a look at them? Or let's say the girl across the street goes to church every Sunday, and when her husband goes out of town, there is some man over there. It happens in every neighborhood—double lives. They aren't walking the walk."

Most evangelicals we interviewed deplored the bad reputation that Christians have inflicted on themselves with such offenses. A few expressed a felt obligation to accept these fellow believers despite the bad reputation they have created.[11] A few others seemed to use these self-criticisms as the starting point for a call to rally recommitted Christians to social activism.[12] But for most evangelicals, this self-aware self-criticism seems to promote two related outcomes: it begets a certain amount of humility and self-restrained caution with regard to the surrounding world, and it fosters an interest in getting the Christian house in order before setting out to influence others. Neither of these are tendencies that encourage evangelical efforts to undermine or overpower cultural pluralism.

CONCLUSION

As we move through this book, we are seeing that one must speak of "American evangelicals" and "evangelical views" with caution. For evangelicalism actually comprises a diversity of views, as well as ambivalence, regarding issues of "Christian America" and cultural pluralism. Even when a dominant evangelical voice is discernible, it is hardly that of the popular Christian Right leaders. Most ordinary evangelicals are tolerant if not comfortable with America's cultural and religious pluralism, and are nowhere near poised to try to assert cultural dominance or uniformity based on their worldview. There are certain issues and groups that do concern evangelicals very much, and these we will explore further as the book progresses. But we can say at this point: it appears that most nonevangelicals have little more to fear from the majority of ordinary evangelicals than being thought of as spiritually or morally mistaken, and thus prayed for, shown a life of good example, and occasionally offered a word of concern about one's relationship to God. These may be things nonevangelicals would prefer to do without. But they are hardly views and practices that threaten civil American pluralism and democracy.

CHAPTER THREE

The Limits of Politics

A FRIEND OF MINE attending an Ivy League graduate program in the social sciences told me about a professor who had remarked in class: "If American evangelicals had had political power during the McCarthy Era in the 1950s, there would have been another holocaust." Not one student, my friend said, raised an eyebrow. The idea appeared perfectly credible to the class, and the discussion moved on.

Are evangelicals really so dangerous politically? Many reports by journalists, book authors, and scholars might lead one to think so. Flo Conway and Jim Siegelman's 1984 book, *Holy Terror*, for example, was among the first responses to Jerry Falwell's Moral Majority. In their book, they described "Holy Terror"—which they said is limited "among America's various religious groups almost exclusively to born-again Christians"—as "mass manipulation on a scale . . . unprecedented in both religion and politics in this country." "Holy Terror," they warned, is "a guerrilla war on our private thoughts, feelings, and beliefs, on our nation's timeless values and historic freedoms, being waged . . . with an arsenal of advanced hardware aimed at the most fragile part of our humanity."[1] This assessment echoed the full-page ad that the American Civil Liberties Union had run four years earlier in the *New York Times*, which claimed, "The new evangelicals are a radical anti-Bill-of-Rights movement. They seek not to conserve traditional American values, but to overthrow them."[2] In his book *The New Subversives* Daniel Maguire described what he calls "Born-Again Fascists": "They admit that they are radicals and that they want to change the system. They are not open to discussion or to compromise, since they believe that the Bible supports everything they hold dear."[3] And Judith Haiven wrote in her book, *Faith, Hope, No Charity*, about the "many evangelical Christians across North America today . . . many ordinary people who could be your next door neighbors":

> I discovered a common thread that . . . unites all the born-agains—a type of intolerance. Anyone who is not born again, or a potential convert, is ignored at best and denounced at worst. . . . Beyond the initial friendliness there is a barrier as hard as steel to those who are not of their thinking. . . . They are holy warriors locked in deadly battle and their Christian charity is carefully preserved. . . . The instant and thoughtless panaceas of born-again Christianity will be seen as a vast sanctuary by millions of North Americans. Is this sanctuary really a recruitment camp for right-wing movements? It would be naive to think otherwise.[4]

Similarly, Arthur Ide catalogued in his 1986 book, *Evangelical Terrorism*, what he saw as rampant hypocrisy, censorship, and totalitarianism within conservative Protestantism. He concluded with this warning: "Censorship does not stop with the closure of one particular magazine or press, but it instead opens the doors to total censorship of all media. Ultimately, this crimson path of calloused clerics culminates into the liquidation and execution of all human freedoms."[5]

Sometimes, these concerns are expressed in less extreme language. Jerome Himmelstein, for example, in his book *To the Right* suggests that the New Religious Right is "not a religious Right, or even a Christian Right, but an evangelical-fundamentalist Right." By the early 1990s, he observes, "determined evangelical activists had gained control of local Republican party organizations" in many states and, in its pro-life politics, "shifted from conventional political activity" to the more confrontational strategies of groups like Operation Rescue.[6] *Washington Post* writer Laurie Goodstein has reported on studies suggesting that white evangelicals express a consistent set of conservative political attitudes, are the most active and cohesive religious force in American politics, and represent the largest share of the Republican Party base. Unlike other Americans, she points out, "among born-again Christians, the power of religious belief is such that the liberalizing influence of education on attitudes about homosexuality is neutralized."[7] The language here is more balanced. But the underlying concern about evangelicals is much the same as that expressed in more alarmist writings.

Our task here is to assess these kinds of concerns in light of what we know from our national study of evangelicals. In this chapter, I am less interested in evangelicals' *political views* (their positions on specific "hot-button" political issues), than in their *views of politics* (their broader understandings of the nature and purposes of political life). This proves much more richly informative than simply counting heads on issues like abortion, gay rights, and prayer in schools.

We asked the evangelicals we interviewed a variety of open-ended questions about politics: Should Christians be actively involved in trying to exert a Christian influence on American society? Why should or shouldn't they? How should they? Should Christians be involved in politics? What should Christians be trying to achieve through politics? What should be their goals? Exactly how should Christians get involved in politics? Are there any limits or dangers for Christians in politics? The evangelicals we interviewed gave us what seemed to be candid and sincere answers.

What we learned is that many conventional assumptions about evangelicals and politics—some of which are reflected in the writings just quoted—are misguided and simplistic. When it comes to politics, evangelical views are replete with diversity, complexity, ambivalence, and incongruities. It is not simply a matter of a dominant evangelical view qualified by internal diversity. Nor is there simply a spectrum of evangelical political views. More accurately, evangelicals express a range of assumptions, beliefs, thoughts, and feelings on a variety of distinct issues that intersect and combine in complicated and sometimes improbable ways. These views, in turn, are frequently qualified by significant exceptions and reservations. All of this intricacy results in complex clusters of views about politics and Christian faith that are arranged along a multidimensional spectrum. In the following pages, I examine this approach to politics by first pulling it apart and examining distinct themes. Then I examine one case to illustrate the way one evangelical holds these assumptions, beliefs, thoughts, and feelings together.

SHOULD CHRISTIANS BE INVOLVED IN POLITICS?

Should Christians be involved in politics? Are American evangelicals even interested in politics? The simple answer is yes, the majority of evangelicals do believe that Christians should be involved in politics.

But beneath the surface of that simple "yes" lies more complexity than the surface yet suggests.

Though the majority of evangelicals believe Christians should engage politics, not all do. A small minority—no more than 5 percent—think that Christians should avoid politics. Some of these evangelicals, like one Church of God woman from Alabama, cited biblical reasons: "I don't think so. We don't have anywhere in the Bible where Jesus got involved in politics." Others, such as a Lutheran woman from California, were simply fatalistic: "Personally, no, I don't think they should get involved with it. I think [that just because] you're a Christian, to go out into the arena trying to change something isn't going to work or do anything." Others, like one Methodist woman from Illinois, seemed uncomfortable with the exercise of force that politics involves:

> I don't think that the two mix, I really don't, just because I'm a Christian and someone else is something else. This is a free country. You get into politics and you cannot help but let your beliefs influence your decisions. And therefore you're trying to influence a lot of people by your beliefs, not by what you think is the best for running the country or for getting a particular problem solved.

But these antipolitical evangelical voices are relatively few and far between.

The next shade on the spectrum of opinion about evangelical involvement in politics is an expressed ambivalence and hesitation that temper an openness to politics. One Pennsylvania woman who attends a Bible church, for instance, said Christians should be involved with politics "if they can." But Christians "have to be careful to be informed and fair, and I don't know if the Christian groups are really fair. They say what is wrong, but do they ever say what is right? I don't know. It bothers me that it is not a balanced kind of thing, and that is why I hesitate." A Baptist man from North Carolina reflected, "Actually my first major in college was political science. I don't know, that's a tough question. I think the way society now views Christians in politics—the same way we view special interests—I don't think so. I think probably we could do more damage than good." And an independent church woman from Georgia wavered:

> Well, I don't know. That's a hard one. Oh boy. You know, it's kind of like a paradox. You usually would not get into those kinds of situations unless you are trying to effect political change from a moral perspective. Yet we've already talked about the fact that you can't change [people]. It's the wrong

way to go about it—to try and get people to change before you get them to be a Christian. That has to come first. So I don't know.

Like the antipolitical evangelicals, this group represents probably less than 5 percent of the evangelical population. But the concerns that evoke their hesitations—about Christians being fair, respectable, and noncoercive in the rough-and-tumble world of politics—as we will see, are quite widespread among evangelicals.

The view one step closer to fully affirming that Christians should be in politics concedes political involvement for Christians, but subordinates it to spiritual priorities. One Evangelical Free man from Minnesota, for example, explained:

> I don't think it would be wrong, necessarily. I look at the life of Christ and I don't see that he was real involved in politics as such. I get the impression that for Christ, whatever your work, country, nationality, language, or government, to Christ it was all so insignificant compared to your relationship with God. I mean, life is so short in light of eternity. We've got to get rid of lesser things, to concentrate on the important things. That's one side of it. But on the other hand, in this country it's within our rights to participate in government. I think you need to do both, but it's a matter of priority.

And notice how one Covenant church woman from California expressed a similar sentiment using passive "permissibility language," based on the absence of a prohibition against politics in scripture: "I don't want to make rules for other people, but it certainly is okay [to be involved in politics]. If you have strong beliefs and want to campaign for them, I don't think the scriptures say you shouldn't do that. [But] I think sometimes it can override your faith, and you can get too involved in the political issues and lose your foundation."

The next step along the continuum of views accepts political involvement, but limits it to those few who feel "called" to politics. According to this opinion, participation in politics is not a fundamental responsibility of all Christians—much less a strategic instrument for widespread mobilization to regain a Christian control of society. It is, rather, one of many arenas in which Christians may or may not choose to participate. A pentecostal woman from Oregon, for example, related, "I am not politically minded, to be really honest. It is never something that I have really been interested in, other than in voting. Christians do need to be involved, [but] it needs to be the ones that have a heart for it." One Bible church man from Illinois remarked, "Christians should support the political process. I think it's up to the

individual to determine whether they are being led to do something politically themselves." And a Baptist man from Minnesota suggested:

> It's different for different folks. Not everyone is called to be involved in pol-
> itics. I would say be proactive in your circle of influence, wherever that
> might be drawn. It might be around politics, or family, a community group,
> a sports group. But not to think you have to do everything, because you
> can't.

A fifth distinct evangelical position about politics is that Christians may become politically involved as citizens, but not as Christians per se, and certainly not through a Christian organization. One
Baptist woman from Michigan, for example, maintained, "I think
Christians should be involved only as the general public should be
involved. I don't think the fact that they are Christians or non-
Christians should have any bearing. But there should be a moderate
involvement percentage-wise." One worry hidden behind this position, and expressed by this Congregational man from Massachusetts,
is that politics will pit Christians against each other and damage their
witness:

> The Christians that I know are in all parts of the political spectrum, so I
> don't think you can say "this is a Christian agenda." We're individuals who
> have differences of opinions. You can have two wonderful Christians run-
> ning against each other and holding different points of views. So I don't
> think there should be a Christian agenda. My wife and I are both very care-
> ful not to get involved in what might be considered a Christian agenda, be-
> cause I know there are some issues that I think are wrong and don't want
> to be associated with. I think a lot of the issues, the way ideas are presented,
> create negativism and discourage evangelism.

Similarly, a man from Minnesota who attends an Evangelical Free
church insisted, "I think Christians should definitely be engaged with
society as individuals. When you talk about politics, I think we should
do so as individuals, not as Christians." We asked him to elaborate,
and he said he preferred this approach:

> It's: "I'm a citizen and I'm a Christian; I need to influence my society as an
> individual as best I can and participate that way." Rather than a structured,
> you know, "Christians are gonna take over the legislature"—which starts
> to look not a whole lot different than any other political group. If we want
> to influence things in our society—individual participation in school
> boards, politics in city government—there's nothing wrong with that. If an
> individual feels led to do that, that's great. [But] I don't feel too good when
> I see, you know—the Moral Majority didn't do much for me.

The most frequently stated position on Christian involvement in politics, however, was said with a different inflection than the preceding ones. Most evangelicals we interviewed replied simply, "Sure, why not? Of course Christians should be involved in politics." These answers were distinctly nonmilitant in tone, expressed with the same ease and assurance one might expect if you asked whether Christians should educate their children or take vacations. These evangelicals viewed participation in political life as a routine aspect of normal American life. Their answers, therefore, did not come with much elaboration. One nondenominational man from Minnesota answered plainly, "Sure," and then commented "just like any group has the right to express their opinions or ideas." One Lutheran woman from Michigan simply said, "I think Christians should. It's everyone's duty." And a Presbyterian woman from Washington State replied, "I don't think there's any reason why they shouldn't be in politics. Christianity should be in every walk of life, so the answer is yes."

In these answers there was little hint of the notion that Christians need to become political activists to champion specifically Christian political causes. The idea was rather that American democracy requires citizen participation and that Christians are not prohibited by their faith from political involvement, so Christians, like everyone else, should be active in American political life. "Active" appears to primarily mean informed voting. Thus, politics for the majority of evangelicals is not a trumpet call to take sides in the much-ballyhooed "culture wars," but a matter of basic citizen responsibilities and rights.

Further along the continuum of evangelical positions on politics, however, were voices that more explicitly argued for Christians to engage politics in order to advocate specifically Christian interests. These were a minority, but they certainly exist and are significant. Some evangelicals, such as one Illinois man who attends a nondenominational church, cast their position in terms of a democratic representation of constituencies: "In this country, government is the people, and the state of the country I guess reflects the people. And if all the Christians aren't involved, meaning voicing their opinion and voting and such, then they are just letting all the decisions be made by people who are hostile to Christianity." Expressed here is a perceived animosity from non-Christians and readiness to take an explicitly Christian stand in politics. But even so, the motivation appears to be the fair representation of Christian views, not Christian domination of all other views.

Others, such as one Baptist woman from Texas, spoke more frankly of Christians taking their fair place at the political table: "Yes, we should be in politics. It's like any other interest group—whether it be the gays and lesbians or the National Rifle Association—that we have someone there representing us, right there representing the cause of Christians, our beliefs." Having accepted the interest-group model of politics, this woman apparently does not expect to silence gay and lesbian voices, for example, only to compete with them.

Many of those in favor of Christians engaging in politics spoke about the need to elect trustworthy candidates into office in order to ensure the passage of good laws. One Baptist woman from South Carolina, for instance, replied, "I would like to see some Christian politicians, and after we vote, to keep in touch with them. Trying to get people with integrity and the Christian faith into a position to make the correct laws."

At the farthest end of the spectrum stood a handful of evangelicals who were prepared for Christians to impose their standards on the country. One pentecostal man from North Carolina used the language of majority rule to explain his view: "We should be dictating. It's fair to say that the majority in this country should rule. The majority should be Christian and the majority should rule." And when we asked one Indiana woman from a nondenominational church how non-Christians would respond to Christians working through the Christian Coalition, or Focus on the Family, to influence legislation—which she advocated—she stated:

They crucified Jesus. The world is going to hate us for doing it. But that doesn't mean we don't do it. Because what are we doing? We're telling them that they have to be disciplined, that they have to take responsibility, that they have to be obedient to a higher being, that there is someone above themselves. It's counter to everything that they want. It's going to be dangerous, yeah! That's what it's all about.

But these more imperious voices were even fewer and farther between than the evangelicals at the other end of the spectrum who said Christians should avoid politics. The vast majority of ordinary evangelicals, even those animated by Christian Right issues, clearly disavowed such aspirations to domination. As we proceed, we will explore some of the reasons why this kind of Christian political supremacy is unpalatable to most evangelicals. But first we should examine another issue on which evangelicals' views on politics are spread in a spectrum—the goals of Christian participation in politics.

WHAT ARE THE GOALS?

We asked those evangelicals who claimed that Christians should be involved in political life to explain what Christians should be trying to accomplish in politics. What are the goals? As with the previous question, their answers fell into a continuum of positions, from having no idea at all to desiring a Christian-governed culture. And again, the majority of evangelicals offered ideas that fell in the middle, most of which had little to do with the stated goals of the Christian Right.

There were evangelicals who believed Christians should be in politics, but had no idea what the goal of that involvement should be. One Lutheran woman from Michigan—whose answer about Christians in politics contained the enigmatic comment "That might keep a little bit of an iron rule"—could only say this when we asked what Christian political involvement should be trying to achieve: "I really don't know. I think it can accomplish something, but I don't know what." And a pentecostal woman from Pennsylvania said Christians should participate in politics, "to make sure the government's run in a Christian manner. How are you going to have a good government if Christians aren't participating?" When we asked her what this might look like, she only said, "They would have a voice in making decisions." And when we persisted and asked her which decisions, she answered, "I don't know. I can't think of anything specific."

Other evangelicals' responses were similarly vague. One Baptist woman from New Jersey remarked:

> Hopefully, [to] present a voice. I feel it would be honoring as a nation—involved in laws that would preserve some of the standards. And I'm trying to think of some specifics [but] I'm not coming up with anything specifically right now. Maybe after a bit.

And one Presbyterian woman from North Carolina offered up nebulous phrases, like Christians "making a difference," "making wise decisions," "going to promote justice," and "not taking America down" in her explanation of what Christians might be aiming for in politics. On the one hand, it's not surprising that some ordinary people simply cannot articulate a political vision. Not everyone knows or cares about politics that much. On the other hand, it signifies that some evangelicals' apparent interest in politics is mostly a matter of stated principle and carries very little substantive policy content. At the very least, these evangelicals are so far removed from Christian Right influence that they could not even think to offer a token of conservative political rhetoric to answer our question.

Most evangelicals who we asked about the goal of Christian involvement in politics, however, did have real answers to offer. Some mentioned goals that had little to do with protecting Christian interests in particular, but instead promoted the common good. One Baptist man from South Carolina, for example, replied, "A better world for all of God's creation. That's what I want to say." And an Evangelical Free man from Illinois answered, "What everyone else is claiming to be doing, fairness for all people. Hopefully, get a better, safer society. Raise the drinking age, stop the drug traffic, help build up the neighborhoods." Likewise, a Covenant church woman from California replied, "So many of the things that Christians want to achieve are really foundational things of the country, as far as equality and nondiscrimination. I would hope that Christians would work toward those ends." One independent church man from Ohio said, "Unity. Balance. Balance is something I think we've gotten away from in society. You have to have balance in life." And a nondenominational woman from Michigan said that Christians need "to try to make changes that would better our communities and make life better for people."

Other evangelicals suggested—in language echoing that of "good government" activists—that the primary purpose of Christian involvement in politics is to make government function more responsibly and efficiently. One Lutheran man from California observed, "Everything would be fair. You wouldn't have all these pork barrel politics." A Presbyterian woman from Ohio said that Christian should be "getting different laws passed, good laws; you know, there's too many people that are bought off today." One Presbyterian woman from Pennsylvania remarked, "Right now I think [we need] a Christian in politics just to show that politicians can live right and morally." And a Lutheran woman from California said the goal was to "try to have a government that is interested in people and not just in greed." These answers presume that Christians have a unique contribution to make in cleaning up the government. But the thrust of these responses reveals little or no concern to reclaim a Christian America. Governmental efficiency and fairness, it seems, would be enough.

In other cases, the evangelicals we interviewed expressed their views in terms drawn directly from standard, institutionalized American politics. We have already heard evangelicals speaking in terms of the political representation of constituencies, and of having a place at the table of interest-group politics. Still others, like one Baptist woman from Virginia, spoke about participating politically in order to sustain democracy in the face of ever-threatening demise: "You should try to help everyone to realize they need to vote. I take people to vote. We are only one generation away from totalitarianism if we don't use our vote." And others answered our question about the goal of Christian politics using the standard political categories of conservative and liberal. They did not talk about Christians battling atheists and secular humanists, but about countering liberal policies with more conservative ones, and their political concerns mostly had to do with the Republican Party versus the Democratic Party.

Many of the evangelicals we interviewed did speak of Christian political involvement as a way to advocate for "better morality" in society. But often when they explained what they meant by morality, it had little to do with specifically Christian morality. They spoke instead of a baseline morality that nearly all Americans agree upon for the general welfare of society. One evangelical Moravian woman from North Carolina, for example, said she thought Christians in politics should work for the "general welfare." She remarked, "If people would live according to the Ten Commandments, we'd have less social problems." When we asked what in the Ten Commandments she wanted to see in American law, she replied, "Don't kill." Similarly, a Georgia man attending a nondenominational evangelical church said about Christians' political goals:

> Whatever the constituency really wants. There are ways to strengthen Christian views of family and society without putting Christian labels on it or being discriminatory against other religions. I think everybody—Christian or not—would like to focus on strong families, relationships, communities, sharing, neighborliness, environmental conscious, job production. I think there is a way for Christians to focus on Christian ideals without turning off non-Christians. Again, no matter what you are, there are some basic truths. The golden rule is not something [only] Jesus said. It has been in societies for ten thousand years prior to Jesus walking in.

And a Presbyterian man from North Carolina argued:

> We should advance policies that we can be proud of, I mean just basic justice. I wouldn't want to set up a theocracy that incorporates things from [biblical] revelation. But there are things that everyone is responsible for and will be judged for not doing, some basic justice kinds of things. I think we can advance those through the state. Foreign policy. We should work for America to be a nation of peace, for example.

The goals of Christians in politics for this subset of evangelicals, then, are things like preventing homicide, building strong communities, and working for world peace.

Yet another sizable group of evangelicals maintained that the proper goal of Christians in politics should be to maintain freedom of religion and speech. They said things like "freedom to evangelize," "freedom to teach your children the gospel, to raise them in the Lord," and "maintain freedom of religious expression." Some cast their answers in terms of a possible antireligious totalitarianism that poses no immediate threat. One Christian Reformed man from Michigan, who, notably, made a careful distinction between public and private property, said, "It can prevent the government from unilaterally sweeping away that which we hold dear and sacred. What would happen if, all of a sudden, the government said there is to be no more public gatherings on Sundays, no more religious displays during Christmas and Easter, not on public property, but *your* property?" Others, such as one California man attending an independent church, spoke in terms of the nondiscriminatory display of religious symbols in public places—a currently contested issue:

> Prayer in our schools, Christ in our Christmas—all of the things that the politicians have removed from our Christian rights that we had before. The idea of not even putting a cross on City Hall at Christmas is infringing on our freedom. Christians should establish that we have the right to be Christians, and someone else has the right to be a Moslem, or to put up the Star of David. Each person should have the opportunity to express his own belief.

Notice how this response begins with a strong "pro-Christian-America" sentiment, but ends by arguing only against the total secularization of public places and in support of general religious nondiscrimination in sacred symbolic displays.

However, most evangelicals who emphasized the goal of maintaining religious freedom focused not on religious displays, but on the simple freedom to share the gospel. A Bible church man from Illinois said, "I assume the standard answer is to use politics to do a lot of evangelism and convert the nation, but I am not sure that is really the role for Christians in politics. I think the goal should be to make sure there are freedoms in the country which allow people to evangelize—the freedom to share the gospel, as opposed to legislating Christianity."[8] Of all the Christian political goals discussed by interviewees, the one of religious freedom was probably the most frequently mentioned. It reflects a very limited view of what politics can accomplish for Christians. It is also a view that shifts the power for change to where most evangelicals think it really belongs: the transformation of individuals through spiritual conversion.

So far, we have seen little in evangelical opinions about political goals that would support a strong Christian Right agenda. The last two categories of responses, however, begin to move in that direction.

Some evangelicals we interviewed said the goal of Christians in politics should be to maintain the nation's moral standards. Often these answers reflected the same vagueness that characterized the "principles and values" meaning of "Christian America," which we saw in chapter 1. For example, one Baptist man from New York said, "Endeavor to present their views according to a moral background. To establish a good moral background in the nation, that's the big thing." An Assemblies of God woman from Ohio answered, "Trying to achieve truth, justice, and morals, depending on the level they're in." And a Wesleyan man from Michigan replied, "Their decisions and votes should be morally and ethically based, to try and turn around the direction of the country." Left unanswered was the question of precisely *how* to maintain exactly *which* standards through politics. And answers like "Stand up for God's rule, God's standards. Show our side— that there is something better," offered by one Illinois woman who attends a nondenominational church, do little to clarify the matter.

Sometimes these "moral standards" answers—such as this one offered by an independent church woman from Georgia—seemed to carry quite modest expectations for change: "Maybe raise the general moral code a little bit. Keeping standards a little bit higher, not just finding the lowest common denominator." Other evangelicals taking the "moral standards" view, like one Congregational man from Massachusetts, simply wanted things labeled wrong that they think are wrong: "I don't know so much what their goal should be. But I certainly like a lot of the things that they're fighting for now, as far as family values and things like that. I guess, try and bring the country's morality structure back a few decades, where things that are bad are known to be bad, and they don't change the name of it to make it sound like it's good now." This man appears to have some connection with a Christian political organization that is promoting traditional "family values."

Finally, a group of between 5 and 10 percent of our evangelical interviewees spoke about Christians using politics to work for laws reflecting explicitly biblical truths and morals. One Congregational woman from Massachusetts, for example, said, "Try to uphold God's order and God's laws. That's a tough thing because it's not the popular choice." These people seemed comfortable talking about instituting biblical absolutes and explicitly Christian morals in American law. Take, for example, a Bible Fellowship man from Pennsylvania who answered our question this way: "The goal is to try and help steer the country in a more Christian, God-honoring direction. In this country, right and wrong used to mean something more than they do now. Let's have the recognition that absolutes mean things in law." We asked him whether this meant, for example, implementing Old Testament civil law today, and he replied, "How are you going to do that? The only way is like these loonies—lunatic fringe people—who fortify their compounds and blame the government when they come in with tanks." Since earlier he had said that real Christians probably make up only about 10 percent of the American population, we asked how he thought the U.S. government could realistically reflect what is a minority religion. His answer revealed a paternalistic readiness to impose Christian morality on an unbelieving majority for their own practical and spiritual good:

> Well, you can fall back on the notion that Christians think they are right in an absolute sense, that the things we derive from the Bible are the right way to live. And to the extent that anyone, even an unbeliever, aligns themselves with that right way of living, their lives will be better. And by their lives being better, they will come closer to an understanding of the God of right and wrong. And there is a hope that the Holy Spirit will awaken something in the individual soul, because the society around them has these Christian touch points, places where Christianity pokes through the muck and becomes something to stand on, a solid place.

This man is evidently unaware that many Americans would consider him a "loonie" also for holding this kind of view. And he seems unaware of having backed himself into arguing a very unevangelical theological position: that people might find God by first living better lives, even if against their own wills.

Typical of these answers was the belief in the Bible as a sourcebook for the substance of American laws. One Presbyterian man from North Carolina, for instance, suggested, "Influence on the making of laws and funding of programs that are more just or biblically aligned, and the elimination of laws that are not biblically aligned." An Independent church woman from Michigan stated, "We should try to become a

godly nation again. It would be nice if they could just live by the Bible."
A Christian Reformed man from Michigan commented that Christians
in politics "should be trying to achieve God's will as they perceive it in
the Bible. They should not roll over and play dead when they can have
an influence and act on their Christian values."

Many who held this view argued that laws based on the Bible would
produce positive, pragmatic benefits for society. One Charismatic man
from Maryland said, "The first thing we need to ask ourselves is 'What
would Christ do?' If in the law you could reflect the law of the Bible,
the way that Jesus has laid it out for us, it's got to be a better place."
Some, like this Nazarene man from Oregon, emphasized the value of
Christians using politics to restrain immorality and protect families:

> We need godly people with a sense of values and integrity to lead our na-
> tion in truth, in establishing laws that would be beneficial to our families,
> and not allowing immorality to be running wild. We need to have restraints,
> because the law was put in place in order to keep us doing good things. And
> where's the definition of good? It should come from the Bible, from God.
> So I really believe that we need godly people in political office.

Others, like one Baptist man from Pennsylvania, tended to stress the
abortion and gay rights issues: "[We should be] focused on moving toward enforcing or keeping in place things that are of Christian value—
pro-life, against homosexuality becoming an acceptable lifestyle."

Evangelicalism definitely includes an element that wants to use political power to promote explicitly Christian values and morals in
American law. But they are a small minority, perhaps no larger than the
proportion of nonevangelical Americans who maintain similar views.
Evangelicals as a whole sustain a broad range of views about what
Christians should be trying to achieve in politics. Some evangelicals we
interviewed had absolutely no idea of what this goal might be, others
espoused only vague goals, and others spoke about working for the
general welfare of society. Some evangelicals seemed most interested in
working for a responsible and efficient state. Others thought in standard American political terms of supporting the general democratic
process, organizing interest-group representation, or taking part in the
usual conservative-liberal party politics. Certain evangelicals spoke
about maintaining basic moral standards, such as not killing, not stealing, community prosperity, and world peace. Many evangelicals focused on defending religious freedom, especially the right to spread the
gospel. And certain evangelicals talked about the need to champion ex-

plicitly biblical or Christian values and laws. Overall, evangelicals express as much diversity on the goal of political involvement as they do on the meaning of "Christian America" and the proper response to American pluralism.

QUALIFICATIONS

Throughout our discussion of politics, our interviewees routinely qualified their views with cautions about politics in general. Some, like one nondenominational woman from Michigan, advised Christians not to expect to accomplish too much in politics: "I'm not sure politics itself will do much for Christians, and that's probably why you detect cynicism on my part. I think people can do more good outside of government." Others, such as a Congregational man from Massachusetts, stressed the need for Christians in politics to be very open and honest about their work:

> If you have Christian beliefs and you're going to vote to favor those types of legislations, you need to be honest with your constituents when you're running. Say "this is what and why I believe." If the people like your stance and vote for you, that's fine. There's nothing wrong with presenting your points of view, as long as you're being honest, saying why you're doing it.

Some, like one Georgia man attending an independent church, argued for the need for Christians to be flexible and compromising: "I think we get into trouble when there is an uncompromising agenda. Fundamentalist Christians get into trouble when they take that all-or-nothing attitude." Others, like one Evangelical Free woman from Minnesota, expressed the importance of avoiding political conflict: "Well, you need to avoid force and strife, you know, saying 'this is my agenda and we're gonna do it.' You can't do that. You have to walk in love and prayer and let the Lord open the way." Certain evangelicals emphasized the need to be tolerant in politics. A Congregational man from Massachusetts said, "You need to be careful of intolerance. If people are intolerant and absolute, you've got a problem. We need to accept— Christ accepted." Others, like one man from Georgia who attended a community church, opposed Christians in politics being exclusionary: "You can separate yourself so much and think you are living a much more exemplary life than everyone else, that you have nothing in common with them. Christianity is inclusionary, not exclusionary." Some evangelicals advised against large-scale political activism and exhorted

Christians to act primarily locally. A pentecostal man from Minnesota pointed out:

> We should focus on your local community. You start with your family and your community because they're what's closest to you. That's where Christianity plays its best role, because these are the things that your church can do. You can only do so much on a large scale, and doing things that mean a lot to you has to be at a local issue. If you get spread out too far, you get all these opposing views—opposing religious views, activist rights or animal rights or humane rights or freedom of speech and things like that, and then it becomes too frustrating.

Some other evangelicals cautioned that simply being a Christian or espousing a Christian position is not enough to make good politics. A Nazarene woman from California commented:

> Christians are fine in politics. That might not make me vote for them, because there's a lot more to politics than what you believe or how you live. There is knowing how politics works. If somebody can do it, I don't think being in politics unchristian, but you have to have more to offer than your Christianity. That can be the motivation, but it's not enough just to say "Well, God says so" or "The Bible says so." That's not gonna fly in politics. There's gotta be more to it than that, because the whole world is not Christian.

And yet other evangelicals, like one Presbyterian man from North Carolina, warned that Christians will not be able to solve the world's problems, since they still have their own problems: "Even if everyone on the earth were genuine Christians, I think we would still have problems. There would still be sin and we would still be living under the curse of the Fall." Thus, even though a few American evangelicals view political power as an important means to achieve Christian goals, many others approach political power with some degree of caution and awareness of its limitations.

BY WHAT MEANS?

While American evangelicals express a broad spectrum of views about the goals of Christian politics, they are relatively united in their thinking about the *means*. The great majority of evangelicals we interviewed think the proper means of exerting political influence are voting regularly, electing good people to office, and perhaps tactfully lobbying elected officials. Very few mentioned the need to mobilize a broad-based Christian political movement to challenge secular humanism in the halls of power. In fact, more often than not, these evangelicals expressed a strong distaste for confrontational, disruptive politics. Most were particularly repulsed by the organized anti-abortion protest groups, with their blockades, shouting matches, and arrests for civil disobedience (not to mention associations with gun violence). Some evangelicals did voice support for groups like James Dobson's Focus on the Family. But they seemed to like the evangelical "voice" it offers in the political discussion more than the mass political pressure it might be able to generate.

Individual voting is the keystone of evangelicals' strategy for political influence. They expressed great faith in the standard mechanisms of political expression through the American democratic process. One Congregational man from California, for example, commented, "I think the vote certainly is important, getting involved. We have a mandate to exercise our role as members of society by voting, talking to officials in Congress, State, Senate, and so forth. Get involved with voting and praying for our leaders." An Indiana woman who attends an independent church explained in the same way how Christians should exert political influence: "Well certainly, you know, with a vote. Letting congressmen know how we feel." And a pentecostal woman from Pennsylvania said, "In voting. I can't think of any other ways but just being active in the community."

Part of the evangelical strategy of voting is electing Christians to political office, as one evangelical Episcopalian woman from Ohio noted: "Getting the right people in office that can express the values and decisions that we want to see done." "Christians are supposed to have the best, I believe, outlook and ideals, morals and ethics," stated one Baptist woman from California, "and if they bring all that into government, I think it can only do good." Likewise, a Presbyterian woman from North Carolina observed: "I need to be a good citizen, to know who I need to vote for. The goal is getting good people in there that are going to make a difference, who are going to make wise decisions."[9]

Also popular in evangelical thinking on politics is the importance of taking a public stand and "speaking up." More prevalent in interviews than talk about actual political accomplishment were comments on the moral need to stand up and have the Christian voice be heard. One charismatic woman from California said, "Go to any meetings that you can, political or school meeting, and speak up for the truth." When asked whether Christians should be trying to make abortion illegal, a Baptist woman from Minnesota replied, "Well, at least let our voice be heard. You feel so much freer and know you've done the right thing to just call and let your voice be heard." Likewise, a North Carolina man attending an evangelical Anabaptist church claimed, "We've got to take a stand politically—we're called to do that. No matter what form or how it's done, there are basic things that we have to stand for that are points of faith on which we have to be firm." To a certain extent, this faith in "speaking out" reveals an optimism about American democracy's capacity to respond to the concerns of all legitimate political interests. As long as Christians make their views known, democracy will respond fairly. It also seems to reflect a need to know one has taken a stand for what one thinks is right, regardless of the outcome or consequences. For when history is written—or rather when all of history is revealed on God's Judgment Day—all parties will know that evangelicals indeed stood up and spoke out for what was right.

What is noticeably absent from the talk of most ordinary evangelicals about the means to effect a Christian influence in politics are visions of mass-mobilized Christian political movements. Occasionally, one will hear a comment something like the view of this nondenominational woman from Michigan:

> I do think it is good that somebody like Ralph Reed is out there representing us. I love it when James Dobson gets people to call the White House on certain issues. It is phenomenal that he is enough involved to get those of us who aren't involved by calling the White House switchboard.

(She immediately noted, however, that "Part of me believes that politics works to a certain degree, and part of me believes you have to do it on a personal level".) But for the most part, evangelicals shy away from mass political mobilizations, especially when they may be confrontational or disruptive. They consider such movements radical, and most are not fond of radicalism. Consider the words of one pentecostal man from Ohio: "I would do it by the rules and policies of the county and government where I live. I would not go out there and just be putting banners all over the place, being some radical Christian." As a nondenominational woman from Massachusetts observed, lobbying is good but mobilized action beyond lobbying is trouble: "Within the church there is a place for taking a stand about political or social issues. I don't think I like the idea of going beyond lobbying. And you do that with a sense of gracefulness." Instead of mass political "activism," then, evangelicals prefer the quiet, standard mechanisms of influence and reform. As one Baptist man from Minnesota expressed it:

Involvement is good, but again, I really am not supportive of protest movements and demonstrations. I think that has not been productive. I think
some of the moves that have been done behind the scenes to promote legislation have been good, and not because of demonstrations, but because of
people working on things, doing things. I think that's more effective. Involvement is good, and Christians are obligated to support our government,
our leaders. You know, voting is a right you get to exercise, and certainly
that is everybody's minimum responsibility.

Likewise, a Lutheran woman from Oregon remarked:

I believe Christians should be active in politics, as active as they can be. But
I despise the picket lines, the marching. I just don't think that's the way to
do it. That turns me off—even though I agree with the principle that they
are marching against. I just don't think that is the way to do it. So, I think,
if possible, even running for office. That isn't me. But certainly supporting
people who run for office who I believe have good, basic, Christian values.
Some are behind-the-scenes workers and some are out front. Whichever you
are called to do, or whatever our talent is, I believe they should be involved
in politics—but not the demonstrations.

MULTIPLE RESERVATIONS

Despite the widespread evangelical belief that Christians should be involved in politics, and despite their widespread faith in the standard
channels of American representative democracy, evangelical talk about
Christians in politics is also peppered with a variety of reservations.
Most evangelicals believe Christians should be politically involved, at
least *theoretically*. But practically, many of them are less sure.

Some evangelicals agree with the nondenominational woman from
Indiana who confessed, "I just hate politics." One North Carolina man
from a charismatic church observed, "I'm kind of disgusted with politics, just disgusted with politics altogether. Unless there is something
really threatening that needs to be prevented, I almost feel like what
needs being done should be done outside of or despite politics." A Congregational woman from Massachusetts said, "I'm sort of apolitical,
but cynical. Politics seems so entrenched sometimes, it's amazing how
much waste there can be." And when we raised the issue of politics
with one Presbyterian woman from North Carolina, she said, "Don't
even jump into the politics, because I dodge that one a lot. I've sort of
been disillusioned with it all." And a community church man from Colorado said, "Well, golly bum, politics is such a nasty thing."

Evangelicals also draw on specific aspects of the evangelical worldview to express their concerns about political involvement. A few interviewees offered a pessimistic view of history—reflecting a premillennial, dispensationalist interpretation of the Bible more typical of fundamentalists—to question the value of taking part in politics. An evangelical Moravian man from North Carolina, for instance, ended discussion of the topic by saying, "I think we will never solve the problems. If you look at the Bible, you'll see a pattern—that things are just going to get worse." And to the question of whether Christians have solutions for the world's social problems, a pentecostal man from Georgia replied,

> That's tough. Yes and no. The things in the world are simply prophesies that have to be fulfilled eventually. End-time happenings are happening all around us. They have to come to pass, every bit of it. But we're not supposed to just sit by and let it go. We're supposed to do all we can, get people converted in the meantime. But we'll never be able to change national events. It's going to transpire according to prophesy.

One Presbyterian man from Georgia even raised the specter of the "Antichrist," prophesied in the Bible, as a reason to avoid Christian politics: "I would not want someone in power who purported to be a religious leader. That's what's going to happen in the end in the Antichrist, and I'd rather not see that, at least in my day. Somebody's going to claim to be a leader of the Christians, and they're not going to be."

Evangelicals tend to be political conservatives, insofar as they oppose "big government" solutions to social problems. And this outlook also disinclines them to look to politics generally to accomplish much of value. A Congregational man from Michigan argued:

> You can legislate almost anything you can get enough votes for in this country. That doesn't mean things change. One of the fallacies of government is that you can legislate morality. You can't. People go and contest it. This country has tried to legislate morality in the past. You don't stop drinking by saying it is illegal. In fact, in a lot of cases you encourage it. Big government is a fallacy, is my point, because you don't legislate those kinds of issues. There are some reasons for government, don't get me wrong. If you throw enough dollars on something you are going to effect some change. The question is whether that is the best way to do it, and in my mind it is not. The federal government doesn't *do* things, they just allocate dollars, and do that flippantly.

More generally, evangelicals often said that there are definite limits on what politics can accomplish for Christians. One Baptist woman from Minnesota, for example, noted, "We have a responsibility to be involved, but there are gonna be limits, and it would be so hard to really turn the government around." A Christian and Missionary Alliance man from Georgia stated, "Politics can help slow down the decay, but the real battle is on the inside of each individual. Politics helps, but to me it isn't the front line." And for some, like this Baptist man from Minnesota, Christians have been too optimistic about their political influence:

> The attempts that have been made by Christians involved in politics are very feeble, very weak. If you're gonna be a Christian and enter that sacrilegious world, you have to realize that you're gonna come under fire and pressure. You can't just stick one foot in and expect that all the morals and values that you uphold are going to be readily accepted by everyone else. I look at some of the politicians that have tried, you know, like Pat Robertson. There appear to be more sacrilegious people in the world than there are Christians. So you're not gonna get into the White House if you're only gonna minister to Christians.

Many interviewees expressed concern about the damage that involvement in politics can do to Christians and the cause of the gospel. Compared with those who said Christians should use politics to uphold moral standards or to promote absolute biblical laws and values, twice as many expressed grave concern about the dirty dealings in politics and their potential to corrupt Christians. One Lutheran man from California, for example, observed about Christians in politics:

> It's all right, but they better remember they're Christians. When they get into politics it seems like there's something that makes them all forget they're Christians. They all look out for themselves and make the deals, like all of a sudden it's a club that they've joined. And they've forgotten everything else except for how to do the other person in, and feather their own nest to make money, and get their own favors.

And an Ohio man who attends an independent church reported:

> There's many dangers. Identifying all [of] them would take more time than we have. There's so much corruption in politics. I worked in Washington for four years as a member of the Presidential Guard for the Air Force. I worked at the Pentagon, I've been in the White House and the Capitol, and have seen things that made my stomach turn. And if you don't follow the mainstream, the power lines there, they'll blackball you, they will leak information about you, get your credibility ruined. So there's many dangers.

Of particular concern is the damage politics can do to Christians' "gospel witness." One Congregational man from Massachusetts observed that "You're more in a spotlight as a politician, so I think you've got to be extra careful, even as a Christian." An Assemblies of God woman from Texas cautioned, "Too often politicians become corrupt and tainted. And if Christians get involved in politics, that could taint and discredit their witness in the community, because politicians are not respected, they are not considered people with integrity. So it could actually hurt Christians' witness to others." One Congregational woman from Massachusetts warned about groups like the Christian Coalition, "We really have to be careful if we are that visible and vocal, raising that much money, that we don't start looking like the other guy that we're opposing. And sometimes I think that they and other similar groups do that." And a nondenominational man from Minnesota maintained:

> It can get corrupted. There's always that possibility of hurting the name of Christianity, because Christians are not perfect. But you get guys like Jim Baaker, and they're just human, no worse or better than anyone else, but they're in the limelight. That can be the draw, being in the limelight of politics. I think there's a lot of corruption there with the power. So there's a need to always be safeguarded that way. Again, you gotta watch the power and corruption type deal.

In a related way, a North Carolina Presbyterian man observed that politics "can't be used as a tool to prop up a church. It should not become an idol that the church props up. Like maybe there's a tendency to see America as a Christian nation, a danger of idolizing the state, of relying on the state to prop you up. Other dangers, power props—maybe there's a danger there of thinking that public religion is Christianity."

For these and other reasons we will explore further, there is a strong tendency among evangelicals to keep a distance from political life, and this counterbalances their desire to become politically involved. For some evangelicals, like one Baptist man from North Carolina, this sense of reservation is expressed as a turn toward personal faithfulness and purity: "The only thing I can be concerned about is myself, to be sure my own house is in order before I start going out and trying to change others." For others, like one independent church man from Minnesota, this distancing from politics focuses on personal evangelism: "I don't want to get sidetracked, you know, fighting this or that idea. Is that where you want to spend all your energies? Or is there something better to focus it on, as far as telling others about Christ and sharing the gospel. It's easy to get sidetracked."

For yet other evangelicals, political activism is displaced by a more important call to pray for the world. One Methodist woman from Illinois, for example, observed, "I think about the best thing you can do for a lot of our social problems is pray. [People like] Pat Buchannan, you know, are overstepping their bounds. When you say Jesus Christ is the answer, you're basically saying you should pray, that's all." Similarly, an Evangelical Free woman from Minnesota said, "I have a hard time saying we should be involved in politics, because social programs don't fix the root causes of the problems. Yeah, we should be involved, but we should be praying too. That's the main thing that we should be doing."

THE EVANGELICAL COUNTERBALANCE TO POLITICS

We begin to see, then, that many ordinary evangelicals feel a deep ambivalence about Christian participation in politics, and vacillate between two countervailing convictions. On the one hand, most ordinary evangelicals believe political life is an important realm for effecting Christian social influence, and they advocate Christian involvement through voting and lobbying. But this view is often counterbalanced, and sometimes even neutralized, by another set of convictions, central to the evangelical subculture, that we noted earlier in this book. These are the beliefs that the world's problems are ultimately rooted in spiritual problems residing in individual human hearts; that solving those problems requires an inner spiritual transformation that cannot be forced but only comes through voluntary personal religious conversion; and that the most effective strategy for real social change, therefore, is personal evangelism, for which the most effective tactics are building personal relationships with unbelievers, living good examples, and sharing the gospel at opportune moments.

These convictions reflect the core of the evangelical worldview, and in relation to them, evangelical political aspirations pale in significance. Whenever these convictions are in force, which for evangelicals is rather frequently, Christians who are seriously invested in politics feel like they are—to use an evangelical phrase regarding the championing of secondary theological matters—"majoring in the minors." In fact, the evangelicals we interviewed expressed these interrelated themes— the spiritual root of social problems, the ultimate need for personal conversion, the futility of forcing the gospel, and the importance of individual evangelism and influence—in connection with politics more frequently and consistently than any other view about politics mentioned. Some evangelical authors, in what may foreshadow a new pendulum swing away from politics, are now starting to emphasize these as well.[10] If we wish to truly understand evangelicals on politics, therefore, we must pay these themes close attention.

The evangelicals we interviewed never carried discussions about the world's social and political problems very far without registering their conviction that both the origin and solution to these problems are fundamentally moral and spiritual in nature. And the related point that inescapably followed was that dealing seriously with the world's problems requires people to change their hearts through conversion to Jesus Christ. According to a Presbyterian man from North Carolina, for example, "A fundamental problem facing the world today is sin. That's why we are here and not in Eden, with starvation and earthquakes and everything else. Jesus is God's solution to that fundamental problem. We are designed to have a full relationship with God, and Jesus is the answer to that." One Baptist man from Pennsylvania stated that "a lot of our social problems are spiritual in nature. If we could turn people who are on drugs and sexual immorality, and the gangs—if we could turn those people to Christ, we would change a lot of the social problems, fix a lot of those problems." Similarly, a Lutheran woman from Minnesota said during a discussion on solving the problems of drugs and welfare, "You're just sort of patching up if there's not a real inner change and dependence on God." And a mega-church woman from Georgia agreed: "I don't think without changing everybody's heart you're going to solve these problems." One Pietist church man from North Carolina remarked:

> A lot of the problems that we face as a nation, which are important problems, really have a moral or spiritual root to them. Society's morals aren't going to be Christian until everybody in society, or the vast majority, are Christian. It's just not going to happen. Even though I would like to see that, but again, it's the deal with free will. You know, I'm not benefiting anyone spiritually by telling them that they must accept my morals.

And a Christian and Missionary Alliance woman from Georgia said:

> People believe the only way things will ever get fixed is if the government steps in. The Christian is saying the only way things are going to get fixed up is if Christ changes the hearts of people and it comes from individuals. Clinton's camp is saying it takes a village. The church is saying it takes an individual who has a right relationship with Christ. That is where you start.

Evangelicals are equally clear about the implications of this view for politics. A man from Michigan attending a Missionary church, for example, noted that "Government just doesn't have the Spirit of God to transform people, so it is really difficult for them to actually make a difference. We end up just baby-sitting people, instead of actually seeing them become more complete."A nondenominational woman from Georgia claimed likewise, "Franklin Roosevelt said, 'If we educate the people, we give them jobs—boom, we'll have a better society,' and it didn't work. Politics can't accomplish that. You see the heart change, you know what I mean? It has to be a heart change."

The great majority of the evangelicals we interviewed were equally forthright about their conviction that it is wrong and futile to try to impose personal spiritual change on people—whether interpersonally or politically. Evangelicals believe that conversion to Christ is a work of God that involves a repentant heart, an individual decision, and a personal commitment, and that no human coercion can accomplish that. One Bible church woman from Illinois, for example, argued, "I don't think you can legislate a heart to be right. You can't legislate your way of life in and send somebody else's down the drain. I don't think Christians can push their lifestyle on everybody else in the United States. God gave them a choice." Likewise, a Congregational man from Michigan maintained:

> We need to allow people to choose other things, as God has given us free agency. Christians need to protect that right. And if it is an anti-Christian choice, so be it. I believe that is God's way. God says, 'Do this because you love me,' and we need to promote that. We have to protect the rights of people to reject it. I think we should try to achieve a movement of people towards a Christian way of life. But I don't think you can do that through legislative powers. You do that through influence ultimately on a one-on-one basis. Politics can't accomplish most things for Christians; it cannot convince one to accept Jesus Christ as their Savior.

This aversion to coercing people has clear political implications for many evangelicals, such as one Methodist man from Washington State: "I don't have difficulty with Christians getting involved in politics, as long as they can stand up to the pressures. But as far as changing laws so that Christians have a benefit, I'm not sure that is appropriate, because what you're doing in that situation is actually using your power to force people into a change." Indeed, for some evangelicals, any use of law to promote Christian morals actually destroys Christianity itself. A Baptist woman from Illinois observed, "Love of God and neighbor should govern our society, not as a law, but as a desirable trait. Not in a law. Once you've done that, you've destroyed Christianity. You

can take it back to the Spanish Inquisition." Outsiders who suppose
that evangelical religion is mostly about fear of hell might be surprised
to hear religious freedom of choice argued by evangelicals. But individual freedom has long been a dominant theme in the American evangelical spiritual worldview. Consider the statement of a woman from
Minnesota who attends an Evangelical Covenant church:

> I get real leery, because whose ideals of what's moral are we following?
> That's scary. Whenever a group has power like that, that's scary. I want to
> be able to choose how I think and what I believe in. I don't want to be told,
> this is how I have to live and what I have to read. You lose all your free-
> dom. God gave us freedom to be great and not to be enslaved again. I'm
> real leery if any group is telling me this is the way it should be.[11]

This kind of approach can foster a tolerant and relaxed element in
evangelical thinking about politics, as expressed in the words of a
Covenant church woman from California: "Christians should not try
to impose their solutions. I feel that in the long run things work out,
so sometimes it's better just to let something run its course."

Given these views, it follows that American evangelicals' regard
sharing the gospel with the unsaved individuals in their lives through
their words and good examples as the chief legitimate means to influence and redeem the world. As an evangelical Moravian man from
North Carolina said, "I struggle with these sorts of issues back and
forth in my mind. Currently, I believe the answer to that question
today is yes, Christians should be involved in politics. But I feel I
should be more concerned about bringing people into the kingdom
than solving all these problems."

Personal relationships, not legislative action, are seen as the key to
this process. Much dearer to the evangelical heart than the ballot box
is personal influence. Right relationships are central to evangelical theology and spirituality. Perhaps the most common buzz-phrase on evangelicals' lips is "a personal relationship with God" or "a personal relationship with Jesus Christ as Lord and Savior." Evangelicals are also
keen on fostering healthy relationships among believers through small
groups in churches and other "accountability" relationships, such as
those encouraged for men by the evangelical men's movement, Promise
Keepers. Family relationships also play a key role in evangelicals' faith
identity and socialization (which helps explain why evangelicals support family-oriented policy issues when they do engage politics). It is
not surprising, then, to find evangelicals emphasizing interpersonal relationships as the fundamental means of Christian influence.

"I can't solve the world's problems, but I can sure love the person next to me that is homeless or beaten up," observed one Presbyterian woman from North Carolina. "Christians do have solutions to the world's problems," she continued, "but I think we are paddling up stream. You know, it's not up to me to solve the world's problems, and yet I know I can on an individual basis. I can deal with that." To the question of how Christians should try to exert their influence, one Wesleyan woman from California replied, "Like I said, reaching out to people individually. That's how I would do it." One nondenominational man from Minnesota remarked, "That can be on an individual basis. Some go off and protest, write letters, express consumer rights. Personally, I like it more on a smaller basis as far as dealing with individuals and relationships, building on those types of things, influencing individuals, rather than group stuff on social issues." Likewise, a nondenominational man from Illinois said, "I think mostly we should be involved in people's lives on a personal level." And a Baptist man from North Carolina argued:

> As far as politics [goes], if we could just start with small groups, if everyone were to be servants to everyone else, those kinds of things are [as important as] politics. And the abortion issue, everything, would take care of itself. We can't heal or change those things until we change people's perceptions of them, and that takes time. It takes relationships. It takes loving and caring about those people. Everybody has their circle of influence in the people they have relationships with. I can't just jump out there and have any kind of credibility with people, because they don't know me. But people that I'm close to do know me. Relationships with non-Christians we try to take to where we can. We can't do everything.

Evangelicals do talk about sharing the good news with unbelievers verbally. But much more often they speak about the value of living a life of good example. As a Four-Square pentecostal woman from Pennsylvania said, "You go back to your actions and language, showing a Christ-like nature, because actions speak louder than words." This emphasis on example suggests a possible historical shift for a religious movement that in the past has so strongly accentuated the verbal proclamation of the gospel. Whether this is indeed a shift, or whether ordinary evangelicals have always placed this much faith in the lived good example, we cannot say. But they clearly do place faith in living good examples today. One Christian and Missionary Alliance man from Maryland recommended, "If they are not Christians, I think we should just try to use our good example. As Christians, we should not have hostile attitudes; we should just be loving and accepting of them. That in itself would create a better atmosphere." A Massachusetts woman who attends an independent church remarked, "Since I'm not in the know in a public way, it's only in the private way. I think we can start living as part of our daily life what we say we believe in, that we can impact those around us." Similarly, a Baptist woman from Georgia argued:

> You can't tell people what to believe. They need to see your example to say, "You know, I would like a little bit of that." You can't tell people to go to church and tithe. But if they see that in your life, it may be a good example for them. But you can't go out and preach morality to someone.

And this Congregational man from Massachusetts stated his opinion: "If Christians were compassionate in their communities, that example would be powerful. It wouldn't have to be dictating laws to do it. People see that as more effective—the whole idea of being an example, being the church, being a witness through an example."

Again, evangelicals we interviewed stressed that all such Christian influence must be noncoercive. When we asked a Baptist man from North Carolina what he thought of the Christian Coalition, he answered:

> There has to be groups like that, to educate people. There is a way to do that, a delicate way to do it. There's no way we can force our agenda. It's just like we feel a lot of times people force their agendas on us. It has to be something of mutual consent. The only thing we do is educate the people why we feel society is in the trouble it's in.

A Congregational man from Massachusetts argued likewise: "I think we should influence through lifestyle, through our lifestyle be an influence. Should we try and push it on people? No. We give them the opportunity. If they don't want it, I mean, they've got to make their own decisions."

For many evangelicals this often means that political power can be dangerous and counterproductive. A Presbyterian woman from North Carolina, for example, observed:

> You cannot legislate morality, I don't think. Morality comes from the heart, from the spirit. You can legislate punishment if people break the law and hurt others. [But] I think our country was founded on freedom and therefore we need to allow that. I appreciate that myself. But you can't legislate morality. It has to come with a changed heart.

The response of an independent church woman from California to the question whether or not Christians should try to exert an influence in society was similar:

> All the way. Not as Christians. I'm not thinking of Pat Buchannan running as a Christian. He was trying to represent Christians only. His idea that anti-abortion was the Christian idea, and you exclude everyone else's idea— I don't buy that. The Christian influence should be there, but without infringing on the rights of others, such as preventing them from having an abortion because you don't think it's right.
> *So what is the best means for Christian social influence?*
> Only by our example.

One may wonder how evangelicals square the view that Christian influence should be noncoercive and voluntaristic with their belief in the importance of Christians being involved in politics. The answer is that they do not always square them. More often than not, they struggle between the two viewpoints. The responses of three interviewees nicely capture this contradiction. In a discussion about morality and cultural pluralism, one Presbyterian woman from Washington State confessed:

> That's the thing I probably struggle with the most, because I think I should vote this [Christian] way, although it would be very dogmatic. But one of the things that as Christians we're supposed to [do is] go out and preach the gospel and convert people. We can't do that if we shove our beliefs down people's throats. I think we're deceiving our whole purpose if we're trying to convert people, [when] all we're doing is turning them off and away. I probably am very inconsistent in that, because I struggle with this all the time. But I don't think that we're ever gonna bring anybody to Christianity by shoving laws down their throats.

Personal evangelism clearly rivals and eventually trumps politics here. Similarly, a Georgia woman who attends an independent mega-church explained the tension she feels between possessing spiritually grounded solutions for the world's problems and putting them into effect:

> We can offer these solutions, but I don't know that we can bring it about totally. God said if you live this way you will benefit and things will be better. We can say, "We think this is the way it can go." And the other side says, "Well, we think this is the way." I think we have solutions based on what God has laid out. But implementing them is another problem.

Finally, notice the way one Baptist man from North Carolina, in a single stream of thought, began by affirming the need for resolute

Christian stands on contested political questions, but ended by talking himself into a spiritually focused political detachment:

> Probably the reason why things are the way they are right now is because a lot of Christians have turned their heads and won't take the stand or the initiative. But I think on major issues, you know, when it comes to abortion or school prayer or things like that, I think we have to. We're caught, and how we do that I'm not sure. We need to do it the best way to accomplish as much as possible, and I'm not sure how that would be done. But there is a need for us to do that. But you have to kind of look back in scripture. How did Christ deal with the Roman government or whatever in politics? He just didn't deal with it too much. He just pretty much said you pay your taxes like you are supposed to and respect the leadership of the government and stick with me pretty much.

EVANGELICAL OPPOSITION TO THE CHRISTIAN RIGHT

The convictions examined in the preceding section, which are deeply rooted in the American evangelical worldview and counterbalance any evangelical aspirations to political power, may help to explain the significant opposition to Christian Right political groups that exists among ordinary evangelicals. For every one evangelical we interviewed who expressed support for a Christian Right leader or organization, there was another evangelical who expressed outright opposition. It is true that, of all Americans, evangelicals are among the most likely to support Christian Right political organizations. But that does not mean that all or even most evangelicals support the Christian Right. In fact, a sizable segment of evangelicals clearly does not, as evidenced in many of our interviews. One Baptist woman from Illinois, for example, contended about Christian political organizations: "They're involved in politics to their own end. They're a nuisance; they bring Christianity a bad smell. I just don't like what they say, and I don't like their role in politics."

Some evangelicals' dislike of Christian Right groups, like that of one independent church woman has a passive and apathetic feel:

> I kind of get sick of hearing about the Moral Majority and Christian Coalition. I just tune it out when I hear it on television. I suppose it's okay for them to do that. This is America. I wouldn't really be a part of it.

Other evangelicals' feelings are more negative and more intense. A California woman attending a Covenant church, for instance, reported:

I get very angry at some of the uncompromising Christian leaders who speak out politically. I get angry because they present a picture that this is the way all Christians are, and I don't like to be stereotyped by them. Once I got mail from the Moral Majority and I refused it. I didn't want the mailman to think I subscribe to their beliefs. I get very angry with those outspoken and rigid and unthinking kinds of presentations of beliefs. I think there's a lot of room for diversity within Christianity, and that should be honored.

Much evangelical opposition to the Christian Right centers on the problem of forcing unbelievers to act as if they were Christians. One Christian and Missionary Alliance woman from Georgia, for example, said:

It is sometimes a problem when Christians get involved in politics; they want to make everything a moral issue: "God said don't do this, therefore what you are doing is wrong. I really don't like how you are living," and going at it with a moral approach. Christians take their morality along with them and forget that they are talking with someone who comes from a totally different way of thinking.

In a similar way, an Evangelical Free woman from Illinois, whose answers about Christian social influence centered largely on caring for the poor, complained:

You can't take people who don't have [financial] means [and tell them] stop having sex outside of marriage and using drugs, and then they're fine. I sound awful cynical and critical, don't I? But that's what they're doing right now, you know, like the Religious Right and stuff. Like I said, I think we should try and influence society in ways that have to do with our obligation to protect the poor and to speak for the voiceless. I don't think we need to try to influence society by making them live right in matters of personal morality if they're not believers.

Similarly, some evangelicals are repelled by what they see as an aggressive or self-righteous attitude on the part of the Christian Right. A Community church man from Colorado commented, "The danger is being [politically] proactive in a threatening way. That is a scary thing. The Christian Coalition scares me occasionally, I worry or get frustrated when they jump in there and start pointing fingers. I am really big on taking responsibility." Furthermore, some evangelicals, such as one Baptist man from South Carolina, view the Christian Right as already corrupted by power:

I have a concern with the Christian Coalition and the Jerry Falwells and James Kennedy and those people. They started out with the very best intentions and with the idea of making this a better world for everybody, [but they] couldn't handle the power and the glory that came with it. That's my opinion. Power became more important than the mission. There are folks like that around.

Even evangelicals who are generally sympathetic to Christian Right causes, like this Baptist man from Pennsylvania, can sour on the actual mechanics of their political mobilization:

It frustrates me when I get a piece of mail three to four times a week from the same organization. They go through a campaign that just keeps sending and sending, and that is a turnoff to me. You support them once and you are constantly barraged. Jerry Falwell was another one that I just kind of shut off on, because I thought it was getting to be overkill.

ONE ILLUSTRATIVE CASE

In this chapter I have pulled apart and systematically thematized evangelicals' views on politics for the sake of analysis. It might be helpful, however, to get a more holistic grasp on the matter as well. So I close this chapter by presenting one case that blends many of the themes and illustrates some of the complexities and tensions we have observed.

Bill Parker is a forty-two-year-old evangelical who attends a Missionary church in Michigan.[12] He is married and the father of two children, seven and eight years old. Bill thinks Christians have solutions to offer the world for its social problems. "Ultimately," he said, "it comes down to the individual caring for their neighbors," but also "being more willing to get involved with the political system and our government. We have a lot of power," Bill noted, "if we just used it." What would it look like, we asked, if Christians were using their political power? Bill answered somewhat ambiguously, "Well I mean, ultimately God comes into the scene with his Spirit and transforms people, and transforms society through people. When we as believers are being transformed—our ethics and morals and behaviors—our society follows suit and will automatically come back to that." Bill then mentioned specific areas where this could work: "things like fidelity, family values, and children being nurtured and cared for as a community," school systems that would assist parents rather than just baby-sit, and "better solutions to social needs like the welfare system." Still, he quickly noted the limits of governmental programs. (Bill was the one who said "Government just doesn't have the Spirit of God to transform people . . . so we end up just baby-sitting people.")

After a long discussion about the historically transformed role of the church in meeting social needs, we asked Bill, what about today? "Well, Jesus said we are to be in the world but not of it," he replied. "That is an oil-and-water blend that has to be very delicate. What it looks like is really very different for every culture; there is no pat solution." So, we pressed, should Christians get involved in politics? "That is another touchy one," he warned.

> We should be involved with politics to the extent that we are using the liberty we have in this country. I think we get in trouble when we become a political instead of a spiritual force. It is really important that you and I as individuals take our citizenship in this country and our rights and privileges seriously, by being active and writing letters and voting, being a participant in the positive things that our society does. But I don't believe we should get to the point where we think we can change this country through basically political interaction.
>
> *So you can't change this country?*
>
> You can make alterations. But my experience is that when we get caught up in the political realm, the spirit of the political realm takes over. We start doing unethical things in the name of our thing. We stop loving. We stop having compassion. We start taking sides. I don't think it's possible for us to take sides against whole parties and groups and be healthy.

Then Bill clarified, "I mean, I support groups like the Christian Coalition and groups like that, which bring attention to issues so we can be informed. But I don't think that we are going to be—as some believe in liberation theology—able to take over the world politically, usher the kingdom of God here." So, we probed, what can politics accomplish for Christians? "Again, that is a hard one." Bill explained:

> Scripture says that God raises up and tears down kings and governments, and as I look through the Bible I don't find a lot of Christian or moral, ethical governments. Quite often Christianity thrived in the most hateful of governments. And I didn't see Jesus go out. In fact he made a specific point not to be a king of this world. So I wrestle sometimes with how much influence we can have.

Bill then detailed how he had been involved through a Missionary church group in helping the evangelical Guatemalan military general Rios Montt become elected as president of Guatemala in the 1980s. The experience, it turned out, tempered his confidence in the Christian use of political power, and made him more cautious about thinking God is doing one thing or another in politics. "His ways aren't our ways. Sometimes I just don't understand what's going on."

Bill then commented that American presidents are "a pretty good reflection of our society's moral and ethical values. We elect people who allow us to do what we want." We had the chance to elect a Christian president with Pat Robertson, Bill noted, but Americans did not want him in office. All of this leaves Bill pretty pessimistic about governmental change: "We have developed a system of government that no one person can alter. You could bring God down himself and put Him in the presidency, and unless the people around the whole system changed with His views, we would still be stuck." And what does this mean for Christians involved in politics?

> You could put a godly man in the presidency, but the president is not as powerful as we want to think. We sometimes think that one politician is powerful enough to do some real change, but it is not [so]. We have a bureaucracy that is founded in deception. We have a government that is just totally based on greed and corruption. And until we get down to the fiber of that and change it, we are pretty hopeless.

The ambivalence, complexity, and incongruities in Bill's comments are copious and dense. Christians could have a lot of political power if they just used it. Yet nobody really ever has the power to change the system. Christians should be involved in a host of social issues and problems, like community socialization, schools, and welfare. But really it all comes down to individuals caring for their neighbors. When God's Spirit transforms individual Christians, society will follow suit. Yet society chooses to elect not godly presidents but ones who simply let people do what they want. Exactly what Bill means by "follow suit" is also unclear. Does he mean voluntarily or not? Bill "supports" groups like the Christian Coalition. But mostly in order to be "informed." In any case, he holds out little hope for changing the country through politics. More importantly, he says, Christians get in trouble when they "become a political rather than spiritual force." Politics turns out to be quite corrupting even for Christians. Still, it is very important, says Bill, that Christians take advantage of their political rights as citizens. Yet it is also true that Jesus rejected worldly political power. So Bill wrestles with how much influence Christians really should have. Bill apparently would have liked to have seen Pat Robertson elected President. On the other hand, what is the point, since even God could not change the United States government? In general, Bill finds the Christianity-and-politics issue "a hard one" and "a touchy one." He started off the discussion relatively positive and confident. But he finished with pessimism and uncertainty.

Is Bill Parker a supporter of the Christian Right or not? The problem is that this question presupposes a coherence of perspective and unity of purpose that is in fact missing in Bill, as in many other evangelicals. In some ways and at some times he is a Christian Right supporter. In other ways and times he is not. Would a Christian Right organizer be happy to have Bill as a core supporter? Probably not. He lacks fire in his belly. More broadly, might Bill's political views represent a threat to American freedom and pluralism? In some ways perhaps yes, in other ways clearly no. Probably most threatening to freedom and pluralism are not any of Bill's religious convictions, but his general despair about the prospects for a vibrant American government. Is Bill Parker prepared to employ the force of law to impose Christian standards and morals on all Americans? Well, he seems friendly to Pat Robertson's 1988 presidential bid. On the other hand, Bill also expressed many of the typical evangelical convictions that tend to neutralize legislative Christianizing: an ultimate emphasis on individual spiritual conversion; anxiety about political corruption and a misplaced Christian mission; a general awareness that God's ways cannot easily be identified with specific politicians, parties, and programs; and a recognition of the limited capacity of politics to accomplish anything of lasting, much less eternal, value.

No one evangelical is "representative" of all evangelicals. In this case, Bill Parker is somewhat more gloomy about the prospects for the American government than are most evangelicals. And his brief excursion into the brutal Guatemalan politics of the early 1980s makes him somewhat more experienced in difficult matters of state than most. But in the ambivalence, complexity, and incongruities that characterize his thinking about politics, some of which appear to counterbalance and perhaps even neutralize any Christian Right tendencies he may embrace, Bill is not atypical of most evangelicals. Those interested in understanding and making claims about American evangelicals and politics, therefore, would do well to remember Bill Parker, and the complex and wide-ranging voices of the many other evangelicals given expression in this chapter.

CONCLUSION

In 1981, Frances Fitzgerald—fresh from a first-hand look at Jerry Falwell's Thomas Road Baptist Church in Lynchburg, Virginia—coined a popular description of evangelical political activists as a "disciplined, charging army."[13] That vivid image has stuck. It is not an uncommon fear in parts of American culture that evangelicals are a uniform body of zealous and obedient devotees now being mobilized by the Christian Right for a massive, concerted political campaign to seize power.

But we have seen that this image of evangelicals is unfounded, to say the least. When we penetrate with open ears beyond the standard and sometimes hysterical depictions of evangelical politics, we find in evangelicalism instead an enormous amount of diversity, complexity, ambivalence, and disagreement. This has important political consequences, for it generates a multidimensional field of complex clusters of views about faith and politics. In fact, only a minority of evangelicals represent anything like the political threat that evangelicals' antagonists fear. Instead, when it comes to politics, the millions of ordinary evangelicals look not like a disciplined, charging army, but something more like a divided and hesitant extended family.

CHAPTER FOUR

Evangelicals on Education

With David Sikkink

EVANGELICAL OPINION REGARDING politics is multivocal and ambivalent. But what about evangelical views on public schools? We would expect, according to the critics, that evangelicals are united in their opposition to "secular" public schools, and strident in battles over religion in public education. In a book review entitled "Schooling for Salvation: Christian Fundamentalism's Ideological Weapons of Death," which criticizes a highly influential ethnographic study of a fundamentalist Christian school, Peter McLaren highlights the social pathologies of "born-again" Christianity, which, he maintains, occupies a "fulcrum position in American society." The review, published in Boston University's *Journal of Education*, inventories among these pathologies: "intolerance and sanctified closed-mindedness"; "strict adherence to authoritarian ideology"; belief in "a loving God who loves most those who truly know their place" . . . and "who is comfortably male and white"; "a thinly veiled disdain for egalitarian democracy and a woeful indifference to diversity and ecumenism"; theological doctrines "wherein [lie] the seeds of all holy wars"; the push for "a religious/state alliance in the name of democracy" and "neotheocracy;" and "a basic distrust of the mind." McLaren concludes: "Shadowed by the logic of totalitarianism, violence has become the purifying aesthetic to many growing right-wing militant factions who wish to purge North America of blacks, Asians, Arabs, and Jews. Such xenophobia is but one of the consequences of the pathological and destructive structuring of relations brought on by the resurgence of fundamentalist evangelism."[1]

Critics such as McLaren argue: Aren't evangelicals part of the Christian Right movement, which sees everything from lower test scores to teen pregnancy as the result of God being "kicked out" of public schools? Aren't evangelicals the shock troops for battles over school prayer and teaching evolution in the schools?[2] Aren't evangelicals making moves to put conservative Christians on local school boards and intimidate textbook publishers?[3] According to popular conception, evangelicals are fomenting a culture war over the direction of public schools at least on schooling issues,[4] and their moral absolutism makes them fervent and uncompromising in their efforts to bring religion back into schools through political means. Many believe that these activities show the true colors of evangelicals, whose ultimate goal is to impose a Christian America through confrontational tactics in local schools.

Further, the argument goes, when evangelicals are *not* involved in battles to "Christianize" the public schools, it is only because they are distracted by their secessionist efforts to build Christian schools or educate their children at home. Thus, they seek explicitly Christian, sectarian schooling either through organized political efforts to "bring God back into public schools," or by fleeing what they see as secular humanism in public schools, in order to unite home, school, and church into a tight web that walls out the secular world.[5] Susan Rose writes in her 1988 book, *Keeping Them Out of the Hands of Satan: Evangelical Schooling in America*, that evangelicals feel that the social fabric is disintegrating and that they are being assailed by satanic forces beyond their control. In response, they turn to Christian schooling to "bring morality back to the United States," and to gain "greater control over the socialization of their young—and thereby greater influence in society. . . . Having felt dispossessed or uprooted throughout much of the twentieth century, contemporary evangelicals have mobilized in an attempt to reclaim control."[6] Elsewhere Rose writes:

> Contemporary evangelicals condemn the liberalism and secularization of American society, arguing that it issues a license of outrageous freedom to people of all persuasions. . . . A politically and socially conservative movement, the New Religious Right wants to restore the common ground that once belonged to white, Anglo-Saxon Protestants who professed a common core Christianity. Evangelicals believe that this old core, replete with patriarchal and patriotic beliefs, was destroyed when it expanded to include the interests of other religious, racial, ethnic, and special interest groups. Their

response has been to call for a return to the practices and values of "Old-Time Religion" and to the authority of the "traditional" American family.[7]

Evangelicals want to secure their children for God, according to Rose, before they are seduced by the secular world and secular humanism. Whether through efforts to impose a Christian America in the public schools, or to unite religion and education in private Christian schools, critics argue, evangelicals disrupt democratic life by burdening it with sectarian religion, and fragment the public sphere by their refusal to participate in public education.

This chapter considers these possibilities through in-depth examination of evangelicals' general orientation toward public schools, the specific changes they would like to see in public schools, and the means they favor for accomplishing these changes.[8]

The results of our inquiry complicate the simplistic story of evangelicals battling in a culture war over the nation's schools. The evangelical movement nurtures a strategy of "engaged orthodoxy"—upholding traditional theological views while actively working to influence or even transform the surrounding society and culture.[9] Evangelicals see involvement in the public schools in terms of this tradition—as an expression of their commitment to a public presence of religious individuals, who are a "witness" to the non-Christian world. While most evangelicals we talked with are attracted to Christian schooling, they are also reluctant to abandon public schools. Opting out of public schools to create an isolated religious world of schooling, family, and church seems to conflict with their sense of a calling to the public world, including public schools. Rather than discouraging evangelical public involvement, problems in public schools seem further to increase the importance of maintaining a presence in public institutions. That is where their influence is most needed, the majority of evangelicals say.

Evangelicals' commitment to public education, however, may depend on their hope for a change in public schools. Among our respondents, a significant minority were quick to bemoan the loss of school prayer, and to argue that Christian views should not be discriminated against in public schools. If evangelicals favor involvement in public schools, we want to know, what do they hope to accomplish there? Do they hope to remake the schools in their own image? Rather than accepting the division between public life and religion that is typical of public institutions in the United States, evangelicals may demand that religion and morality follow their children into the classroom. But we will see that most evangelicals have something quite different in mind for public schools than their cultural critics fear.

In fact, we found that most ordinary evangelicals tend to associate problems in the public schools with problems in the home, and do not spend much time talking about secular humanism as an insidious force in the schools. Though wanting greater attention to morality and ethics in public schools, they do not seem fundamentally opposed to the structural divide between knowledge and morality that is institutionalized in public schooling. Thus the changes ordinary evangelicals would like to see in public schools often sound little different than those the average American wants: teach the "basics" well, avoid "social" issues, reduce safety problems in the schools, and so on. Beyond these concerns, there is a generally expressed wish for more respect for authority from students, and more consistent and severe punishment for offenders. Oftentimes the loss of student respect for authority is pinned on unsupportive parents who are "sue-happy," as one evangelical put it, and a legal system that encourages this. How evangelicals understand these problems, however, does not appear much different from the perception of the average American parent, who, like parents of many earlier generations, bemoans a decline in respect for authority among youth. Regarding issues of morality and religion in public schools, most of the changes that evangelicals would like to see are framed in a way that at most calls for "equal time" for the Christian viewpoint, rather than the "Christianizing" of public schools.

We examine as well the strategies favored by evangelicals for introducing changes in public schools. These strategies show marks of the evangelical preference for interpersonal strategies of change and uneasiness with organized attempts to institute change that characterize the evangelical tradition. They also reflect a particular, evangelical version of religious individualism, as well as the idea of a custodial relationship between evangelical religion and American culture. Evangelicals think that the presence of Christians in public institutions in itself provides a preserving effect ("salt and light," in evangelical code) on American culture and society.

Efforts to transform public schools, in the view of most evangelicals, must be made through individual Christians, who appear somehow different in their personal relationships with others in the schools. Evangelicals believe their "presence" will have a positive impact—almost by some kind of hidden osmosis—on teachers, parents, and children at school, and therefore on the schooling institution as a whole. Evangelicals almost never spell out the exact means by which this presence works its wonders on public schools, but they do emphasize that truly effective change comes through personal, one-to-one influence, rather than through organized, power-centered, over-arching strategies for structural change.

A MINORITY OF RADICAL VOICES

The first thing that we noted in our interviews is that evangelicals, while broadly supportive of involvement in public schools, are divided over issues of schooling. The growing legitimacy of alternative schooling for children creates dilemmas for evangelical parents. For example, a woman from a nondenominational church in Illinois expressed evangelicals' typical reservations about separating themselves from the world through private schooling:

> Kids are going to go out in the world sometime. You can't totally shelter them from everything. I am not against home schooling—and my kids are talking about doing that—but we're separating [from the world]. Kids eventually are going to get out there.

At the same time, she also fit the culture warrior mold. When we asked her how public schools are doing, she responded in no uncertain terms:

> Lousy. They're going downhill more and more. In grade school, homosexuality doesn't need to be taught. I am not against sex education in school, since school is the only place [many children] are going to get it. But the way they're doing it now is very immoral—providing condoms and things like that. I just don't think that's right.

A small number of evangelicals we interviewed had decided to abandon public schools, but cited not religious reasons but the general dysfunction of public schools as the reason for their choice. When we asked one independent church man from Ohio how he thought the public schools are doing, he replied:

> Horrible, in our area. Absolutely atrocious.
> *What's the problem?*
> Money is poured into everything but our school systems, it seems. If the mayor wants a raise, he gets his raise. If a rich community needs to have their roads repaved, they get them repaved. But our school systems may be overcrowded, not enough teachers, less books, violence in our school system—kids carrying guns and knives. The school system scares me. That's

why my child is going to private school. I'm not sending my child to a public school.

An equally small number of evangelicals regarded schooling issues as a key front in a culture war. The response of one Presbyterian woman from Ohio to a question about what Christians should try to achieve through politics was that schools need God, prayer, and Christian leaders:

> Change the way things are! They need to bring God back into the schools, they need to bring prayer back into the schools. We need to just put Christian leaders in there. I really think that a lot of these problems we're having would be solved.

Yet after making such a classic culture-war statement, she qualified her views on school prayer by saying that she primarily supports the idea of voluntary Bible studies outside of school time.

A small minority of evangelicals we interviewed supported the infusion of a religious ethos and explicitly religious instruction into schooling. Some of these evangelicals felt that prayer should be imposed in schools because they believe America is a Christian nation. A Baptist woman from New Jersey defended her support for teacher-led school prayer, even when we pressed her about whether mandatory school prayer is fair to atheist parents:

> It's doing more good than harm, you know.
> *So you think it should remain and they can just kind of adjust to it?*
> Uh huh. If they want to close their ears or whatever. That's what our nation is. That's what it was founded on, and that's what it is. They would have to totally throw out everything that the nation began with to have a nation without any religion or any God in it.

Others went beyond the issue of school prayer. A Wesleyan woman from Michigan thought that in public schools "you have to have prayer, and I think you need to be able to talk about the Bible and use it in class." A black woman from Georgia who attends a nondenominational church, for example, had no doubt about how she would like to see her faith reflected in public schools:

> You know, I would love to see a class taught on the Bible. I mean, we got black history, we got evolution, we got all this other stuff—why not? Mandatory. It's like reading, writing, and arithmetic: make it mandatory.

A Michigan woman who belongs to a nondenominational church, when asked how she would like to see her faith and values reflected in public schools, replied, "School prayer. I would like to see a class taught about Christianity, about Christ. I would turn it into a Christian school, basically." A Nazarene man from Oregon was clear that schooling for children should directly integrate religious interpretations of historical events:

> We believe that there are tremendous accounts in history that give validity to scripture, give validity to the Christian teachings, and they're being ignored in the public schools. For instance, George Washington—when you read about him in a secular school you don't hear anything about his Christian faith. But in the Christian school setting you hear about how God divinely helped us during the revolution, and without some divine miracles we would not have won the revolution. Things like when the British were coming in to attack and the fleet was wiped out in the storm, it came out of nowhere. And if that hadn't happened, if the fog hadn't moved across the river when George Washington took his troops and escaped to Valley Forge—just one thing after another that you say, "that's not coincidence." But it's not taught in the public schools and so you lose the value of understanding how God has worked in our history. You lose perspective on the purpose of scientific investigation: to confirm the truth that's in the Bible, not to contradict it.

While this man started with a general concern that public schools ignore religion in history classes, he went on to link the propagation of faith directly with the teaching of history. This prescription for schooling seems to imply that Christians should turn schools into something closer to Sunday School than public school.

Yet even among those interviewees who wanted a major incorporation of religion into public schools, very few advocated equally drastic means to achieve school reform. Almost all evangelicals we spoke with were sensitive about the extremist tactics of some Christian organizations. When we asked a Michigan woman from a Presbyterian church how Christians should bring about change in schools, she favored "table discussions, meetings, versus, say, riots and picketing and that sort of thing."

But these various minority, radical voices do not drown out the dominant, more moderate evangelical opinion regarding public schools, which emphasizes the need for the presence of individual Christians in the classroom. The dominant evangelical voice, in fact, is very uncomfortable with the idea of imposing religious perspectives on public schools through official policy, and is ill at ease with the notion of turning public schools into Christian schools in disguise.

BEING THERE

The dominant evangelical viewpoint regarding public schools that emerged in our interviews was one of feeling "called" to public schools despite—and sometimes because of—the "downfall" of the schools. The response of one woman from Massachusetts who attends a Congregational church and has a young child exemplifies this general view:

> We're feeling led right now to send our kids to public school to be a positive influence. If you just took all Christians out of public anything, how is the truth going to be spread and how are people going to become Christians? They're not. I just don't think we can run away from it. What I'm hoping is that my child will have a strong enough foundation at home to be able to go out into a public school and decipher right from wrong and to stand up for what he believes and to be a positive influence and to be a light. That's kind of what I'm hoping for and that's my goal. And I just feel very strongly that we need to be missionaries and our children do, too.

This response epitomizes evangelicals' view of their relationship to American culture and public life. It reflects the value they place on integrating their faith into their everyday lives, especially in the "secular" world. According to this respondent—and consistent with the evangelical missionary impulse—evangelicals have a personal calling to take a stand in public institutions, not withdraw from them. And in public schools this should happen through individual evangelical children, who non-Christians should see as somehow different from non-Christian children because of their religious training in the home.

Evangelical support for public schools was not always expressed as a calling. For some evangelicals, it follows from their belief that public schooling provides Christian children with a needed time of trial so that their faith does not fall apart when they enter the "real world." When we asked one woman from a Presbyterian church in Michigan if Christians should send their children to Christian, home, or public schools, she expressed this "boot camp" view of public schooling:

> I think you have a better chance of instilling good Christian values if you keep your children in a totally Christian environment, and not expose them to the non-Christian values out there. But if they are going into the real world to work, they are going to be flattened because they have not developed through the years the protective mechanisms that they need. And it would make it very tough for them to enter real society if they had not been exposed to any of it.

Similarly, a man from an Evangelical Free church in Minnesota commented that evangelical children need the social skills gained through public schools, and that while Christian schools have some advantages, "in a Christian school, kids are kind of sheltered in their holy huddle, and when they come out I think there is a tendency just to go crazy."

The differences of viewpoint between evangelicals and public insti-tutions are not a threat to religious faith, nor do they create a bound-ary to overcome. Rather than causing evangelicals to withdraw from public schools, the conflict between the "secularity" of public schools and the religious orientation of the family can be an asset. For engag-ing one's faith with secular American public life is a positive and im-portant way of solidifying evangelical religious identity. A woman from an independent church in North Carolina claimed, "We're glad for the kinds of life experiences that our kids have [in public schools], and to the exposure they have that isn't necessarily Christian. We use that sometimes to define the differences." A man from an Evangelical Free church in Minnesota agreed that public schools are important for Christian children:

> They are going to grow up in a secular society that isn't going to be the way they want it to be. And they have to learn that they can't run away from that and hide. Part of what they learn as they grow up is that there are a lot of differences and a lot of different people, and you don't have to buy into someone else's view. You can take your own views and carry them with you. You learn everything you can in the course work you do, and when it be-gins to violate the principles of what you believe in, then you gotta be alert to that.

Religion has a custodial relationship with public life, according to most evangelicals. Evangelicals typically see public institutions—along with society and culture in general—as naturally inclined to deterio-rate, and they think religion can have a preserving effect. In the con-text of the public schools, this is conceived of as being a presence within, rather than exerting reform from without. One Nazarene woman from Oregon explained, "God calls us to be light and salt in the world, and I think if all Christians take their kids and put them in Christian schools, then who's gonna be over here to be salt and light to the rest of the world?" Evangelical custodianship of public schools is centered on the actions of individual evangelical children in school. As a woman from an independent charismatic church in Illinois put it, "Well, if you take all of the Christian children out of the public schools, that's a sad thing for the other kids." So, just by "being there," Christian kids are "salt and light." When we asked an Evangelical Free woman from Minnesota if she thought Christians should send their children to public schools or Christian schools, she replied, "Basically they should go to public schools, because if they're out of the public school there isn't going to be any influence—there's not gonna be anybody there even. [Christian school] is just like hiding in a church and not getting involved. Even if it's kids [in the public schools], they have a strong witness." The preserving effect of individual Christians in public schools extends to parents, according to a pentecostal woman from Oregon:

> If your kids are in any school, whether it is public school or private school, the school is a good place to be. I have friends that have given up having a job and a second income in their family to be there in that school. To try to be an influence, to be an aid for the teacher. And, without the kids knowing it, pray for those kids. [My friend] walks around and just prays in her head sometimes. She will see a kid having trouble, and she walks up behind them and just prays for peace and a cooperative spirit in that classroom, for a cooperative spirit within the teacher and themselves. Just that, just being there.

The preserving influence of religion on the public schools comes through individual evangelicals acting as citizens rather than explicitly as Christians. As we have seen already in this book and will see again as well, in the evangelical subculture the custodial nature of the relationship between religion and society does not imply that religion should provide the basis for transforming public institutions through large-scale structural or political change. Rather, evangelicals see religion contributing to the support of public institutions through interpersonal relationships. "Being there" as individuals is the dominant evangelical strategy on public schooling issues.

FAMILY MATTERS

The general orientation of evangelicals toward public education—that they should remain a preserving presence in public schools and have a positive effect through interpersonal influence—shapes evangelical talk about the problems in public schools and what changes are necessary. The majority see the public schools as a leading social problem, but they articulate their specific concerns in "secular," not religious, terms. For instance, a large majority of the evangelicals we interviewed regarded public school problems as a reflection of problems in the family. They also expressed concern that drugs and violence are making the schools unsafe, and that schooling is not focused on basic education—

"reading, writing, and arithmetic." Concern that secular humanism is infiltrating textbooks and curricula was in fact not a dominant theme.

Since evangelical traditions provide cultural tools for seeing social problems as interpersonal issues,[10] it is not surprising that the most common response we heard to problems in public schools is not that religion and morality have been removed from public education—though that is also a concern—but that morality and values have broken down in the family. One Illinois woman from a nondenominational church identified "the problem of children not being responsible" as the biggest problem in public schools and explained, "Parents are not making them to be responsible." When we asked a woman from a Lutheran church in Michigan what causes problems in the schools, she responded, "Parents aren't teaching the children at home. You can't blame the teacher altogether. It starts at home; it starts with the family, with Mom and Dad instilling proper morals." The results of family problems come to school through the children. One Evangelical Free man from Minnesota summed up the evangelical view on the centrality of the family when we asked him what he thought was the biggest problem in America:

> Breakdown of the family. There are so many divorces and single-parent families. It's just amazing now what the school does today. Anything that comes up is all added to the school—"let the teachers do it." And they're just overwhelmed with all this stuff from the families. If there is a family, both the mom and the dad are working. Or maybe as a single parent, the kids are "latchkey," and that whole business. So much of the responsibility of raising children has been given up by the family and taken over by something else, like the school, and that's what the biggest problem in our country is.

If family breakdown explains public school problems in general, it also lies behind specific educational problems. We asked a Presbyterian woman from Colorado what was causing lower test scores:

> Lack of interest on the parents' part. Kids are not coming home and doing their homework. There is no family unit involved at home. There are too many people working, too many moms working. And then by the time they get home they are tired, they are making dinner, and there is an hour before they need to go to bed.

An evangelical Moravian man from North Carolina explicitly avoided placing blame on educators and educational methods; rather he linked discipline problems to the lack of parental support:

I think public schools are having a tough time. I really do. And I credit the breakdown of the family for that. I don't think that the educational institution is really the problem. You know, they're dealt a tough hand. Let's face it: it doesn't matter if you have good educational theory or bad educational theory if you've got bad raw materials. If you have discipline problems, and whatever you try to teach isn't being reinforced [in the home]—that is the problem. Not that the children themselves are bad.

But in terms of the troubles public schools might be having—do you think much of it is traceable to your earlier concern about federal government regulation?

I honestly think that the problem is a problem at home. It's a problem of discipline.

It would not be difficult to find fifty or more similar responses among our interviews. The most frequent evaluation of school problems was in terms of family breakdown. Change must start in the family if problems in the school are to be solved.

Secular School and Sacred Home.   Even when evangelicals talk about changes that need to be made within school walls, they generally respect the cultural divide that exists in America between a "private" world that includes morality and religion, and a "public" world of economic and political life that is supposed to operate according to secular, rational logic.[11] Most Americans, including evangelicals, make a distinction between the "sacred" role of families and religion, and the complementary, "secular" role of public schools. In fact, evangelicals seem to hold an exaggerated version of the concept that the family is a particularly sacred space, distinguished by direct, interpersonal, and normatively governed relations. We asked one Evangelical Free woman from Colorado if Christians should try to make public schools more Christian, or more open to incorporating Christian beliefs or practices. Notice the structural divide between the "sacred" family sphere and the "secular" schooling sphere in her response.

No. I say that because I think people who want to make schools more Christian have an agenda that we want to say prayers when we say the Pledge [of Allegiance]. And there are certain kinds of things they want to be teaching in the classroom that we don't need to get into in public schooling. It's something that belongs in Christian education, our churches, and our families. You're not going to be able to teach everything kids need to know in school.

According to most evangelicals we interviewed, the family is expected to give the children a foundation of morality and values upon which the public schools can accomplish their primarily secular work. The public sphere is not expected to mirror the private world of family, friends, and church. A woman from an independent evangelical church in Michigan affirmed the association of the sacred with family and church: "I think to take a position that we want to have prayers recited in school by teachers is a wrong-headed approach. I think we need to be looking more at our lives and making sure that we're immersing our children in church and Sunday School, making sure that our children have a prayer time." An Ohio man who attends a nondenominational church, said that "it would be the moral obligation of the parents to teach Christian standards, not our school system. That is my belief. Now it is also my belief that if they want to exercise their Christian beliefs at school they should be allowed—as in prayer." An Illinois woman from an independent church, when asked how she would like her religious values reflected in public schools, seemed to go out of her way to say that traditional Christian attitudes about sex education are not as important as the value of "information" on resolving conflictual relationships for children:

> I don't know if you're familiar with conflict resolution, but it's a strategy for teaching children to resolve conflicts in a nonviolent manner. I think that's one thing that parents are not opposed to. I wish that when people who tend to be more on the religious right oppose sex education, they would understand that there are parents who are not doing the right thing as parents in the home. So the proper information is not getting out. And those children need that information. But, the [Religious Right] gets wrapped up in, "I don't want my child to hear this [sex education] stuff." That's a problem. If [only] we could help those people understand that it would be okay to teach that.

There are many examples from our interviews demonstrating that most evangelicals' complaints about public schools are not driven by the sense that the divide between religion and public life is illegitimate. In fact, as we have seen, evangelicals tend to regard the "worldly" aspects of public schooling as useful for strengthening the faithful. Acceptance of the sacred-secular divide is reflected in the response of a Presbyterian man from Colorado. When we asked if there was any way that he would like to see his values reflected more within public schools, he answered:

> Probably not. Because if I send my child to public school, it is no different than him or her going to work after college in the world. The world is corrupt. Public schools are corrupt. They are going to see that. You can't build

a shelter around your child. All you can do is give them the tools to defend themselves or to escape harm on their own, and then throw them with the lions.

Struggling with Morality.   Most of the evangelicals we spoke with framed the major changes that they wanted to see in public schools— such as greater emphasis on morality and "basic" education, and "equal time" for religious perspectives—in terms that respect the sacred/secular divide. A significant minority even considered morality and religion out of bounds for public schools. A Christian and Missionary Alliance woman from Georgia, for example, thought that "morality should be taught at home, and it's something they should see in the life of their parents. I don't want anyone teaching my child morality." An Ohio woman from a Presbyterian church, when we asked her if she would like to see a specifically Christian morality taught in the public schools, responded, "I don't see where you could teach it unless you were a Christian yourself." These evangelicals either do not trust public school teachers to teach particularistic, Christian morality correctly, or they think that public schools are not the appropriate arena for teaching it. A Presbyterian woman from Michigan made a distinction between giving instruction in Christian sexual morality, and teaching "facts" about sex. Her response was actually to the question: what are your main concerns about American society?

> Schools—how the government wants schools to educate our children on sex. That bothers me. They are going to take over a job that I think should be handled in the home. They want to educate my children about what they think is right versus what we as a family think is right. I don't have a problem with [teaching] certain facts. But when they get into condoms and birth control, and what [people] should do and shouldn't do, I have a real problem with that.

Both the evangelicals who voiced the view that particularistic religious morality is inappropriate for public schools and those who would not entrust that morality to public school teachers respect and maintain the cultural distance between a "sacred" private space for family, friends, and faith, and a "secular" world of competition and technical efficiency. For many evangelicals, this view of the relation between public schools and morality extends to their understanding of the relation of public schools and religion. A Baptist woman from Texas stated that:

> Whenever I send my [eighth-grade] son to school, I expect him to get an education in the eighth grade. I don't expect the school to teach them religion. That is my job and the job of the church. I send them to the public school to learn to read, to write, to be able to do math problems, to learn the history of the world. I don't send him to that school to be moralized.

These examples show that evangelicals' great concern about moral and religious truth does not lead, as some analysts would have us think, to a desire to impose religious perspectives in public schools. Rather, among a significant number of evangelicals we interviewed, the particular regard with which they hold their perspectives on morality and religion created greater reluctance to leave these areas to those without specific religious credentials—including school authorities.

Many evangelicals we interviewed said that public schools *should* place greater emphasis on upholding the morality of the family sphere—or at least should not denigrate the morals, values, and religion that families are trying to teach their children. But they more usually framed morality in public schools in terms of a general moral sense that would seem uncontroversial for any public institution, and lead to little debate with most nonevangelical American parents. An Evangelical Free man from Minnesota wanted public schools to teach "just the Boy Scout/Girl Scout code of ethics kind of thing . . . some fundamental values like respect, hard work, honesty, discipline—those kinds of things." We asked a Presbyterian woman from Ohio about the Christian goals she would like to see in the schools, and her response did not go beyond the concern for greater discipline and respect for others that is common everywhere.

> I think that respect and discipline are pretty much the only Christian part that you can get in there. We have to learn to respect human beings, and because we don't, we have so many problems. So, if we can enforce that more in the early education years, hopefully it will carry over.

A California woman who attends an Evangelical Covenant church expressed the view that general morality, rather than Christian morality, should be taught in public schools, as a response to pluralism: "Christian teaching—I don't think it should be taught in the public schools. I think it's a reality in Southern California that we are so diversified that it's unrealistic to try to promote only one point of view. But as far as the moralities and the ethics of Christianity, certainly."

The evangelical demand for greater moral training in school is often not far removed from the now widespread push for "character education" in public schools. A California man who attends a Nazarene church, for example, explained what he would like to change in the public schools:

> I would like to see more of an emphasis on teaching character as opposed to information, especially these days when we're in an age of technology where information is so radically changing, and will in the future become so rapidly available to us in different ways, that the need to learn that the way we did when I was in school is totally unnecessary. So I would say there could be much more emphasis on character. People [with character] are gonna be way better prepared for the future, because that's really ultimately what they have to sell.

The kind of general character education this man suggests, which has value in the marketplace, is unlikely to offend anyone. A Baptist woman from California spoke even more explicitly about instruction in general character:

> Of course they need to learn how to add and subtract, but I feel like manners—just common respect for others—should be expressed. I feel like this should all be brought up in the classroom, too. It's like a mini little world in there, and I think that all of this needs to be addressed at home and at school.

Other evangelicals said that the schools should instill general morality in children, but then spoke about morality mostly in terms of the morals of the Ten Commandments. We asked the question: "Should Christian morality be taught in the public schools or just in the home?" One Southern Baptist woman from South Carolina replied:

> I do think that most people feel it is wrong to steal, and to lie, and to kill, and things like that. To that extent, I can't see that morality being turned down by anybody. I think those things are acceptable to everybody.

A Presbyterian woman from Maryland responded: "Just morals, right from wrong. I am not saying public schools should force every kid to pray, but things that would be basic for society—don't steal." And a woman from an independent evangelical church in Michigan answered:

> I don't think you can teach exclusively a Christian morality from the Bible. But I think you can teach virtues and morals that come from the Ten Commandments about not hurting people or killing people. And these are moral absolutes. And I think virtues should be taught more in schools: a work ethic, responsibility, caring for your neighbor. Those are absolutes and they are universal.

Each of these evangelicals recommended a general morality that is unlikely to bring much protest from the average American, rather than a more "sectarian" morality, for public schools. When evangelicals talk about wanting more emphasis on morality in the public schools, they nevertheless generally accept and honor the cultural divide between "private" morality and religion, and the "public" duties of public schools.

Putting Basic Education First.   Many evangelicals we spoke with recommended that public schools focus on "basic" education, and avoid what are considered "social" matters. An Ohio man from an independent church wanted public schools to "go back to the fundamentals—the reading, the writing, the arithmetic." A Presbyterian woman from Michigan thought that "liberal" educators are getting "away from guidelines, and moving into 'how you feel' and 'let your mind expand and make your own decisions.' They're into a lot of touchy-feely stuff versus learning the basics." In some cases, the endorsement of basic education was the flip side of the evangelical sense that nonevangelicals could not appropriately handle the particulars of evangelical views of morality and religion. A Georgia woman in an independent church made this argument explicit in her discussion of the most important things that children should get out of their elementary and high school education:

> They should know how to read, to write legibly and logically. And they should be able to do relatively simple math. That's the function of the school.
> *Are there any Christian goals that the schools should have?*
> I have never thought that that was the function of the public school system. I think that is my function. They should not do anything that is against what I believe, and what I'm teaching my children morally and spiritually. But I've never thought that that was the function of the school system. To be the religious teacher for my children—that's my role as a parent. I want [the schools] to teach them how to read, write, and do math.

A North Carolina woman in an independent church agreed, and added that too much emphasis on social issues also gets in the way of what schools should really be about: "Well, I don't think you go to school for life experiences as your primary goal. I think you go for a solid education in core knowledge kinds of things, as opposed to values or something like that." When we asked a Michigan woman from an nondenominational evangelical church what schools should focus on, she constructed a divide between social issues and general knowledge: "The basics. History—true history—reading, writing, math, English. What they are teaching them now—women's studies, African-American studies—is creating divisions among people. I would rather schools celebrate what we have in common." Other evangelicals did not create such a strong divide between schooling and morality, but the outcome was much the same. A Christian and Missionary Alliance man from Georgia thought that "there should be a morality taught, but public schools need to concentrate on reading, writing, and arithmetic. And stay away from [things like] 'Heather's Two Mommies.'" His wife chimed in that public schools are distracted by teaching environmental issues:

> Or even the whole environmental issue. Stop teaching that a spotted owl is worth more than a human being. Stop waging all these save-the-whale campaigns, when we need to have save-the-baby campaigns. Placing the value of an animal or tree above that of a human! Let's just teach the basics.

Some evangelicals criticized the concern in schools for children's self-esteem, if it takes away from educational basics. A Presbyterian woman from Colorado stated:

> The whole self-esteem movement—I don't think a child should not feel good about themselves, but I don't think that should be the focus of education. It should be the traditional elements of learning, reading, math, science. I feel those should be the focus. Social issues, this whole recycling—I work for an oil company so I have a particular sensitivity to the girls coming home talking radical environmental stories. I just have to tell them, wait a minute; that is an issue that did happen, like the Valdeze oil spill, but you have to see where we use petroleum products. There needs to be a balance. I think in some of the schools' environmental radicalism as well as the social—you know, feel good about yourself—that is kind of silly.

While these arguments for the value of basic education show some strongly held political and moral views, they also accommodate the cultural boundary between a rational public sphere, in which education includes a separation of knowledge and morality, and the normative sphere of family and church. The remark of a nondenominational woman from Illinois illustrates the ambivalence of many evangelicals on the relationship between religion and public schools, and the view that, in a pluralistic society, basic education is the way out of that dilemma:

> I'm not sure how much Christian stuff should be put in school. I think it's not right when the non-Christian people get the upper hand and teach chil-

dren things that we don't agree with. So it's probably safer for them to stick to the "three R's" and career skills and things like that. 'Cause if we don't want them to teach what they want to teach, then I don't guess we have the right to teach Christian stuff either.

Focusing on the "three R's" means that evangelicals do not need to either withdraw into a Christian school that unites religion, family, and schooling into a neat package, or bring their religion directly into the public sphere. The opinions of the evangelicals we interviewed on the relation of morality, religion, and schooling do not call into question the divide between public institutions, and family and religious life. The cultural divide between private and public remains intact in their ways of thinking about their relationship to public schools.

EQUAL TIME FOR ALL

The fact that evangelicals do not call into question the boundary between public and private, between faith and schooling, is challenged, however, on the topic of schooling issues in which evangelicals perceive some form of discrimination against a religious perspective. But even here the large majority of evangelicals we spoke to did not wish to return to an earlier day when white, Anglo-Saxon Protestants ruled the schoolhouse roost. Instead, most of them called for some kind of pluralistic time-sharing that would accommodate diverse beliefs.

An Illinois teacher in an independent church explained how she would like her faith reflected in public schools: "I would like to be able to talk openly about my faith. Not in a way that I'm trying to influence them, but just in a way where I can tell them. Because it's who I am. And there's a whole big part of me that they don't know. I can't tell my kids about me."

Issues of free expression are important to evangelicals because their identity is rooted in individual expressions of faith within the public world.[12] Ironically, one reason evangelicals are particularly sensitive to issues of religious discrimination is because they treat rejection from the outside world as a badge of honor. Therefore issues of equal time arise out of—and become an important part of—evangelical identity formation. Evangelicals' response to discrimination is not a call for "Christianizing" public schools, however, but for equal representation of and openness to diverse perspectives. A Presbyterian woman in Michigan responded to a question about how she would like her faith and values reflected in public schools by saying, "No different than if

a Japanese person comes into the school, or a person from India. That
they are respected for their religion and their country, and they wear
their set of clothing, and they can do a report on their background.
Fair treatment." As a woman from an Evangelical Free church in Illinois put it: "I think there should be equal access, that you should be
able to have Bible studies, that you should be able to have the crazy
stuff that I think is awful, you know, like an astrology club or whatever. You should be able to have all those different things."

Interviewees complained that public schools do not give "equal
time" to Christian beliefs across a large number of issues. One key
issue was the treatment of religious holidays in the schools. A Presbyterian woman from Georgia considered public schools hostile to her
faith because "On holidays teachers aren't allowed to put up anything
about Christmas or Easter. You can't even say 'Merry Christmas.' It
has to be 'Happy Holidays.'" A Presbyterian woman from Michigan
was concerned about her daughter's fourth-grade classroom at Christ-
mastime:

> They will have a Jewish child bring in candles and discuss their beliefs and
> Rosh Hashanah, or whatever. But my daughter's not allowed to stand up
> and talk about her beliefs in Jesus Christ.
>
> *How does that make you feel?*
>
> It makes me feel angry. It should either be in the schools or leave it out.
> We're denied our Christian beliefs, but yet they allow in all the religious
> groups—all the nationalities. I don't have a problem with my daughter
> learning about [other religions and nationalities]—it's not that I don't want
> any of it there. I just feel like she should be able to get up there and talk
> about her background and her religious beliefs.

One Ohio man who belongs to a nondenominational church was concerned about discrimination against a Christian standpoint in what
children are allowed to wear to school:

> A young lady wore a pin that said "Jesus" to school, and the principal made
> her take it off. When she wouldn't, he suspended her and sent her home!
> There was a big stink about that—and should be! Now they say they don't
> allow gang members to wear their colors to school, but they do! They get
> away with it! Kids wear rock T-shirts all the time. You know, the most dis-
> gusting T-shirt I've ever seen a kid wear to school—a shirt that had lizards
> on it in different sexual positions. I mean, if they let somebody wear that in
> the school, let me tell you, wearing a Jesus pin is not bad!

Even the issue of human origins—the so-called creation-evolution
controversy—which receives much press as evidence of a "culture war"

being waged in the schools, was constructed by evangelicals we interviewed as a matter of equal time, rather than a call for eliminating instruction in the theory of evolution from the classroom altogether. In the following illustrative quote, a man from Illinois who attends a nondenominational Bible church brought together his concerns about the need for a separation of Christian morality and schooling, a focus on basic morality, and the need for equal time for different perspectives:

> I don't think that Christian morality should be taught. I think that there are a lot of by-products that should be taught—honesty, integrity, values, that can be taught and held by people who are not Christians. And I think in a public school they should be encouraged, but they shouldn't necessarily be taught. I don't expect the science teacher to teach Christianity any more than I would expect the science teacher to teach two dozen other religions. What I would expect the science teacher to present would be different theories of how something had happened. And to maintain an environment where people who had different views could express those views openly and freely.

While arguing for including diverse perspectives on the origin of life in the classroom, this man also supported pluralism in the public square by making religious perspectives one among many options. And he seemed more concerned about whether teachers present scientific material undogmatically than whether they offer a specifically "Christian" perspective in the classroom.

Some evangelicals may use "creationism" in the classroom as a symbolic issue to express their concern about the tendency in public schools to squelch Christian perspectives. But this does not imply that they long for a political solution that would drive out other viewpoints. A Michigan man from a Christian Reformed congregation said, "I don't have a problem with evolution being taught in schools. That is history; that is fact. But don't use evolution as the only way to [explain the world]. If you are going to do it, do it with creation also." A Presbyterian woman from Georgia, who wants to see creationism taught in the schools, said:

> Well, I think just having equal time. If they are teaching evolution, they should teach creationism. If they are teaching about history, why not have some of the religious things? And it doesn't just have to be the Christian faith—even educating children on what the different holidays are. And again it is part of our pluralistic society. If we are truly a pluralistic society, then why aren't we learning about each other?

The concern for change in the public schools seems not so much a call for radical restructuring of curricula, than a call for an openness to Christian viewpoints alongside others. An Evangelical Free man from Colorado, when asked whether public schools are hostile to his Christian faith and beliefs, said:

> I don't know. I guess I would have to say there is some hostility that way. It would be hard to pinpoint. I suppose you can get a teacher who is a liberal or an atheist, and they are teaching your kids the theory of evolution and not even offering that there could be a creation.

When we asked a Southern Baptist man from Texas if Christians should be trying to "redeem" public schools, to make them more Christian, he initially answered yes, but then qualified his answer by advocating openness instead:

> Yes, I think that in all areas there should be an attempt to allow the freedom of clear and open knowledge about Christ to be there. A decree, or a dictate, or a pushiness, or a requirement: no. But an openness: yes.

Evangelicals are generally not asking for a science class that excludes evolution from the syllabus. Many evangelicals see God's hand in the evolutionary process. But they do want room for alternative perspectives. One Presbyterian man from Colorado explicitly rejected "Christianizing" public schools, but did want to see a balanced presentation of different viewpoints on human origins. When we asked if he thought Christian moral views should be incorporated into sex education or science classes, he replied:

> Not in the public school. It is not reasonable that you expect that you are going to go in and ask your superintendent to make sure they get Christianity classes in public school. They are going to say you are nuts.
> *So should Christians get involved at different levels at trying to influence schools?*
> Sure. But again it is in terms of helping the school achieve a reasonable balance. It is not from the standpoint of "Let's make sure Johnny hears about Christ at school."

This is clearly not a view advocating the secular neutrality of schools. But it also seems a far cry from a call to impose evangelical views in the classroom. One woman from Oregon who attends a nondenominational church pointed out that different views deserve equal treatment in the curriculum, and even indicated that she would not want to go back to the days when religious perspectives dominated the classroom:

> I think it would be nice to see them just acknowledge Christianity. It's such a big part of American history. They should really be teaching that. Let them teach evolution along with creation. Let the kids make the decision. Give both points of view, since they are both "theories," you know. Some people think evolution is a fact, and some people think creation is a fact. Let them both be presented. Just show both sides of the coin. It is so one-sided now. I suppose some years ago it was one-sided the other way. Let them both in. Let's not exclude one or the other.

Advocating equal time for different theories and viewpoints in the schools does not seem more radical than the recent calls by some educational philosophers for humility on the part of scientists as our postmodern age calls even scientific certainties into question.[13]

Some evangelicals we spoke to extended the desire for "equal time" into subjects such as history, where they claim religion has been unfairly discriminated against, but they stop short of using history for religious indoctrination. These claims are often couched as demands to tell "what really happened," rather than explicit demands for religious indoctrination through religious interpretations of history. A Nazarene woman from Oregon associated teaching about the influence of religion in history with "equal time" in science class:

> I'm offended that some of our history books don't even tell the story about the Pilgrims correctly anymore—that things have been altered so that the Christian aspect is not there. I don't mind teaching evolution if you're gonna teach the theory of creationism along with it.

Similarly, when one Presbyterian man from North Carolina was asked to comment on the major problems in American society, he said that students should learn about the influence of religion in history:

> A large issue is educational materials. Much of early American history— the historical background of some of our early leaders—has simply been written out of the books. Left out. And yet many of them had strong Christian backgrounds and were the people they were because of what they believed in.

This man was clearly presenting a rather one-sided view of early American history himself. Still, for him and for most of the evangelicals who expressed concern about equal-time issues, the argument was not that history must be told from a religious perspective, but that history teachers should apply the standards of historical narrative fairly. The call for an appreciation of religion's role in history is a far cry from the perspective of the man quoted in the previous section who thought that the American Revolution should be taught as an example of Divine Providence at work.

We cannot say that evangelicals have no interest in bringing religion back to public schools in some way, for in fact a sizable minority of them do. However, most evangelicals' view of the relationship between schooling and their faith is not as radical as is often assumed or portrayed. Many interviewees seemed to draw on cultural beliefs about democratic pluralism to support their view more than they drew on the idea of Christianizing the public schools. For example, an Illinois woman from a nondenominational church spoke about school prayer this way:

> I am not sure that I am looking for a school system to teach Christian goals necessarily. I guess I may be looking for a school system not to do anything that would be in conflict with Christian standards. I want a school that would see cheating or breaches of integrity and address it. And I would be very supportive of a school where they wanted to have a moment of silence. I could understand why people could have a problem with open prayer. And I am not sure that I really want them to have an open prayer. Because if it is a moment of prayer today, fifteen years from now when the political environment could be different, it could be a moment for facing east and bowing to who knows what. But a moment of silence could be supportive of diversity.

The responses of our interviewees indicate that evangelicals are generally supportive of non-Christianizing changes in the schools, such as teaching "the basics" or giving equal time to diverse perspectives. For the most part, these options hardly thrust sectarian religion into public schools; rather, they assume that public schools are and should be positioned in the "public" world of competitive individualism and technical rationality. Public knowledge is acceptable to evangelicals even when it is not colored with particularistic morality and religious beliefs.

STRATEGIES FOR SAVING SCHOOLS

If evangelicals believe that public schools should adopt an equal-time policy regarding diverse viewpoints, concentrate on teaching "the basics," and instill a general moral sense in children, what steps are they willing to take to bring these changes about? As on other issues such as "Christian America," strategies of personal influence define the evangelical approach to "redeeming" public schools. The evangelicals

we interviewed showed a fairly strong distaste for large-scale, organized efforts to change public schools, and said little about advocating
broad institutional changes in public education.

We have seen that evangelicals support teaching a general morality
in public schools. But would they work to pass and enforce laws to
bring this about? A political solution would not be appropriate even on
the issue of general morality, according to one Baptist man from Texas:

> As [a political official], I don't have public prayer in our meetings, because
> I don't want to feel that I am forcing anything on anybody. So, that there is
> private. Again, forcing is not God's way, but He's not left us unclear about
> what His ways are like. So, for example, I'm tuning in to what Focus on the
> Family is saying about the divisive thing about sex education, and coupling
> that with enablement of education about values. And, apparently, the ap-
> proach they've taken is: common values that people of great diversity can
> agree upon is good as an enablement for people to choose abstinence, for
> example, as a value system in sexuality. So their view is that it's really mean-
> ingless to say "We're teaching an alternative lifestyle which includes absti-
> nence" when nothing in the person's training or background equips them to
> make that a reality. So that's an example of walking this tightrope of not
> forcing things, but yet trying to bring a level of structure that will benefit all
> of society. It's to me a difficult area but an important one. So I think that to
> say that we shouldn't try to get a high level of values [in schools] is the
> wrong answer. But there is obviously a point when we've gone too far in
> trying to force something. [We should focus on bringing about] an empow-
> ering education that brings a commonly agreed set of values to bear with
> the education.

The means by which general morality is brought into the schools is important to evangelicals. "Forcing" a value system in the schools would
destroy the meaningfulness and effectiveness of that system, according
to most evangelicals we spoke with. For one Baptist man from Minnesota respect for the ideas of the Ten Commandments is important,
yet enforcing school prayer would be imposing beliefs on others. When
asked if Christian morality should be the commonly accepted morality
in our culture, he replied:

> To the extent of having school prayer, no. To having stuff in the schools, no.
> I think [morality] needs to be practiced in the home and the churches. To
> force it upon "other people"—I don't think it's Christian to do that. We live
> in a pluralistic society, and we need to show respect for other cultures.
> Again, I think what the scriptures talk about in terms of the Ten Com-
> mandments are very basic, and they should be practiced by all people. But
> to force it upon people—no, I don't think so. Are we a Christian nation
> where we all believe the same? No. I'm never the type where I'm very vocal

about my beliefs in terms of forcing it down people's throats. That to me is a turn-off. And I trust it is for other people, too. So it should be almost like friendship evangelism: developing relationships with people so that you build trust, and you show that you do care about other people's needs. Not forcing your beliefs upon them, but seeing where they're coming from and trying to understand their position. So being compassionate, I think, is very key. That's another characteristic of an evangelical: doesn't just have the right theology, but demonstrates that in a compassionate way.

Note the contrast he made between forcing compliance through political means, and attempting to change people through relationships. A Nazarene man from California expressed a similar opinion when we asked him how Christians should be trying to exert influence in public schools:

To go out and volunteer your time—to help a teacher, to be on the PTA, to be in a booster club, to be in any level of visibility where you can be salt and light, pure and simple. And donate and make it easier for someone else. Not to get petitions, not necessarily to tell them how to do it. Just get in and make their job easier. Help them do it, and then they'll be much more receptive. Christ says that if you want to lead, you have to be a servant. So if you want to impact something, you go in at the bottom level and you serve and you give yourself away in whatever you can do. People notice. You don't even have to say, "Hey, look at me." You should do it in the closet where your right hand doesn't know what your left hand is doing.

In fact, turning to political, mundane solutions, according to our respondents, tends to ignore the spiritual root of school problems—and spiritual problems are a matter of individual hearts. A woman from an Evangelical Covenant church in Minnesota believes that she is "contributing to God's kingdom" as a public school teacher. She does this through prayer, which in her view sets her apart from non-Christian teachers:

I am called to be a teacher, and I pray for all my students in the classroom, especially for the really challenging ones. They're the ones that need it. Sometimes school is the only place that they're safe. It's the only sane thing in their lives. I have a powerful tool praying for students at the school. I'm there to be able to pray for them, to lift them up. And only the Lord knows what they're really going through. If I was there just for me, I'd be grumbling about this kid, grumbling about that kid, you know, thinking my life is hard. Well, I'm not there for hard or easy; I'm there for whatever the Lord wants me to do, or whatever lives I'm supposed to touch at that time. So your focus is different, and that's important.

Efforts for political, structural change miss the spiritual dimension entirely. A Colorado woman who attends a community church argued, "I don't know if we should try and redeem the public school because it's a spiritual thing as people's hearts get changed." A California man from an Evangelical Free church maintained that the "removal of God from education, from political and social life" cannot be "tackled collectively." Instead, he "tries to do it individually as much as I can." In the schools, the individual approach is often not a matter of parental influence at all, but means the witness of individual Christian students. When we asked a pentecostal woman from Alabama whether Christians should try to make public schools more Christian, she replied:

> The way we are going to win it is through the students. Yes, the answer to that [is] yes. Student-to-student that is how they are going to get reached. The Christian student can teach the young people.

A North Carolina woman from a nondenominational church combined in her response a sensitivity to the public-private boundary with a personal calling to be active in her children's school:

> I don't think public schools are all going to become Christian. But I feel a sense of responsibility to be involved in public schools. That helps to redeem them, if you want to use those words. So, I don't feel called to be a politician. I do feel called to be very active in my kids' school. So I feel that what I'm doing is partly out of obedience towards the Lord, what the Lord wants me to do—not just my desire to be involved in my kids' education.

Even for those evangelicals who are in favor of political involvement at the local level, a strategy of changing laws seems to run counter to the influence of relationships, which evangelicals treasure. A Baptist woman from New Jersey put it this way when we asked whether Christians should be trying to redeem public schools:

> That's another one that I have trouble about really. Ideally, I would like to see it happen. But what's right? What's the right way to go about it? Is it going to happen naturally as Christians living within that community are living out the life of Jesus Christ and caring about the school that their children are attending? Being an influence in the way that schools run—you know, parent associations or support the teachers—there's a lot of ways of influencing the schools for good without making a law to do it.

Evident in this woman's answer is the common evangelical view that change should come through interpersonal means, while institutional solutions run counter to the personal touch. With this set of cultural tools, it is more difficult for evangelicals to regard strategies for political, institutional change as meaningful.

Even efforts to place Christians on school boards—which look like political strategy—may be limited by the sense that all influence is accomplished ultimately through relationships. A Christian and Missionary Alliance man from Georgia considered membership on a school board as part of a personal influence strategy. When we asked what would be the best way for Christians to exert Christian influence on their environment, he said:

> Again, one-on-one. There are many ways to do that. Raise your kids right, be on the school board, whatever. Until you get to the individuals and get them redeemed, it is going to be pretty hard to redeem the schools.

The accepted division between religion and public life is called into question if Christians attempt to organize a political pressure group. Evangelicals we interviewed saw this as a threat to their personal influence strategy—which they considered more meaningful because it is not "structured." A woman from Georgia who attends a nondenominational church combined her reservations about political solutions with her value for the personal strategy of changing individuals when she described what Christians should be doing about safety in the schools:

> [Trying] more [to] change individual hearts. You can't legislate attitudes. So you do have to change on one-to-one, as each person changes. [Evangelicals] need to be involved in the inner city, helping lead some of these young people when their families aren't doing [it].

The example of a strategy to make changes in the schools offered by one Congregational woman from Massachusetts was very revealing:

> One of my favorite ways to be involved is a group called "Moms in Touch." These are women who get together to pray for the public schools, the teachers, and the children—that's all they do. They don't, as a result, tromp into the schoolroom and interfere at all; it's strictly a background praying type of thing. That kind of influence I think is great, because in a society like ours they can't really waltz in and demand that Christian values be taught, and things like this.

This prayer group has all the traits of acceptable evangelical public engagement. It avoids large-scale, organized efforts at institutional changes in favor of indirect means of personal influence—in this case, the petitions of individuals in a personal relation to God. Individual interaction is considered the key to exerting a "leavening" influence on society. When we asked the same woman what she meant by her concern that Christians should be salt and light in society, she said, "I guess to me it means living so that you have a subtle but hopefully powerful influence on people you interact with."

Some respondents mentioned their personal faith as a strategy for dealing with social issues and linked it to an increasing sense of personal peace. When asked why her faith is important to her, a Georgia woman from an independent church answered:

> It makes dealing with things just a lot easier. And it's brought just a peace. I can go out and get really disturbed about the way things are going in the schools, or courts, or whatever, but my faith has just brought me a peace, in that I know things will be dealt with in a righteous and just way eventually.

Though critics have decried evangelicalism as a launching pad for organized political attempts to challenge the secularity of public schools, there is evidence from ordinary evangelicals themselves that religion causes them to discount—or at least not put hope in—participation in culture war struggles to "save" America. The evangelical tradition tends to be uncomfortable with organized political efforts and attempts to bring about broad, institutional changes in the public schools, especially when these changes would require any form of coercion. It seems more likely to promote individual involvement and interpersonal influence strategies to work toward change in public schools.

CONCLUSION

Our personal interviews with evangelicals from around the country show that evangelical self-identity is associated with a strong sense of a calling to public life, especially to public schools. The majority of evangelicals are reluctant to abandon public schools and set up countercultural educational institutions. Evangelicals' engaged orthodoxy involves an active presence in the secular, competitive public world, which includes the public schools, even while religious life is conceived primarily as a matter of family, friends, and church. Of course, some evangelicals are sending their children to nonpublic schools, but the dominant evangelical schooling strategy requires a presence within the public schools.

But what kind of presence? A small minority of evangelicals want to pursue some version of a Christian America within public schools, including mandatory Bible classes, religious interpretations of historical events in history class, and an explicitly Christian ethos, such as teacher-led school prayer. But the majority of evangelicals see their role as just "being there." By "being there," they are "salt and light to the world."

The changes that evangelicals advocate generally respect the cultural divide separating public life from religion, morality, and values. Contrary to the picture painted by some theorists of conservative religion and politics,[14] "deprivatization," or bringing religion directly into the public sphere, has some fairly clear limits when it comes to ordinary evangelicals' views of public schools. For example, many evangelicals do not criticize the institution of public schooling at all, and instead focus on the failings of the family to do their duty to instill morality and values. Other evangelicals advocate a general morality, which most Americans support. And the evangelical call for schools that teach a "basic" education—the "three Rs" rather than "social" concerns—provides little challenge to the separation of sacred and secular.

Evangelicals are concerned about what they see as unfair discrimination against religious viewpoints in the public schools. The evangelical demand for equal time in the schools for Christian holidays, for religious perspectives on science, and for attention to the role of religion in history, may provide the most concern for critics about what the evangelicals really want from public schools. But the evangelical desire for equal time is couched in terms of a pluralistic conception of the public square, which does not call for Christianizing the curriculum. Even evangelicals who call for a balance of evolution and creation in the science classroom seem to want a token place for creationist views, and have little stomach for the radical "six-day" creationist views advocated by a few vocal religious leaders.

The evangelical strategy for influencing public schools seems a far cry from any behind-the-scenes political maneuvering to stack school boards with Christians. In fact, evangelicals specifically contrast such organized political strategies of Christians with the witness of evangelical children in schools and volunteering by parents. It seems likely that the much-publicized efforts of religious conservatives to take over school boards are isolated and short-term events—at least if most ordinary evangelicals have any say about it. The evangelical sense that large-scale institutional change is not meaningful because it does not involve interpersonal influence or "changed hearts" makes it difficult for them to sustain support for a Christian political solution over the long haul. Evangelicals' belief that social problems have spiritual roots and that the spiritual is a matter of individual hearts reduces their trust in political, cultural-war solutions. They tend to favor subtle forms of change through individual involvement, such as prayer. They believe that real, lasting solutions require voluntary changes of heart and will. Rather than creating shock troops for a culture war, evangelical religion generally provides resources for accepting, rather than fighting at all cost, the status quo in education.

Embedded in a movement that focuses on communication with the outside world, evangelicals open up a cultural tool kit that allows them to see their presence in the public realm as a religious duty. But evangelicals in fact are not focused on transforming public schools in their own image. Rather, evangelical traditions are reconstructed in a way that calls for active involvement, a continuing "moral presence," but ultimately little fundamental change.

CHAPTER FIVE

Male Headship
and Gender Equality

With Melinda Lundquist

ON 9 JUNE 1998 the Southern Baptist Convention, in a national meeting of 8,500 delegates, amended its essential statement of beliefs, the *Baptist Faith and Message Statement,* to include a declaration that a woman should "submit herself graciously" to her husband's leadership, and that a husband should "provide for, protect, and lead his family." This was only the second amendment to the Southern Baptists' *Statement* in its entire history, and its first-ever declaration dealing with a social—and not strictly theological or church—issue. With it, the nation's largest Protestant denomination officially disavowed the idea of egalitarian marriage, in favor of functionally hierarchical marriage relationships in which husbands stand as authorities over and leaders before their wives. R. Albert Mohler, Jr., president of the Southern Baptist Theological Seminary in Louisville, Kentucky, stated that the submission of wives to their husbands is "not a modern idea," but "is clearly revealed in Scripture." And Paige Patterson, president of Eastern Baptist Seminary in Wake Forest, North Carolina, declared that the amendment was a response to "a time of growing crisis in the family," and that those who disagreed "happen not to be real familiar with the Bible."[1] Two days later, James Dobson, head of the conservative Christian organization Focus on the Family, exhorted the Southern Baptists in his keynote address to "defend righteousness in the culture." "If the church won't stand up for morality," he said, "there's no one to take our place." Dobson predicted that Southern Baptists "will be vilified and marginalized" for their declaration, but encouraged them not to be deterred, since, he maintained, "We answer to a higher authority."[2]

This formal policy declaration by a sixteen-million-member conservative Protestant denomination seems to clearly substantiate a long-standing criticism of evangelicals on family and gender issues: that evangelicals are militant, nostalgic patriarchs attempting to "turn back the clock" to a bygone era when women were happy housewives who obeyed their sole-provider husbands, who ruled with authority. Critics charge that American evangelicals in general are resolved to reinstate the traditional, nuclear, "Leave-It-to-Beaver" family of the 1950s. They are cultural reactionaries struggling on behalf of male privilege, and are genuine enemies of freedom, equality, and women's rights. Worse yet, they underwrite and justify their vision through appeals to sectarian religious absolutes, which they are intent on imposing on all Americans without compromise, since they, in their own words, "answer to a higher authority."

Take, for example, political progressives' apprehensions about the evangelical men's movement, Promise Keepers, which numerous journalists have surveyed with grave suspicion. *The Village Voice*, for example, has criticized Promise Keepers' "sanitized multiculturalism," calling its "policy of racial diversity so overt that it reeks of insincerity." And *GQ* magazine has called Promise Keepers' founder Bill McCartney a "lop-eyed loon" and a "raving lunatic," repeatedly using Nazi imagery—such as titling the article "Triumph of His Will," in reference to the infamous Nazi film, "Triumph of the Will"—to describe the movement.[3] Russ Bellant, of *Free Inquiry*, sees in Promise Keepers "manipulation and control," "anti-democratic views," and "the strongest, most organized effort to capitalize on male backlash in the country today." "While projecting an image of spirituality," Bellant suggests, "leaders of Promise Keepers seem to be bent on gaining social and political power. . . . Men are to submit to a cell group that in turn is closely controlled by a national hierarchy. Most important, women are to submit absolutely to their husbands or fathers."[4] Similarly, Nancy Novosad described Promise Keepers in *The Progressive* as "a male supremacist conservative religious organization that strongly advocates gender bigotry."[5] John Swomley has written in *The Humanist* that Promise Keepers is "one of the most dangerous of the fundamentalist Christian political groups active in the United States today," and that it is "preeminently a commercial enterprise" that is "designed to provoke a backlash to the women's equality movement."[6] And in a

1996 cover story for *The Nation,* Joe Conason, Alfred Ross, and Lee Cokorinos wrote that Promise Keepers is the "new 'third wave' of the religious right"; "ostensibly nonpolitical, it is a movement of unmistakable political importance." Promise Keepers, they suggested, promotes "regressive racial politics," shows "hints of theocratic ideology," and is associated with "controversial, ultra-right-wing organizations," one of which advocates "the curtailment of the Bill of Rights and a hostility to democratic institutions as incompatible with its vision of a theocratic state." The authors conclude:

> The success of their religious revival has gone hand in glove with the growth of conservative Christian political power. In conception and execution, in fact, Promise Keepers appears to be one of the most sophisticated creations of the religious right. . . . Now, mobilizing hundreds of thousands of men into a disciplined, hierarchical, nationwide grass-roots formation with significant military connections but a subtle presentation, Promise Keepers poses a new challenge. Its promise may be our peril.[7]

What should we make of all of this? The Southern Baptist declaration on the family seems clear enough, as do the views of Southern Baptist leaders like Paige Patterson and R. Albert Mohler, Jr. But, one might wonder, what do ordinary Southern Baptists, or more broadly, ordinary evangelicals, think and feel? Do they, too, support a hierarchical view of marriage? Do they want husbands to rule their wives? Are they also concerned about a "growing crisis in the family" and prepared to mobilize forces through something like the Promise Keepers movement to recreate some mythic 1950s happy nuclear family? This chapter attempts to answer these kinds of questions, and illuminate more clearly the feelings, beliefs, concerns, and experiences of ordinary American evangelicals on the matter of gender and family relations.

GRAVE CONCERNS ABOUT FAMILY

The first thing that became clear in our interviews was how deeply dismayed evangelicals are about contemporary family life in America. The family is very dear to the evangelical heart, and grave concerns about the breakdown of the American family are widespread among evangelicals. One reason for this is that evangelicals draw a close connection between their faith and their family lives. One Baptist man from Minnesota, for example, observed about family life: "To me, it is where the essence of Christianity is lived out—the patience, the understanding, the perseverance, all these traits." An Assemblies of God woman from Texas likewise noted, "It all starts there: you learn all your morals and values through your family, learning from your family and those who are around your family. And you take those values with you. So it really starts with the marriage and having and raising children." And one Southern Baptist woman from Georgia drew an explicit connection between spiritual and family relationships:

> The breakdown of the family to me is one of the biggest things that I really hate to see.
> *Why should Christians be concerned about that?*
> Because to me that is the basic fundamentals of religion. I mean, God our *Father*—we are His family, and it's our purpose in life to do the same thing for our families and for other people. Not just necessarily our specific families, but our church family, our community family.

In addition to drawing a strong connection between family and faith, evangelicals also generally view the family as the basic social unit of society, the foundation of its survival and health. Broken families, then, automatically produce broken societies. A Christian and Missionary Alliance woman from Georgia expressed a common evangelical sentiment when she said, "I think a lot of problems in the country come right back to the structure of the family, because of the pivotal—you know, like the atom, it is one of the smallest building blocks of society." The condition of the family is therefore used as a litmus test for the general health of society. A man from Minnesota who attends an Evangelical Free church stated, "If I could pick out only one problem in our society, the crux of all the problems, it would be the breakdown of the family." Similarly, a woman from an independent seeker-church in Georgia commented, "A lot of the social problems come from the disintegration of the family. So if you can keep the family strong, then society ought to be better off."

But what exactly do evangelicals think is harming the family in America? And what do they think should be done about it? A few of the evangelicals we interviewed accused groups they viewed as hostile to families—such as feminists, liberals, homosexuals, etc.—for causing the breakdown of the American family. But the majority did not point fingers at such groups. Instead, they talked about pervasive economic pressures and easy divorce as the primary forces eroding the strength of the family.

Some evangelicals we interviewed put the blame for economic pressures on the fact that women are leaving the home in search of careers. And some respondents were critical of two-income families, claiming that the parents' selfish motives for status and material goods hurt their children. But most evangelicals simply accepted that families today have to earn two incomes to survive. One Covenant church woman from California, for example, said, "I think the breakdown of the family is dramatically evident, and I think the fact that most women are forced to work out of economic necessity causes difficulties in the family, so that children aren't raised with as strong a sense of values as they might have been if one parent had been home." A Mennonite man from Ohio echoed her sentiments: "I think the home is a problem, discipline is a problem. I think our economics have a lot to do with it, because the mother and father are both out working to put a roof over their kids' heads, and I think they don't have enough input in teaching the kids how to behave and discipline." And a woman from Massachusetts who attends an independent church said much the same:

> Parents worry about how they're going to take care of their children. When mother and father go out, the children are left alone. Parents feel guilty because of this, and so they try to buy things to replace the needs of love and attention that their children are asking for. And I see it as a breakdown.

Many evangelicals agree that the fact that both parents have to work means that children are often given inadequate attention and guidance. And since evangelicals see the family as the primary means of instilling faith and morals in future generations, they fear for the consequential loss of moral stability and religious roots. Thus one Evangelical Free man from Minnesota related, "If there is a family [in which] both the mom and the dad are working, or maybe a single parent, so much of the responsibility of raising children has been given up by the family and taken over by something else like the school, and that's what the biggest problem in our country is."

The problem of inadequate time for children, the interviewees often commented, is compounded in single-parent homes. So, high divorce rates that create single-parent families are also a major concern. Many evangelicals we interviewed criticized the increased social acceptability of and easy access to divorce. A Christian and Missionary Alliance woman from Georgia, for example, remarked:

> Getting a divorce is easier than [terminating] a contract to fertilize your lawn. That's wrong. In a country where it is easier to break up a family than to get out of a simple business arrangement, that's wrong. The family has not been given the place that it needs to have.

Many others also lamented the way divorce has, in their view, all too often become an easy and nearly automatic solution for married couples whose relationships hit hard times.

What particularly troubles evangelicals is the harmful effects they see these strains having on children. According to one Presbyterian woman from North Carolina, for example, "I think that part of the breakdown in the whole family system is that there's no involvement with kids." One Baptist man from Minnesota agreed, saying that "Probably the most [important] thing is the time constraint we all have, and I really see the break-up of the family as a result of parents doing their thing and not spending time with the kids." And a Southern Baptist man from North Carolina commented, "You think about all the kids who grew up without a father. Just the fact that they have to deal with not only their family life, but then education and everything else—it's unbelievable that they have to do that. And that is a direct reason for the way things are." Many evangelicals argue furthermore that all of this produces in children poor self-esteem, lack of self-discipline, inability to distinguish right from wrong, vulnerability to peer pressure, and various forms of illicit behavior. These in turn contribute to larger social problems, such as juvenile delinquency and lack of basic skills to function in society among children. Social problems are then perpetuated into the next generation through these children, as they grow up to reproduce a society that neglects the family. As one evangelical Episcopalian woman from Ohio observed, "The breakdown of the family is probably the biggest [problem], because I think it's a snowballing effect. When parents break up, it affects the kids, it affects them and their kids. It's snowballing." Explaining the problem in a more positive light, a Baptist woman from Texas said, "If you can help fix the brokenness in the family, if you can keep a marriage from breaking up, then you can keep children from being hurt because of it. They are saying a lot of juvenile crime—those kids are products of a separated home. If you can keep a family intact, who knows what [other social problems] you could prevent down the road?"

FOCUS ON *MY* FAMILY

If these are the problems plaguing the American family, what do evangelicals think are the solutions? One might easily expect these discontents to drive evangelicals into fervent political activism, in an effort to

counter the social changes that have caused family decline and somehow "reinstate" the traditional, male-headed, nuclear family. Some
evangelical leaders definitely do talk in these terms, and a minority of
ordinary evangelicals certainly do embrace this political agenda. But
for most, the strong evangelical preference for individual and noncoercive influence prevails even on the deeply felt issue of the family. The
majority of evangelicals turn out to have little interest in imposing a
general social order in which everyone else must conform to their supposed ideal of the traditional family.

No more than a sizable minority of the evangelicals we interviewed
mentioned politics in relation to their concerns about the family.
Among these, a handful spoke about targeting political leadership—
supporting Christian politicians, or writing to political leaders and
pressuring them to take actions that bolster families. However, half of
the evangelicals who did mention politics said that, while political involvement was generally fine, it was not something *they themselves* felt
comfortable with. For many, like one California woman who attends
an Evangelical Covenant church, voting in elections was often the extent of their desired political involvement: "I'm sure there are many
Christians that feel they should be politically active. I'm not, but I take
voting very seriously, and I talk to people I know about how I feel
about issues." At the same time, a small group of evangelicals in the opposing camp spoke directly against active political mobilization. One
Assembly of God man from Minnesota, for instance, argued that politics would simply be ineffective: "If we get involved on public issues
and national issues, I think you're gonna have the same thing all the
time, a constant struggle going on. I think it would be more damaging
than anything else."

Contrary to many media accounts, we did not find ordinary evangelicals eager to mobilize politically against the forces seen as threatening the family. Most recognize that society is not going to be changed
overnight by political strong-arm tactics. Instead, the majority of evangelicals think about dealing with family breakdown primarily in terms
of individual—not political or institutional—influence and change.
They want, first, to make sure that their *own* families are strong. Sec-
ondarily, they hope somehow to persuade others about the importance
of "family values" and Christian faith.

When we asked interviewees, "What should Christians be doing
about concerns such as the breakdown of the family?" by far the most
common response was to look to their personal commitments to their

own families. In other words, the typical evangelical response was not so much "focus on *the* family" in some activist sense, but "focus on *my* family" in a very personal sense. A Wesleyan man from Michigan, for example, argued, "I think most important is my family and what my kids grow up to believe, what their moral values are. [My role] is to make sure my family has a solid foundation and is really in the work of God and has high moral standards." So, just as many social ills begin with problems in the family, so too do solutions to these problems.

A few evangelicals we interviewed thought it necessary to focus on their families in a defensive way, to protect them from the negative influences of society. But most regarded focusing on their families and doing their best to pass on good morals to their children as their primary, positive means of contributing to social change. One North Carolina man who attends an evangelical Moravian church, for example, stated:

> If you have children, I think the most important thing you can do is to raise children to be godly grownups. I have two children, and I can take care of myself. I can have them grow up to be good upstanding citizens that aren't going to be causing any of these problems, and now there are going to be three people in the future that are not going to be contributing to the problems [in society].

Similarly, a Presbyterian woman from North Carolina observed, "I don't think every Christian is called to picket. I think they should teach morality to their own children and feel a responsibility that their children know God's word." And an Assemblies of God man from Minnesota suggested, "You start with your family and your community because they are what is closest to you. I think that that's where Christianity plays its best role." Echoing the same, one Missouri Synod Lutheran woman from Oregon reflected:

> Rather than pointing our finger at other people, I think we have to first start in our own home, our own local church, and not sit with my fingers [pointing] around [at] the rest of the world. Because it can only start with me, with me and my family, my local church. That is what "evangelical," the good news, means: to set an example.

Many evangelicals argued, sometimes in self-critical tones, that the influence of the Christian faith can only come after the Christian community is practicing what it preaches regarding family. For instance, a woman from California who attends a Congregational church observed, "I think Christians have a real opportunity to rebuild their families here. I think we've neglected them in past efforts to get the gospel out, and I think there's a new sense that we have to strengthen what's at home, as well as reach out to the world." And a Christian and Missionary Alliance woman from Georgia said:

> Once you've [dealt with] the family, then you can build the church. Once the church has dealt with its sin, then they are able to go out to the community in love, and the community is able to respond. I think it does take a village [to raise a child]. But before that, it takes a family, a church, a community that is willing to make a difference.

The next most common evangelical response to concerns about the family, after "focus on *my* family," was to get involved, not in politics but in a local church. This seems to serve a two-fold purpose. First, evangelicals see church participation as a source of support for families seeking to raise their children in the Christian faith and with Christian values. Fellowship with other believers is a source of encouragement for evangelicals, who often perceive many of the forces they encounter in society as contrary to their own beliefs. Second, the church serves as a tool to help its members reach out to their communities. For instance, one Lutheran woman from Minnesota said, "In our churches, we can reach out to help people. I know we do in ours." We asked if this meant helping single parents or helping families be better parents. "Either one," she replied. "Wherever it's needed. I think sometimes people just need some help." Another woman from an Assemblies of God church in Texas offered this response:

> I think that the best way to address some of these social problems is for Christians to offer support. Particularly with single[-parent] families and the breakdown of the family. The best thing to do would be to have a shelter for families who need help, to offer financial assistance to those who need it.

Helping families in need and hoping their help will affect deeper, underlying problems beyond the immediate difficult circumstances is another way evangelicals believe they can address family breakdown in society. Recognizing that their family ideals are not accepted by everyone in society, most evangelicals tend to put their hope for change not in political activism, but rather in influencing individuals so that they freely choose correct attitudes and behaviors. By reaching out to the people around them, they exercise the "strategic relationalism" that will bring others to the faith and strengthen the family. One Free

Methodist man from Washington State, for example, viewed the local church as the starting point for a broader example to the community: "I guess our theory has always been to have a connection with the local church, but to be able to be outside of that church setting, meeting people one-on-one in business situations, in community situations, and, again, allowing people to see our lives for the way that we are; to set an example, but not to be condemning with where they are." In this way, evangelical concern about family breakdown often circles its way back to a concern with personal evangelism and the prevalent evangelical individual model of influence. Thus, the Assemblies of God woman from Texas quoted above continued:

> I think if you help people in need, then that might open up a door for a relationship in which you could evangelize. If people start coming to church and if they accept Jesus as their Lord and Savior, then they will start changing some of their values and their lifestyle. Then some of these social problems will start to disappear. If a husband or father becomes a Christian, then he will understand that he has a responsibility to be involved in the family, so the breakdown of the family will start to diminish.

And a woman from a Vineyard church in Colorado pointed out that the introduction of Christian values

> is not an overnight process, it is not an instant Band-Aid. It is more of a long-term process, where the changes are effected in the home, with their children, with their job, with their priorities, and that just affects people throughout their circle, whether it is their friends, family, or neighborhood. When a person gets involved in accepting salvation and then living a Christlike life, it spreads.

To summarize, most American evangelicals consider economic pressures and the prevalent system of easy divorce as the primary causes of family breakdown. But they do not generally respond to these causes in an institutional, legal, or systemic way. Instead, the response of most evangelical responses is: first, to maintain the integrity of their own families, protecting their values while upholding their responsibility to raise children who will contribute positively to society; second, to set an example through their lifestyle that might lead others to accept the Christian faith and to choose voluntarily to raise their own families according to Christian principles. Underlying this entire strategy is the deep evangelical commitment to effecting voluntary, individual change through interpersonal influence.

ON THE HEADSHIP OF HUSBANDS

The fact that most ordinary evangelicals are not interested in mobiliz-ing political power to impose their version of "family values" on America speaks directly and significantly to the broad concerns of this book. However, it answers only part of this chapter's larger question. For while the Southern Baptist *Faith and Message Statement*, for ex-ample, with its declaration of wifely submission and husbandly leader-ship, is not a formal political platform to be legislated for all Ameri-cans, it nevertheless represents a clear model for family relations that presumably may shape the family lives of Southern Baptists and any others influenced by them or their *Statement*. Many Americans who are committed to full gender equality, therefore, might still be legiti-mately concerned about the family norms and practices within the evangelical subculture. Whether or not most evangelicals are trying to impose their "family values" on everyone else politically, there is still the question of the model of marital and family relations that those val-ues represent. Don't evangelicals believe in and practice a form of pa-triarchy that more egalitarian-minded outsiders would find objection-able, perhaps even offensive and repulsive?

To try to answer this question in an illuminating way, we next ex-amine in greater detail the key concept around which any evangelical practices of patriarchy are constructed: the "headship" of husbands. The following pages explore what "headship" means to ordinary evangelicals, both in an ideal, theological sense and in everyday expe-rience. What does it mean, we asked evangelicals, that the husband is the "head"? And how does that work out practically in one's mar-riage?

The biblical text on which most evangelical notions of the headship of the husband are based is this New Testament passage from Saint Paul's epistle to the Christians in Ephesus (Ephesians 5:21–28):

> Submit to one another out of reverence for Christ. Wives, submit to your husbands as to the Lord. For the husband is the head of the wife as Christ is the head of the church, his body, of which he is the Savior. Now as the church submits to Christ, so also wives should submit to their husbands in everything. Husbands, love your wives, just as Christ loved the church and gave himself up for her. . . . In the same way, husbands ought to love their wives as their own bodies. He who loves his wife loves himself.

Ordinary evangelicals, it turns out, interpret this somewhat am-biguous text in very different ways. Not surprisingly, minorities of evangelicals take firm positions at opposite ends of the spectrum. One fairly small group of evangelicals, for example, argues that this passage and other biblical texts (for instance, 1 Peter 3:1–6; 1 Corinthians 14:33–35) clearly support male authority and leadership without qualification. An Assemblies of God woman from Texas said, "I would like the idea of equality, that would be ideal. But I don't think it's reality. The idea that the husband has been given headship does mean that he ultimately has authority." And one woman who attends a Vineyard church in Colorado replied similarly:

> I used to think they should [be equal], but just recently I have learned that they shouldn't. Whenever you are equal partners, there is no way to resolve a dispute of any kind. If you are equal and you have two different opinions, how do you resolve it? You can't.
> *So, you think it is better for the well-being of the family if one person has the ultimate authority?*
> Right.

For this minority of evangelicals, "headship" may mean, variously, being the primary breadwinner of the family, having more authority in decisions, or simply being the family's unmistakable "leader." In any case, in their view, headship is primary and equality is absent.

At the opposite end of the spectrum, another fairly small minority of evangelicals believe this passage ("Submit to *one another*. . . .") and others in the New Testament (such as Galatians 3:28; 1 Corinthians 7:3–5) stand as clear endorsements of gender equality and mutual submission in marriage as God's highest calling. This group talked about marriage as an equal partnership, and regarded male headship as incompatible with equality. When asked if he believed that husbands are to be the "heads" of their wives or families, for example, one Evangelical Free man from California replied: "I think overall, in general, they are a team, they do things together. They go through life together, help each other. So I think in general, equality, you know, submit to one another out of love for Christ." And one Evangelical Free woman from Illinois emphasized that the woman is not the only one to whom submission applies:

> Well, first of all, they're equal, no matter what. I know for sure it says wives submit and husbands love. Now that makes it sound more like the wife is in the subordinate position there, but when we're saying [husbands should] "love as Christ loved the church and gave himself up for it," that's pretty heavy submission [on his part].

And a Nazarene man from California remarked, "In terms of an equal commitment to the end result to whatever that task is, wherever that journey takes, and whatever the price that has to be paid, absolutely, both partners pay the whole price. I think when the two become one, you can no longer delineate those lines."

The majority of evangelicals, however, did not take either of these opposing positions. Most embraced more complex views that fell somewhere along the spectrum between the extremes. What follows attempts to lay out some of these diverse viewpoints and convey some of the texture of ordinary evangelicals' perspectives on the matter. In the process, we make two important general observations: First, the majority of ordinary evangelicals believe that headship and equality are entirely compatible, not contradictory, commitments. Second, while discussing headship, very few evangelicals emphasized the submission of the wife; rather, most stressed the burdens and restraints headship places on the husband.

Gender-Impartial Headship.   The strategy a few evangelicals used to reconcile headship and equality was to affirm the occasional need for a head who can lead the family, but to argue explicitly that gender should not determine who is the head. Taking a pragmatic rather than an ideological approach, they said that either the wife or husband could play the role of leader, depending on their relative strengths and on the situation. One Lutheran woman from Wisconsin gave this example: "In our situation, I would say I have to be the head, just because—not that I know better or anything, but I seem to be stronger when things go astray. I think a lot of the headship—it's whoever is the strongest one." Another woman from an independent church in Indiana said that in her marriage the husband is the head, but that the head "wouldn't have to be the man. For me, I'm comfortable with it being him. But, I've been married before, and it hasn't been that way, I've had to be the one with the final say." And one Congregational woman from Massachusetts linked ideological egalitarianism with pragmatic headship:

> I think they should both be subservient to Christ—Christ should be the head. I think that this business of the man ruling—he may not be the better one. I think that the couple has to come to terms within themselves as to who is the head, if there has to be a head.

Equal but Different.   A more common approach—one which holds perhaps the greatest potential to legitimate male-privileged marriage through the rhetoric of equality—was to contend that husband and wife are equal in value and spiritual importance, but are *functionally* different. One Illinois woman who attends a nondenominational Bible church, for example, said, "I believe men and women are equal in the family and everywhere else. But I think God has given man the responsibility for the leadership role." Drawing on Saint Paul's corporatist language regarding the church to combine ideas of equality and male authority in decision-making, an Evangelical Covenant Church woman from Minnesota argued:

> We all have different talents and different ministries. [Some think that] because you're not a hand but a foot, you're less, and because you're a finger you're less than if you are a brain. I think if we lose any part, we're missing something. It all fits together to work for good. I think it's the same with having mutual responsibility, mutual respect, being equal. You can still be equal and have one person make the final decision, but the decision is usually made equally.

Similarly, a Presbyterian woman from Pennsylvania used an equal-but-different approach: "We are mutual and we are equal. But my husband in the end is responsible before God, so he has to make sure that the decisions he is making are right."[8]

Evangelicals who took this perspective were often concerned to clarify that in marriage "equal" does not mean "sameness." Each partner, rather, is unique and brings different strengths to the marriage. One Bible church man from Illinois noted: "They are equal and different. We have to remember that." Does headship, we asked, undermine equality or not? "It shouldn't," he replied. "In some cases it would. I guess it can make equality, because men and women are different and each has a role that is equally important." A man from Minnesota who attends a nondenominational church responded to the idea of husbands and wives being mutual and equal partners: "I think so in most ways. Different roles, though. I don't think that men and women are supposed to be exactly the same. I think that there's definitely different roles. As far as being equal, yeah, that's okay." Likewise, an Evangelical Free woman from Colorado answered:

> Yeah, I guess equal, but not like the same. But valued equally. I don't think you would need a husband and a wife if they were going to be the same

person or have the same role. There is a reason you need both. There are specific things each are called to, but they are equally valued.

Likewise, an Evangelical Free man from Minnesota stated that "Headship has nothing to do with being better. I mean, it's like when Christ describes two different roles: it's not that one is better or one is worse; they're equal as far as Christ is concerned." A Congregational woman from Massachusetts made a similar comment:

> We are all created equal in God's eyes, and we are equal partners to a point. We just have different responsibilities. Neither the husband or the wife are more important; we're both just as important. You can't function really without the other. But we just have different responsibilities.[9]

For some, such as one Presbyterian woman from Colorado, the idea of equal partners in marriage suggested a rigidity or formality that she didn't like:

> I see the benefits of [equal partnership], I do. But there is no flexibility in that. There is some love lost when everything is equal. It's like, "Oh, it is your night." Everyone has their strengths and weaknesses. It is good to play on those.

In these ways, many respondents who talked about equality and mutual partnerships also endorsed male headship. Rather than holding them as contradictory, many wove these two concepts together as they spoke. A Presbyterian man from South Carolina who agreed that the man is the head of the house also said about marriage: "I view it as equal partners in all endeavors. We are a partnership. When we were married, we became one. We have different roles, but we are one in the goal of making our marriage work." Some, such as one Assemblies of God woman from Ohio, even went so far as to merge equality and headship into a unified whole:

> Well, equality and headship are the same thing in that sense. I think when you have equality, headship is intact. I think when you have headship without equality, then you have domination. And that's when you're becoming not submissive to your husband, but you're becoming a servant to him, you're opening yourself up for abuse.

Burdens of Responsibility, Accountability, and Sacrifice.   The biblical idea of husbands as heads of their wives easily evokes images of male domination and privilege. To be "the head" of something in this culture, after all, means to be the boss, to have authority to order others around.[10] Most interesting, therefore, was the fact that many of the evangelicals we interviewed construed "headship" in ways that explicitly undermined male domination and privilege. In fact, of the variety of positions evangelicals took on the meaning of headship, the most common interpretation emphasized not male authority and leadership, but the burdens of responsibility for, accountability to, and sacrifice on behalf of others that headship places on husbands. In this view, headship appears to function not so much to privilege husbands, but to domesticate and regulate them and to extract energy from them for the sake of their wives and children.

Evangelical men and women spoke frequently, for example, of the *responsibilities* of headship. Emphasizing both the husband's responsibility and the final authority of Christ, which limits the husband's authority, one man from Minnesota who attends a nondenominational church commented:

> Being the head doesn't mean that you're a ruler or something. It's more of a responsibility, and you're the one that's responsible. But you're not being a dictator. So it's easier that way, because the scriptures say that Christ is the head of the man, and the man is the head of the wife. So it's more that Christ is the ultimate head, you know. We're both under Christ.

Echoing the idea of responsibility without extraordinary authority, a Presbyterian woman from Ohio commented:

> Basically, he is to be the pillar of the home. It doesn't mean that he controls everything. It actually makes his burden even heavier, because he is also supposed to be the kind of man that can hear his wife's needs, that can be there for his wife, that can respect his wife. So a head just basically means that he has to be able to handle everything that comes to him, and that's a big responsibility. It doesn't mean that he's the boss, but it means that we go through him, you know, to solve our problems. We lean on him. He's like our rock. So I need to respect his wishes as well as he needs to respect mine.

Clearly, this is not a straightforward egalitarian ideology. Yet while this language carves out a distinct family role for husbands, it also places weighty obligations on them without obvious compensating privileges. Husbands are to solve problems, but they ought not to control things. Husbands must "handle" all situations that might arise, but they are not their families' bosses. Husbands are to be strong and reliable for others and must meet their wives' needs, but respect for differing desires between marriage partners is to be mutual, not husband-centered.

Arlie Hochschild has written insightfully about "economies of gratitude" that marriage partners negotiate.[11] Perhaps in our case it is helpful to consider the "economies of responsibility" involved in evangelical constructions of "headship." So far we have seen that headship obliges evangelical husbands to be responsible for attending to other family members' needs, while at the same time, this obligation is not counterbalanced with distinct power and privilege. Indeed, in almost every case, evangelicals explicitly say that headship does not bestow control or superiority. What do evangelical women appear to receive in return? One independent charismatic woman from California indicated that she receives love and protection she seems to value very much:

> Well, the man is head of the wife as Christ is head of the church. But he's not better than her, and he's not supposed to say "submit," you know. But he is head of the wife and the wife comes under his protection. This is so much more than, you know, women's lib. She has his loving protection.

Similarly, one Presbyterian woman from North Carolina explained that for the "privilege" of final responsibility without absolute control, a husband must take responsibility for the welfare of everyone in his family:

> When I say "head," I do not mean domineering or controlling. I see it as the one responsible for the well-being of the family. The-buck-stops-here kind of thing. But also with that privilege comes the responsibility of being a loving, caring parent, of caring for their spirituality, helping each person in the family to be the best person they can be.

Evangelicals also widely believe that, besides exacting responsibility, headship calls for the *accountability* of husbands both to and for their families. Many evangelicals we interviewed regard headship as ordained by God and believe that the man must answer to God for how he has handled his responsibilities. A Baptist man from Pennsylvania, for example, said, "I think God will hold every man accountable for his family. That is part of the headship. God has given the responsibility to the man to lead his family, and will hold him accountable come Judgment Day for how he led that family—be it good, bad, or indifferent." And an Evangelical Free woman from Minnesota stated, "I think although we will both stand before Christ and answer for what we did within our family with our children, I think the man will stand before God with a little bit more of a heavier hand on his shoulder perhaps, because it does say that the man is the head of the wife as Christ is the head of the church."

The evangelicals we interviewed commonly emphasized that, besides accountability to God, headship also means husbands are accountable to their wives, families, and others. One Presbyterian man from Colorado observed:

> Men have not taken responsibility, because I think they don't feel they are accountable to anybody, least of all their wives. He is selfish and doesn't recognize that he is accountable to her. In scripture, it talks about "Husbands, love your wives as Christ loved the church." It is talking about accountability. In the prior verses it is talking about being subject one to another.

An Evangelical Covenant woman from California elaborated on this idea:

> Well, the picture that we have in scripture is that he puts his wife's needs above his own. I think that being the head has incredible responsibilities to be considerate of those that you are leading. There's always somebody else to be accountable to, and that's a nice picture of Christianity in a marriage. But my husband is not the final authority. He still has Jesus and the church and society to be accountable to.

The "economy of responsibility" with respect to accountability means that the husband receives acknowledgment as the "head" of the family and of his wife; and yet, though he is regarded as leader, he does not have final authority. In return, the wife acquires a husband who is responsible and considerate of others, who privileges his wife's needs above his own, and who is accountable for his conduct to God, the local religious community, and the wider society. This is clearly not egalitarian ideology or practice—it is indeed formally patriarchal. Yet it is a marital bargain that many American evangelical women appear happy to strike. And the costs of the role of headship are not lost on evangelical men. A Christian and Missionary Alliance man from Georgia, for example, spoke of headship as "a horrible responsibility in a way, because when I stand before God I will be responsible for my wife's actions and my child's actions."

Another theme respondents frequently elaborated upon is the obligation of *sacrifice* for the sake of their wives that headship places on husbands. In this context, the model for how husbands ought to treat their wives is Jesus Christ, who, as the Bible says, came "not to be served, but to serve," and who "laid down his life for the church." A woman from Indiana who attends a nondenominational church described headship in these terms:

> Headship is like Christ. Our model for that is Christ. He's a servant—the servant leader, the loving, sacrificial love. That's how I see headship.

Likewise, a Southern Baptist man from North Carolina observed, "The scripture says that we're supposed to be the head of the family, just as Christ was the head of the church. I see the way he is the head of the church as being a servant, and that's what I see I need to be with her." A Southern Baptist man from Texas not only agreed, but voiced a view that almost places wives as masters in relation to their servant husbands:

> It means that he is to love the wife as Christ loved the church and gave himself for her. And so if the wife says, "You're not meeting my needs," then I think that no matter how well he thinks he's following the Lord—and I'm really speaking about myself here—he is, to a fair degree, a failure. So I think the ultimate grade comes from how the wife scores it. I think what the wife has to say shows where the husband really has assumed the proper servant role.

A nondenominational Bible church man from Illinois argued similarly, explicitly setting aside the idea of domination:

> Headship should be modeled after how Christ is the head of the church. Christ loved the church. He gave himself for the church. Sometimes it seems to be an issue of who is in control of the family. That shouldn't be the issue. He should love his wife and care for her, and they are a team. They work together, and of course he respects her opinion. They discuss decisions.

Closely tied to the image of Christ loving the church is the idea of the husband "loving his wife as he loves himself." Evangelicals often cited this part of the "Ephesians mandate" in support of self-sacrifice on the part of the husband. One Presbyterian woman from Georgia, for example, observed:

> Scripture says that a woman must submit to her husband. But then it also says he is to love her as Christ loved the church, and he has to be willing to die for her. I think people sometimes forget that. So yes, he is the head. But in that role, that is the kind of attitude he has to have.

Similarly, one Baptist man from Texas explained:

> See, we don't think of leadership and responsibility in terms of serving. But that's what Christianity and Christ are all about.
> *And that's what a husband should do?*
> That's what I'm espousing, what I believe the Bible espouses. So just the opposite of lording it over somebody, commanding or demanding, is serving

in an attractive enough way, again, so that this person wants to be around me rather than can't stand me.

Headship understood in the light of service means that husbands are not automatically granted respect. Rather, husbands must *earn* the respect and affection of their wives through sacrificial service. This concept of headship, argued some evangelicals, naturally produces fair and mutually respectful relationships. A Southern Baptist woman from California pointed out: "The Bible says that the man is supposed to love his wife as he does his own self. Well, if he loves his wife as he does his own self, then why or how in the world would he want to make all the decisions and not give his wife her rightful place?" Evangelical women often evaluate this aspect of the "economy of responsibility" in favorable terms. One Presbyterian woman from North Carolina, for example, observed, "In Ephesians, it says to love your wives as you love your own body. So when a husband loves the wife with that kind of love, then it is not a problem for the wife to let him be head of the family." Evangelical men, like this Presbyterian man from Pennsylvania, often commented on the weight that this interpretation of headship places on them:

> Headship has been abused so much over the years. Men have used those scriptures to put [women] into submission and to justify power for themselves. So I feel I have to almost make up for sins of the past. But I still believe that's the way it ought to be. That means the husband lays down his life for the spouse. It's not a good thing to have that responsibility, to have to be putting kids and the wife above you. And yet at the same time it has to jive with what honors Christ.

In their comments the evangelicals we interviewed often combined several of the themes discussed here into multifaceted descriptions of headship. One Congregational woman from California described headship this way:

> I really think that this comes with that protectorate role. I really appreciate a husband who takes accountability and responsibility very seriously. I think the problem in the past is that headship has always been associated with being the authoritarian, and I don't think that's the way it is. I believe it's servant leadership.

A Nazarene man from California also incorporated several ideas into his description of headship:

> It's providing for the emotional needs, for the sense of identity and security and so many things that men haven't even considered. It's to be the servant

of, to make sure that the woman is provided and presented to Christ at his return as spotless and perfect or unblemished. And that's a huge task, a huge responsibility to nurture in such a way that that woman or that person is whole in every dimension in her life—in self-esteem, emotionally, spiritually, physically—that every area of her being is met by the husband.

Evangelicals' common constructions of male headship primarily in terms of responsibility, accountability, and self-sacrifice at times shaped their discussions of headship in an interestingly *conditional* way. Very rare were explanations of headship that unconditionally established the rights and authority of husbands. More often, as we have seen in the quotations from interviews, talk of husbands as "heads" of their wives and families contained the subtle but perhaps important conjunction "if." One pentecostal woman from Oregon, for example, explained:

> I believe in headship, that the man needs to be the head. There is a verse in the Bible that says "Wives, be submissive to your husbands." Women just go "whoa!" I am a very independent person, always have been very strong-willed. It's like, "I'm not being subordinate to somebody." [But] you need to understand the scripture: what it really says is that *if* your husband loves you like Christ loved the church, you are going to want to follow him—he is going to be a wonderful man. You are going to know he is praying for you, that he has a relationship with God, that he wants the best for you. He wants to do things unto the Lord and you are going to follow him gladly. My husband would never, never ask me to do anything that was wrong. I would not want to follow an ungodly man. It is a neat relationship when your husband really does what the Bible says.

An Assemblies of God woman from Oregon stated this conditionality in fairly exacting terms. Under those terms, headship begins to sound a lot like an equal partnership. "*If* he were the head of the household as Christ is the head of the church, in every aspect of what that means, then my being submissive to him is not even an issue, because we're in agreement, because we're both seeking the Lord and his will for the decisions that we have to make." Similarly, a Maryland man who attends a charismatic church pointed out that "*If* you love your wife as Christ loved the church, then you could be the head of the house, but not the superior of the house." In this context, many other evangelical women we interviewed commented, "Why wouldn't I be happy to submit to someone if he were willing to die for me?" It is a bargain, with mutual obligations, that appears to many evangelical wives as well worth making.[12]

Functional Egalitarianism.   A significant number of evangelicals admitted that, although they believe in the headship of husbands theoretically, their daily experience reflects de facto an egalitarian model of marriage. Though the husband should be the head, in lived practice that idea makes very little difference. One Congregational man from California, for example, conceded, "I guess ultimately the husband is the head, but working it out day-to-day, I guess it's a mutual working relationship." A Presbyterian woman from Colorado said both that marriage partners are to be equal and that husbands are to be heads, and then explained:

> I think we can call Dad the leader of the family because I know we share the same perspective. So we can do it in that sense. But it is countered with the reality that I am out working. As the girls get older, I think these distinctions are going to become a little more obvious to them than it is right now. I want to say that the father is the head of the household. What does that mean? I don't really know. In our relationship it's not like he is saying how we are doing everything.

We asked her if in her daily life it feels like she and her husband are actually mutual and equal partners. "Yeah," she said, "it does. It really does."

Similarly, a Congregational man from Massachusetts struggled to explain what practical difference his headship makes in his marriage: "I feel as though I'm responsible for the spiritual welfare of the family. I'm not sure what that means. But I think scripture is telling me I'm responsible for it. But my wife and I do things pretty evenly." And in a revealing comment another Congregational man from Massachusetts remarked, "I think in actuality it is equal. I just think I have the final responsibility. She does pretty much whatever she wants to do, but I think God's holding me responsible for the end result." The relationship is equal, the wife is autonomous, and the husband is responsible—not a particularly bad bargain for the wife in this marriage's "economy of responsibility."

Against Authoritarianism.   Before moving on, it is worth noting again a theme that ran throughout our interviews and across much of the spectrum of evangelical views on headship: While almost no evangelicals stressed the obligation for wifely submission to husbands, the majority of interviewees—particularly women who defended headship—were at great pains to declare that husbands as heads were not to be authoritarian. One pentecostal woman from Oregon, for example, observed: "Just because he's the head doesn't mean that he's the boss. He's not the boss. He's just there to answer for situations. To be the strong leader, the responsible person. To depend on." Likewise, one Presbyterian woman from Pennsylvania said: "I don't mean a dogmatic situation, but be a leader. A leader does not have to be dogmatic. A leader can encourage, build up, support, encourage, and bring out qualities in the other person." And a woman from Oregon who attends a nondenominational church contrasted headship as it should be with the behavior of many men:

> It means he is more like a manager of the family. I don't think he is king or boss and tells everybody what to do. But he is more of an example. He shows the family what is the best way to go and how to do things, and kind of holds us all together and encourages and supports. I don't think it's with an iron fist—"you do this, you do that." That's where a lot of men have trouble. They think they are head of the family and "I am just going to tell everybody what to do," and so on. Wrong! I don't think so.[13]

In the case of many evangelicals, constructions of headship as benevolent appear to derive from positive experiences of marriage. For others, however, insistence that headship should be nonauthoritarian seemed founded on bad personal experiences. One Presbyterian woman from Michigan, for example, explained decision-making in a way that fully involved the participation of the wife and children, and then noted:

> I did not grow up in that environment. I grew up more in a dictatorship environment where my father was the head of the house and my mother and us children basically had no say. Not that my father was mean and nasty to us, but I think it could have been a friendlier atmosphere. I have a different outlook on the way I view the Bible as wanting a family to be.

And a Presbyterian woman, a professional counselor from North Carolina, observed: "I've had a lot of patients who grew up in homes with tyrannical heads of family, and I certainly don't want to leave any room for that as a possibility in this headship idea."

DECISION-MAKING IN THEORY AND PRACTICE

Decision-making in a marriage or a family inevitably involves the exercise of power. How, we might want to know, do married evangelicals actually go about the business of making decisions, whatever ideological spin they may put on the notion of headship?

In Theory. Most of the evangelicals we interviewed who spoke in support of headship said that the husband should have the "final say" in decision-making. Thus, with regard to arriving at decisions, most evangelicals clearly affirmed, in theory, a nonegalitarian, patriarchal model of marriage. However, as with nearly every other issue we have examined in this book, matters quickly became complicated as we began to explore evangelical beliefs in greater depth. For even within the view that husbands should have final say in decisions, we discovered a significant diversity among evangelicals in both their ideas of how that should function, and in their experiences of how it works out in daily life.

Perhaps predictably, there were minorities of evangelicals who took polar-opposite positions on this issue. Those few who said that authority in the decision-making process clearly lies with the husband tended to emphasize not so much the wife's need to submit to her husband as the burden of responsibility the husbands face. Having the final say in decisions is not flexing authoritarian muscle, but is the fair corollary to taking responsibility for the welfare of the family. One woman from a large seeker-church in Georgia said, "If God is going to hold him responsible, then I think he should make the decision that he is going to be responsible for. But in the end, I think a husband is foolish that doesn't listen to his wife. I think ultimately there has to be one that is going to have to take the final responsibility, and I'll let him have that." A charismatic woman from Minnesota said she preferred to have her husband take the lead: "I could never make any major decision without going to my husband. I always liked him to be the one to make the final yes or no on things. It was just easier for me."

Almost all of the evangelicals who expressed this view, however, were quick to point out that even if husbands do have final say, they should not exclude their wives from the decision-making process. One woman from an Assemblies of God church in Minnesota, for example, commented, "Even though I am talking about the husband having the final word, that doesn't mean that he's not influenced by his wife, not listening to his wife, and that's influencing his decision or compromise. Or maybe his final decision is not what it would have been before he talked to his wife." An Evangelical Free man from Georgia reflected, "Somehow the weight of that decision might lay on the guy, but not without getting input first from his wife. I think that is the key: to hear what she has to say and then pray about it. Make sure you have everyone's feelings and concerns." And a Presbyterian woman from Georgia clarified: "It doesn't mean that she is his doormat. He should be asking her opinion on things and he should consider her. She should be his first priority." So even those who maintained that husbands should have clear authority also said the men should feel a certain accountability to their wives and to God for the decisions they make.

At the other extreme were a minority of evangelicals who denied the husband any right or responsibility in making final decisions. When we asked one Ohio man who attends an independent church if headship allowed him the final word in decision-making, for example, he answered emphatically:

> No. And if any man thinks that, I'm here to tell them "not a chance." If any single man is listening to this tape, don't even think it. Communication and cooperation are fundamental in a relationship. If you think you are going to have the final word in everything, it's not going to happen. Your relationship will not survive that way. God communicates with us. He talks to us and we talk to him. He forgives us when we mess up. But in a [marriage] relationship, neither of us are perfect, so we can't look at each other through that magnifying glass and try to pick each other apart. You have to cooperate and you have to communicate. So, no final words.

An Evangelical Free man from Minnesota explained in a similar way:

> I don't make any decisions without consultation and agreement. If she says "I don't think that's right because of this principle or because of what the Word says," then I want to back off. I want to make sure we're doing things [together]. And we go to the Lord every day and we ask the Holy Spirit to reveal to us through the Word, you know, truth and right. And all those— every decision, we know when the decision is right. It's very clear to both of us.

This man's wife, who also participated in this interview, followed up by saying, "I think it's very fulfilling in life for me to go together as a team. We've done it without [working together] and that's really tough. But it's very rewarding and fulfilling when you do work together as a team."

The majority of evangelicals who explicitly connected headship with marital decision-making, however, fell somewhere between these opposing positions. They tended to agree—with varying levels of certainty and intensity—that husbands should have the final say in decision-making, but they also, almost always, were quick to qualify that idea. Some interviewees expressed a fairly strong sense of the husband's ultimate responsibility and accountability for decisions made in the family. They usually regarded both partners as full participants in the process, but the responsibility of the husband as the head seemed to carry more weight in their view. One Presbyterian man from North Carolina related:

> There's a certain authority that God grants the man of the house, and I see it exercised to different levels. The understanding we operate under is that we will discuss a lot of decisions, but if it comes down to the point where a final decision needs to be made and we can't come to agreement, then I have the final say.

A Baptist man from Pennsylvania put it this way:

> If there is a right balance there, the husband and wife will talk about decisions. And, yes, the husband will probably ultimately make the decision. But it is always a dual, not singular, activity. If there is a major decision to be made and we don't totally agree on it, we're going to talk about it until we can come close to some agreement. But ultimately somebody has to make a decision. The notion of headship says that the man ultimately has to make that. But you know what? He ultimately also has to answer for it.

Others agreed but presented the ultimate authority of the husband even less strongly, emphasizing instead that the final decision is the husband's only as a last resort. One Evangelical Free woman from Illinois, for instance, stated that the biblical mandate for husbands to love their wives normally encourages mutual submission in marriage. However, "if it really, really, really, really, really, really comes down to it, then yeah, the husband ultimately in some cases will end up having the last [word]. But I don't think that that's like an automatic thing." In this view, the final say of the husband is more an ideological safety net than a routine reality. The basic decision-making model is one of mutual input, discussion, and compromise. And only if they have tried everything and still cannot agree, then as a last resort the husband should be the one to break the tie. A Nazarene woman from California explained:

> When it gets down to it, there are some times when a decision has to be made. And I tend to think that when it gets to that point where both parties have listened to the other person's point of view, and they've negotiated as much as they can, somebody's gotta be responsible and make the decision. I tend to see that as ending up on the male doorstep, but again I couldn't make that an absolute—that that's always the way it's gonna work out.

In Practice.   Whether the respondent's ideological position on decision-making was relatively patriarchal or egalitarian, however, one fact that clearly emerged from nearly all interviews is that the "final say" male privilege is actually almost completely irrelevant in practice. That is, last resort "final says" almost never come up in the pragmatics of evangelical marriages. Time and again, when we pressed even the more ideologically rigid evangelicals to be specific about these tie-breaking scenarios, they had great difficulty giving concrete examples.[14] One Congregational man from Massachusetts, for instance, related:

> In general, [my wife] and I reach agreement. If we had a major decision that we couldn't agree on, I think I would be responsible to make that decision. That's never happened. And I personally think that if both people are in the Holy Spirit, it's not going to happen.

A woman from Illinois remarked, "I think that ultimately if you completely reached an impasse, ultimately there's cases where you could say, 'okay, well, you have to [break the tie] with this so. . . . ' But how often is that going to happen?" One man from a nondenominational church in Minnesota explained why he has never had to have the final say in his marriage:

> I think that's because neither of us are trying to be right, or "Mr. Big Stuff," or anything. We both face things and talk about things and pray about things. And I think that the right thing is both of us have got to submit ourselves to the Lord. And the final decision, hopefully that's the one the Lord leads us in, and that's all. It's never a conflict as far as, you know, I've got to override something that she's decided, or she has to override me. You know, we're always in agreement. We're both under Christ, and if you're both submitting to the Lord then things should work out.

Most evangelicals we interviewed, then, clearly do feel the need to maintain a meaningful ideology of headship within the subculture. But according to the vast majority, one of the most frequently mentioned aspects of male headship is rarely, if ever, capitalized upon. In the words of sociologist Sally Gallagher, headship's "final say" authority is a trump card that male heads of families simply do not play.[15] It remains formally in the evangelical repertoire of action, but is very rarely used. An Evangelical Free man from California explained the need for headship: "Whenever there's a disagreement and a final decision needs to be made, I think God has put the man to make that decision." Yet he immediately qualified this: "But I think those kind of decisions should be really rare." And when he began to describe the way he and his wife actually make decisions, the "final decision" model of headship vanished; what emerged instead was a model of mutual negotiation and consensus:

Something we've started doing is, you know, there's veto power. Both of us have veto power. And so, we're looking at houses, and I may have really liked one of them but she didn't, so fine, it's dead, and we're on to the next one. I think that's a good way to do it.

At least three factors seem to play into the functionally egalitarian practices of most evangelical marriages. First, many married evangelicals appear to have satisfactory if not happy relationships that seldom come to total disagreement and ultimatums about decisions. As a Bible church man from Illinois observed: "Well I think that to me it means that at a very practical level you are in tune with each other, you share common beliefs, you have common priorities. Then very seldom are you going to be in conflict with each other." Similarly, a Nazarene woman from California noted, "The headship part is kind of innate. I mean, it's just there and we both know it's there, but we don't abuse it. He doesn't step on me." And an Assemblies of God woman from Minnesota explained the compatibility of headship and equality thus: "Yeah, I would say, it's hard to explain. But I think I very much saw it with my parents. They always just did stuff together. They always made decisions together. I'd say they were partners in everything, but yet I can still say that my dad maintained the head of the household and my mom let him do that. She let him have that say." When we asked if she saw partnership and male headship as contradictory in any way, she said "no."

Second, evangelicals, like most other Americans, seem to naturally rely on pragmatic expertise when it comes to decision-making. Thus, one man from a Nazarene church in Oregon reflected, "If we can recognize which one of us is stronger in that particular area that we're working on and give more weight to that opinion, that seems to help us make better choices as we go along."

Third, like other married American men, evangelical husbands are not in a position to regularly assert extra authority in the decision-making process, since evangelical women as a group are participating just as much in the paid labor force as other American women.[16] Recall the observation of the Presbyterian woman from Colorado quoted above:

[Dad's leadership] is countered with the reality that I am out working. . . . I want to say that the father is the head of the household. What does that mean? I don't really know. In our relationship it is not like he is saying how we are doing everything.

And so the picture that emerges from our interviews is one of evangelicals working to integrate headship ideology into marriages that are actually quite mutual and equal in practice. Time and again in our interviews, evangelicals expressed the need for male headship while simultaneously describing the functionally egalitarian practices of their marriages. As one Christian and Missionary Alliance woman from Ohio described:

> Well, I feel my husband is the head of the household and he would make any final decisions. But, we have a very equal relationship in that respect, that we virtually both make the final decision in things. I mean, my husband is not going to make decisions without talking to me about it or vice versa. So, he is the head of the household, but we have a real kind of equal relationship.

Later in the interview she remarked, "We both feel that he is the head of the household, but we divide things. How things get worked [out] ends up being very equal as far as any decision that's made." A man from a community church in Colorado also mixed together headship, mutuality, and equality:

> My wife's decisions or thoughts have just as much weight as mine do. We come to agreement. Sometimes we agree to disagree on things. But she has just as equal work as I do. But as far as if there was a decision to be made and she could not make a decision about it, I would take the lead and make that decision.

The response of one Presbyterian woman from North Carolina started off supporting clear male domination yet ended up in favor of mutual submission:

> I love the word "interdependent." Even though someone needs to be head, I like the idea of submission to be this: a woman should submit herself totally to her husband—not just her body, but all of her ideas too. As a loving head of the family, he is going to listen to them. He may not do everything she wants done, but she feels free to share with him. They really do share back and forth. I think he would be submitting to her as well—mutual submission, talking about what is important to them. It seems to me if there is a problem, they should talk and come to a mutual decision on it.

WHAT IS GOING ON HERE?

Marriage relationships in which the husband is the "head" are also equal? Wives defer to husbands a final authority in decisions that husbands do not exercise? Husbands may not rule their families, but are still ultimately entirely responsible for them? What is going on here?

The tensions, contradictions, and ambivalence we see among evangelicals on issues surrounding marriage relationships are not unique to this area of life. Throughout this book, we have seen similar complexities and incongruities in evangelical approaches to "Christian America," politics, pluralism, other religions, education, and related topics. Evangelicals, we have learned, negotiate their lives with cultural tool kits containing a mix of tools that do not necessarily all work neatly together. Contemporary evangelicals are heirs of diverse historical and theological legacies, the multiple strands of which provide logics, impulses, and inclinations that often contradict each other.

On the one hand, when it comes to marriage relationships, few evangelicals are committed egalitarians ideologically. Rare is the ordinary evangelical who stands up and fights for full equality between the sexes in marriage as a matter of basic human rights. Most evangelicals are quite comfortable with the idea that the husband should be head of the family. They believe the Bible teaches this, and they very much want to take it seriously.

On the other hand, most ordinary evangelicals are also very comfortable thinking about marriage as an equal partnership. They stress the need for mutual respect and participation in the relationship. They conspicuously avoid talk of wifely submission and take great pains to stress that husbands may not rule their families as superiors. Indeed, when most evangelicals discuss the meaning of headship, it has little to do with male privilege or domination, but instead means, for husbands, extra responsibility for, accountability to, and sacrifice on account of their wives and children. And when they describe their lived experiences of marriage, their practices tend to sound more egalitarian than patriarchal.

Part of what is at work here is the influence of the gender-egalitarian values of the surrounding culture. Evangelicals, too, are moving along with the cultural current propelled over the past thirty years in part by the women's movement. Contemporary evangelicals may be suspicious of the feminist movement, and may even sometimes denounce it, but their thinking has nevertheless been at least somewhat shaped by it.

Another factor at work here is the very same set of social structural conditions that other Americans face, which have given rise to changing gender relations in the United States: the stagnation of average real family incomes since 1973 (measured in constant dollars); the demise of the single-paycheck, male-breadwinner model of employment; the massive entry of American women into the paid labor force; the opening up of many professions and occupations to women workers; the increased availability of effective methods of birth control; and the erosion of legal bases of gender inequality. The fact that evangelical women participate in the paid labor force at rates no lower than other American women is also telling.

At the same time, we think it would be a misinterpretation to argue that an essential evangelical patriarchy has been corrupted by entirely external cultural and social forces, pushing evangelicals toward a more egalitarian practice that is in fact alien to their true faith. Evangelicalism is a multivocal religion, comprised of a variety of subcultural resources that can move evangelicals in many different ideological and practical directions. In fact, evangelicals do possess more than a few indigenous subcultural tools—whether specific biblical passages or more general theological themes—on which they can draw to legitimate gender equality. The plethora of evangelical books on egalitarian gender relationships—such as Gilbert Bilezekian's *Beyond Sex Roles*, Letha Scanzoni and Nancy Hardesty's *All We're Meant to Be: Biblical Feminism for Today*, Patricia Gundry's *Heirs Together: Mutual Submission in Marriage*, Craig Keener's *Paul, Women, and Wives*, and Richard and Catherine Kroeger's *I Suffer Not a Woman*, to name a few—signals this fact. It is likely, then, that the "external" social and cultural forces described above have not so much "contaminated" evangelicalism, but rather have created a broad social context within which the tradition's more egalitarian subcultural tools have become relevant and meaningful to a greater degree.

Still, it is clear that evangelicals have not adopted en masse a purely egalitarian marriage ideology. Instead, they have largely integrated an older ideology of headship into newer egalitarian languages and practices. In sometimes amazing rhetorical couplings of gender equality and male headship, evangelicals manage to salvage the symbolic image of the husband as head, while simultaneously embracing and expressing the more egalitarian values and practices of their own tradition and the broader culture—and all of this in the context of lived relationships that appear much more equal in practice than evangelical headship rhetoric would suggest.[17]

Should we expect, then, that the majority of contemporary American evangelicals will line up behind the leaders of the Southern Baptist

Convention and their new *Baptist Faith and Message Statement*'s declaration that wives should submit themselves to their husbands, and that husbands should provide for, protect, and lead their families? Perhaps yes, insofar as this language does resonate with part of what ordinary evangelicals think about the matter. But they would not endorse the Baptist statement with great conviction. And how they would interpret some of the key terms (for instance, "submit" and "lead") would often be significantly at odds with what the Baptist leaders appear to mean. Furthermore, by the time the principles behind these key words are actually worked out in ordinary evangelicals' daily lives, their marriages do not look much like what one imagines the Baptist leaders were hoping to produce. Finally, had the Southern Baptist declaration read instead that "Marriage should be an equal partnership involving mutual submission between husbands and wives in all things," the majority of ordinary evangelicals would probably be happy to sign onto that pronouncement as well. It would just as easily fit their views.

Are the mass of ordinary contemporary American evangelicals cutting-edge champions of women's rights and gender equality? Certainly not. Then, are they fervent proponents of a patriarchal system of marriage? Certainly not. Evangelicals generally do want to hold onto the discourse of male headship. But they also happily embrace the soft rhetoric of mutuality and equality. They also find their marriages shaped by social forces that tend to undermine male authority and promote egalitarian practices. In the end, the picture that emerges is much more complex and muddled than the rhetoric of certain evangelical leaders would suggest. It is not a picture that will convert the cultural critics of evangelicalism to a new opinion of great sympathy and approval; neither is it one that verifies their worst fears and condemnations.

CONCLUSION

Demythologizing
the Angel/Demon

AMERICAN EVANGELICALISM NEEDS a good dose of demythologizing. In the American media, in the popular imagination, and often in academic scholarship, American evangelicals are routinely cast as either angels or demons. The angel myth is fostered by many religio-political conservative activists who posture American evangelicals as the country's last bastion of righteousness in a decaying society, a mass constituency of morally upright and outraged citizens prepared to "take back America" for Christ. This image may abet political mobilization and power-brokering, but it is mythological. It is not the real truth about evangelicals.

Likewise, many liberal-leftist activists imagine American evangelicals as demons. They cast evangelicalism as an ominous resurgence of religious oppression, a movement of radical, intolerant, and coercive zealots determined to undermine basic American freedoms in the name of narrow religious supremacy. The demon image may abet political mobilization and power-wielding of another sort, but it too is mythological, not the truth about evangelicals. In the so-called "culture wars" drama—played out mostly by small parties of activist cultural and political elites of both persuasions—American evangelicals are too often projected "larger than life" as angels or demons. But in fact, we have seen, they are neither.

This cultural analysis of ordinary evangelicals has uncovered some of the diversity and complexity present in the American evangelical subculture. Its portrayal of evangelicals is life-sized—as mostly ordinary Americans of a particular religious bent who are beset by the same kinds of incongruities, made interesting by the same kinds of complexities, and tempered by the same kinds of ambivalences that characterize other Americans. We have seen that, like most people, they maintain a variety of diverse and sometimes conflicting beliefs and ideas among and within themselves. And we are led to conclude that most ordinary American evangelicals are not very fairly represented by many of the single-minded and often self-appointed conservative Christian leaders who claim to speak for them.

Be that as it may, mythologies about angels and demons sell exceptionally well. We humans, after all, are fundamentally story-telling creatures who make sense of our lives and our world through the tradition-grounded narratives that construct our identities and practices. Despite lingering Enlightenment ideologies about strong objectivity and universal rationality, our lives remain fundamentally governed by the imaginative narratives of the historical traditions that encompass them. Since humans are roused well by drama, rivalry, and conflict, the narratives that resonate best—whether recounted as scientific analyses or not—are stories of darkness and light, of crisis and victory, of angels and demons. These typically offer simple and entertaining story lines for the many journalists (and sometimes academics) who compete for the attention of a reading public that wants uncomplicated, engaging stories. Mythologies about angels and demons also make great fundraisers for political activists. There's nothing quite like the Manichean threat of a desperate struggle against darkness to keep the constituents' checks rolling in. Thus, angel and demon stories continue to maintain an alluring grip on the human imagination today—even, apparently, for some of the most secular of moderns.

THE TRIUMPH OF AMBIVALENCE

But American evangelicals are neither angels nor demons. They are much too diverse, complex, ambivalent, and inconsistent for that. The vast majority of ordinary American evangelicals are not particularly interested in cultural warfare; they do not share many of the assumptions and proclivities that make such warring attractive. Nor are more than a few of them, in Frances Fitzgerald's words, a "disciplined, charging army," ready and eager to follow their alleged leaders into battle.[1] If anything, our interviews with ordinary evangelicals reveal not the triumphantism of the Christian Right, but the triumph of ambivalence.

Since dramas about angels and demons are rousing and engaging, there is a certain anti-drama in this book's story. But it is a demythologized anti-drama that might serve well both American evangelicals and our common American public life. Both will be better off if conservative religio-political activists realize that "their" alleged mobilized constituency is not really very much *theirs*, nor much mobilized. And both will be better off if liberal-left-wing activists realize that "those" radical zealot evangelicals are not quite as alien or radical or mobilized as they fear. This demythologization is not a story that will make arresting headlines or raise big political funds. Yet it may help to de-escalate needless cultural conflicts and open the way for groups of very different Americans to work together more successfully toward a common life of civility and justice in a genuinely pluralistic society.

IMPROVING ON "SAMPLE SIZE" AND "SAMPLE BIAS"

As it stands, American evangelicals remain one of the last social groups in the United States that people can speak disparagingly about in public and get away with it—at least in the general circles in which I move. Who among the well-educated is going to speak well of evangelicals? It's like standing up for the Crusades. Some people openly deprecate evangelicals. Others speak of them with a vaguely irritated tone of voice, or a certain barely perceptible look of pain on their faces. Either way, the underlying view of evangelicals is about the same.

This book makes clear the fact that most of those who disparage evangelicals in general terms really don't know what they are talking about. In fact, many don't have significant personal relationships with enough ordinary evangelicals to inform their views of what evangelicals are actually like. So, often they are left to base their views on media reports, organizational newsletters, ideas about what evangelicals *should* be like based on the few things they think they do know, and the general sense about evangelicalism they pick up from others like themselves. From a sociological perspective, these people are working with too small and too biased a sample to be able to draw valid, generalizable conclusions. They need, in sociological jargon, to "increase their N" and address their "sampling biases."

Most people agree, in theory at least, that those who have strong negative views and make strong public statements about groups of people ought to know what they are talking about sufficiently to warrant such views and statements. Otherwise, those views and statements are what we normally call ignorant and prejudiced. Especially in an increasingly pluralistic society like ours, the less genuine understanding people have of others who are not like themselves, the less opportunity there will be for everyone to figure out how to construct a common, civil life together. This will continue to be the case as long as some people easily denigrate others with whom they are not really familiar. To be sure, many evangelicals are often quite guilty of this themselves. But they are not alone.

This book has attempted especially to broaden outsiders' familiarity with evangelicals—to provide a larger "sample size" to better understand this significant group of Americans. It has also attempted, for ordinary evangelicals themselves, to wrap words around some things that most of them already know but may have a hard time seeing on a big scale or articulating in a way they find satisfactory. I hope that for both, and for all people of goodwill, this book serves as one helpful step toward figuring out how to build, despite our many differences, a just and civil common American life together.

What Surveys Tell Us

WHAT CAN WE LEARN from telephone surveys about conservative Protestants, pluralism, tolerance, and politics? I suggested in the introduction that descriptive survey findings on such matters are often superficial and incomplete. Nevertheless, relevant survey data are available, and reviewing them here may add a somewhat helpful, even if limited, dimension to our investigation.

In this appendix I examine findings from five national-level telephone surveys that contained questions about religious identity, affiliations, and beliefs, and about pluralism, tolerance, and politics. The first is the Religious Identity and Influence Survey, funded by The Pew Charitable Trusts and conducted by a research team from the University of North Carolina at Chapel Hill, between January and March, 1996.[1] The second is the Religious Right Survey, commissioned by the American Jewish Committee and fielded by the Gallup International Institute in 1996.[2] Third, I analyze data from the 1996 General Social Survey, conducted by the University of Chicago National Opinion Research Center.[3] Finally, I examine evidence from the Southern Focus Poll, Spring 1996 and the Southern Focus Poll, Fall 1996, conducted by the Institute for Research in Social Science at University of North Carolina, Chapel Hill.[4]

All of the findings in the following tables compare differences between various subgroups of conservative Protestants and all other Americans on matters such as tolerance, political pluralism, and race relations. Whenever the survey data allow, I have used multiple measures of conservative Protestantism—including self-identification, denominational affiliation, and theological beliefs—for comparative purposes. I have used logistical regression procedures to determine whether differences between conservative Protestants and other Americans are statistically significant. All regression models control for age, sex, race, education, income, regional location, marital status, and urban-rural residence. We can be confident, therefore, that the observed differences between religious groups do not spuriously represent other more fundamental demographic influences and differences. Differences between groups that were not found to be statistically significant are noted as such in the tables as "n.s."

One of the goals of this appendix is to present results in a way that is readily comprehensible to an audience of readers broader than those who know how to interpret logistical regression results. Therefore, I do not present in this appendix's tables the actual logistical regression betas or log odds, since their meaning may be unclear to the statistically uninitiated. Instead, all findings are presented as differences in *percentages* of comparison groups that hold some attitude, affirm some belief, or engage in some action. To compute these more easily comprehensible descriptive percentages while still controlling for demographics, I have used a multivariate statistical procedure known as multiclassification analysis. This procedure compares differences in dependent-variable means between groups, while controlling for differences in the survey respondents' age, sex, race, education, income, regional location, marital status, and urban-rural residence.[5] Using this procedure with dichotomous dependent variables, computed means are directly convertible into percentages. These converted percentages are the figures presented in the tables that follow. Readers should bear in mind, then, that tests of statistical significance were figured using logistical regression models, but the results for statistically significant differences are displayed as percentages, calculated through multiclassification analysis. Both forms of analysis are multivariate, and in this analysis both were controlled for the same demographic factors. Tests of statistical significance by both procedures showed results that were nearly always identical for the same dependent variables.

In interpreting the tables, we should focus attention both on the absolute support for different views within specific groups (for example,

how intolerant are evangelicals themselves?) and on relative comparisons between groups (for example, are evangelicals *more* intolerant
than other Americans?).

To put this appendix into perspective, then, what follows is merely
a quick summary of quantitative data, with little commentary or interpretation. The goal is a broad overview of the "lay of the land." If this
feels like a whirlwind tour of a mass of numerical data, that is because
that's exactly what it is.

RELIGION, MORALITY, AND PUBLIC LIFE

At the heart of many people's concerns about American conservative
Protestants are apprehensions about their views of the role of religion
and morality in public life. Are fundamentalists and evangelicals cultural imperialists who want to impose their religious and moral views
on everyone else? Survey data provide some—even if not conclusive—
answers to this question.

Christian Right rhetoric contends: America was founded as a Christian nation and prospered under God's blessing. Having recently abandoned its commitment to God's unchanging truth and morality, however, America is now suffering social breakdown. Unless America
repents and returns to "traditional" values and morals, America will
suffer God's judgment. Turning America around from its anti-Christian
moral drift will require the active struggle of Christians and supportive
allies—the moral majority of Americans—against hostile forces comprised of secular humanists, feminists, the liberal mass media, and so
on. At the very least, traditional Christians, whose views are typically
excluded and attacked by liberal cultural elites, should insist on a place
for their voice in public debates. This is the story expressed by many
conservative Christian social and political activists. To what extent do
ordinary conservative Protestants appear to subscribe to this view?

Examining table 1,[6] we see that not only conservative Protestants
but the majority of Americans believe that America was founded as a
Christian nation. The vast majority of evangelicals and fundamentalists affirm this belief, but two-thirds of all other Americans do also.
Similarly, we see a widespread perception among all groups that American society is suffering a serious breakdown. More than 80 percent of
nonevangelical Americans and more than 90 percent of evangelicals
and fundamentalists believe this.

But conservative Protestants and other Americans begin to part

TABLE 1 Conservative Protestant Views on Morality and Public Life, Compared to All Other Americans

(percent)[1]

	Self-Identified Evangelicals	Self-Identified Fundamentalists	All Other Americans	Members of Conservative Protestant Denominations
The U.S. was founded as a Christian nation	87	82	66 66	77
We are seeing a serious breakdown of American society	92	93	83 82	91
Morals should be based on an absolute, unchanging standard	68	63	31 29	58
Religion is a private matter, to be kept out of public debates over social and political issues (disagree)	69	62	30 29	54
Christian morality should be the law of the land even though not all Americans are Christians	55	50	25 23	49
The federal government should promote traditional values in our society[2]	68	70	50	NA[3]
Feminists are hostile to respondent's moral and spiritual values	66	55	30 29	51
The mass media is hostile to respondent's moral and spiritual values	77	72	47 48	63
Abortion should be illegal in all cases	36	28	14 13	29
Women should take care of running their homes and leave running the country up to men[4]	22	26	14 14	21

Source: 1996 Religious Identity and Influence Survey.
1. Controlling for age, sex, race, education, income, region, marital status, and urban residence, using multiclassification analysis; dichotomous dependent variable means converted to percentages; all differences significant at the $p < .05$ level.
2. Source = Southern Focus Poll, Spring 1996.
3. NA = variable not available on the dataset.
4. Source = 1996 General Social Survey.

ways when it comes to the role of morality and religion in public life. About two-thirds of evangelicals and fundamentalists believe in an absolute, unchanging standard upon which morality should be based. But only about half that proportion of all other Americans—one-third—agree. In almost exactly the same proportions evangelicals, fundamentalists, and all other Americans disagree that religion is a private matter that should be kept out of public debates over social and political issues. About one-half to two-thirds of conservative Protestants disagree, viewing religion instead as a publicly relevant matter; while less than one-third of other Americans do so. Similarly, about one-half of conservative Protestants believe that Christian morality should be the law of the land, even though not all Americans are Christians. But only one-quarter of other Americans think this. Likewise, about 70 percent of evangelicals and fundamentalists believe that the federal government should promote traditional values in our society; compared to only 50 percent of other Americans. A majority of evangelicals and fundamentalists view feminists as hostile to their moral and spiritual values, whereas only one-third of other Americans agree. Well more than two-thirds of evangelicals and fundamentalists view the mass media as hostile to their moral and spiritual values, whereas about one-half of other Americans do. More than twice the proportion of evangelicals and fundamentalists compared with other Americans believe that abortion should be illegal in all cases. And evangelicals are more likely to say that women should stay at home and leave running the country up to men.

In sum, this survey evidence suggests that ordinary conservative Protestants do tend to be significantly more supportive of some of the claims of the Christian Right than other Americans—often 20 to 40 percentage points more so. Evangelicals and fundamentalists are, indeed, distinctive in these ways. This general conclusion, however, should not mask other interesting findings in this data. We should notice, for example, that about half of conservative Protestants do *not* believe that Christian morality should be the law of the land; and that the vast majority of them do not think that women should leave running the country up to men, nor do they believe that abortion should be illegal in all cases. These are minority views among conservative Protestants. We should also remain aware that fully one-half of Americans who are not conservative Protestants share evangelicals' and fundamentalists' concerns that the mass media are hostile to their moral and spiritual values, and believe that the federal government should

TABLE 2   Conservative Protestant Religious and Social Views, Compared
to Other Churchgoing Christians
(percent)[1]

	Self-Identified Evangelicals	Self-Identified Fundamentalists	Other Christians	Members of Conservative Protestant Denominations
Christian values are under serious attack in the United States today[2]	93	88	79 80	88
Everyone should have the right to live by their own morality, even when it is not Christian morality (disagree)	35	32	24 21	37
Christians should try to change American society to better reflect God's will, even using ways they know may cause conflict and set people against each other[2]	32	26	20 23	n.s.[3]
The only hope for salvation is through personal faith in Jesus Christ	94	89	57 61	73

Source: 1996 Religious Identity and Influence Survey.
  1. Controlling for age, sex, race, education, income, region, marital status, and urban residence, using multiclassification analysis; dichotomous dependent variable means converted to percentages; all differences significant at the $p < .05$ level.
  2. Comparison with other churchgoing Protestants only, not Catholics.
  3. n.s. = logistic regression procedures show differences between groups are not statistically significant at the $p < .05$ level.

promote traditional values. Conservative Protestants are not alone in
these views.

Continuing to review our survey evidence on religious and social
views, we see in table 2 (which, due to data limitations, compares conservative Protestants not with all other Americans, but only with other
churchgoing Christians) that an overwhelming majority of evangelicals
and fundamentalists perceive that Christian values are under serious

attack in the United States today. But the great majority of churchgoing mainline, liberal, and other Protestants also share this perception. Evangelicals are about 10 percentage points more likely than other churchgoing Christians to disagree with the view that everyone has the right to live by their own morality, even when it is not Christian morality. Self-identified evangelicals and fundamentalists are also 12 and 6 percentage points, respectively, more likely than other Protestants to affirm that Christians should be actively trying to change American society, even using ways they know might cause conflict. Those in conservative Protestant denominations, however, are no more likely to believe this than other Americans. Finally, conservative Protestants of all kinds are significantly more likely than other churchgoing Christians to make the claim that only through personal faith in Jesus Christ can people be saved.

Once again, we see that conservative Protestants tend to be more religiously exclusivist, and perhaps more defensive and contentious, than other Americans. Yet, at the same time, we ought to note that the vast majority of evangelicals and fundamentalists do, in fact, believe that everyone should have the right to live by their own morality. Similarly, the vast majority believe that Christians should not cause conflicts in their attempts at social influence.

Well-publicized, contentious battles over textbooks, sex education, prayer in schools, and so on have left many Americans wary about what appear to be evangelical and fundamentalist attempts to force distinctively Christian views in public schools. What does survey evidence on the matter tell us? We see in table 3 that evangelicals and fundamentalists are more likely than other Americans both to see public schools as spiritually hostile, and to want to bring Christian religion back into the public schools. Conservative Protestants are about three times more likely than other Americans to believe that public schools should teach Christian values and morals. They are more than twice as likely to think that the biggest problems with schools are the removal of prayer from classrooms, the influence of secular humanism or secular values. Evangelicals and fundamentalists are also twice as likely as other Americans to view the public schools as hostile to their moral and spiritual values. They are much more likely to want to see public school instruction include Christian views of science and history. And they are significantly more likely to want public school teachers to lead their classes in spoken Christian prayers.

Once again, however, we should not let the relative differences

TABLE 3   Conservative Protestant Views on Religion and Education,
Compared to All Other Americans
(percent)[1]

	Self-Identified Evangelicals	Self-Identified Fundamentalists	All Other Americans	Members of Conservative Protestant Denominations
Public schools should teach Christian values and morals	18	16	5	13
Biggest problems with schools are removal of prayer, secular humanism, or secular values and morals	29	27	11 / 10	25
Public schools are hostile to respondent's moral and spiritual values	58	50	24 / 23	47
Public school instruction should include Christian views of science and history	90	83	57 / 57	77
Teachers should lead their classes in spoken Christian prayers	20	22	12 / 12	18

Source: 1996 Religious Identity and Influence Survey.

1. Controlling for age, sex, race, education, income, region, marital status, and urban residence, using multiclassification analysis; dichotomous dependent variable means converted to percentages; all differences significant at the $p < .05$ level.

between groups overshadow the significance of the absolute proportions within groups. For these data also show that the vast majority of evangelicals and fundamentalists do *not* think that public schools should teach Christian values and morals; do not believe that teachers should lead classes in spoken Christian prayers; and do not blame schools' problems on secular humanism, secular values, the removal of prayer, and so on. Those conservative Protestants who do so are in the distinct minority. Furthermore, it is worth noticing, for example, that nearly 60 percent of Americans who are not conservative Protestants also believe that public school instruction should include Christian views of science and history. The desire for a more religiously inclusive curriculum apparently is not limited to fundamentalists and evangelicals.[7]

RELIGION AND POLITICS

What do these surveys tell us about conservative Protestants and politics? According to table 4, about 90 percent of conservative Protestants (measured denominationally and theologically) believe that the main cause of America's problems is moral decay. And 76 percent of theologically defined conservative Protestants think Christians should get involved in politics to protect their values. (Denominationally defined conservative Protestants were not significantly different from other Americans on this issue.) Thus, the majority of conservative Protestants appear prepared to engage in politics with explicitly religious interests in mind. Furthermore, 15 percent fewer conservative Protestants than other Americans believe that a person can be a political liberal and a good Christian; and 12 percent more conservative Protestants than other Americans say that on most political issues there is only one correct Christian view. In these ways, conservative Protestants reflect what many would consider a narrow and inflexible approach to faith-based political involvement. Conservative Protestants defined theologically (though not denominationally) are also more likely than other Americans to favor constitutional amendments permitting school prayer and declaring the United States a Christian nation. They are also less likely to think that the religious views of a politician are not relevant in determining fitness for public office. However, conservative Protestants are not more likely than other Americans to admire right-wing and Klan-associated 1996 Louisiana candidate for U.S. Senate, David Duke.

But again, to keep our discussion in perspective, we should attend not only to comparisons between groups, but also to the absolute support for different political views within specific groups. The responses of Conservative Protestants do reflect some attitudes about politics that appear religiously narrow and inflexible. But the relative difference between conservative Protestants and other Americans on these matters is not nearly as large as the total support for the same views among those other Americans. Solid majorities of Americans, we see, agree with evangelicals about moral decay as the cause of America's

TABLE 4   Conservative Protestant Social and Political Views, Compared
                 to All Other Americans
                 (percent)[1]

	Members of Conservative Protestant Denominations	All Other Americans	Conservative Protestants Theologically
The main cause of America's problems is moral decay	92	80 76	85
Christians should get involved in politics to protect their values	n.s.[2]	62 57	76
A person can be both a political liberal and a good Christian	60	75 75	n.s.
On most political issues there is one correct Christian point of view	32	20 19	30
Respondent favors a constitutional amendment permitting prayers to be spoken in the public schools	n.s.	62 55	72
Respondent supports a constitutional amendment declaring the U.S. a Christian nation	n.s.	25 22	36
The religious views of a politician are not relevant in determining fitness for public office	n.s.	54 56	46
Respondent admires David Duke	n.s.	4 4	n.s.

Source: 1996 Religious Right Survey.
   1. Controlling for age, sex, race, education, income, region, marital status, and urban residence, using multiclassification analysis; dichotomous dependent variable means converted to percentages.
   2. n.s. = logistic regression procedures show differences between groups are not statistically significant at the
p < .05 level.

problems; about the legitimacy of Christians becoming involved in politics to protect their values; about the incompatibility of liberal politics
and Christianity; about the need for a constitutional amendment on
school prayer; and about the relevance of religion in determining fitness for political office. One may certainly believe that most Americans
are terribly wrong on those issues. But at the very least we would be

misled to think that conservative Protestants are wildly out of the cultural norm on these matters. Conservative Protestants merely accentuate tendencies that are widespread in the American population generally. Moreover, we should note that, of conservative Protestants (depending on how they are measured), about 70 percent do *not* think there is only one correct Christian political point of view; between 64 and 75 percent do not favor a "Christian nation" amendment; about half do not think religion matters in determining fitness for public office; between 28 and 38 percent do not favor a school prayer amendment; and between 25 and 40 percent do not think Christianity and political liberalism are incompatible. Conservative Protestants—especially those defined as such theologically—are significantly more likely than other Americans to support these ideas. But it is also true that very large numbers of conservative Protestants do *not* support them.

Looking beyond the general political attitudes and orientations observed in table 4, to what degree are conservative Protestants more likely to support and defend the Religious Right? According to table 5, conservative Protestants measured theologically (though not denominationally) are somewhat more likely to have heard a moderate amount or more about the Religious Right, and (at 32 percent) nearly twice as likely to consider themselves supporters of the Religious Right than other Americans. Furthermore, evangelicals are four times and fundamentalists and denominational conservative Protestants twice as likely as other Americans to say that their vote is influenced *a lot* by conservative Christian political organizations, such as the Christian Coalition, while conservative Protestants of all kinds are more likely to say that their vote is influenced *some* by such groups. Finally, conservative Protestants measured theologically (though again not denominationally) are less likely to believe that criticisms of the Religious Right are legitimate, and more likely to believe such criticisms raise exaggerated fears. Overall, then, conservative Protestants tend to be more aware and supportive of, more influenced by, and more defensive about the Religious Right than Americans at large.

But that conclusion again must be placed in broader perspective by considering the following points: One-half of conservative Protestants have not heard much about the Religious Right. More than two-thirds of them do not consider themselves supporters of the Religious Right. Well more than half of conservative Protestants say their voting is never influenced by the Religious Right. And the majority of conservative Protestants think that criticisms of the

TABLE 5 Conservative Protestant Views on the Religious Right, Compared to All Other Americans
(percent)[1]

	Self-Identified Evangelicals	Self-Identified Fundamentalists	Members of Conservative Protestant Denominations	All Other Americans	Conservative Protestants Theologically
Have heard a great deal or a moderate amount about the Religious Right	NA[3]	NA	n.s.[2]	45 / 42	50
Considers self a supporter of the Religious Right	NA	NA	n.s.	22 / 17	32
Vote is influenced *a lot* by conservative Christian political organizations such as the Christian Coalition	19	12	12	5 / 5	NA
Vote is influenced *some* by conservative Christian political organizations such as the Christian Coalition	29	25	25	17 / 17	NA
People who criticize the Religious Right for its political activities are raising legitimate concerns about this movement	NA	NA	n.s.	37 / 43	31
People who criticize the Religious Right for its political activities are raising exaggerated fears about this movement	NA	NA	n.s.	34 / 32	40

Sources: 1996 Religious Right Survey, 1996 Religious Identity and Influence Survey.
1. Controlling for age, sex, race, education, income, region, marital status, and urban residence, using multiclassification analysis; dichotomous dependent variable means converted to percentages.
2. n.s. = logistic regression procedures show differences between groups are not statistically significant at the $p < .05$ level.
3. NA = variable not available on the dataset.

Religious Right raise legitimate concerns, not exaggerated fears. Support for the Religious Right, in other words, although stronger among conservative Protestants as we would expect, is located nevertheless among only a minority of conservative Protestants. The majority appear to be uninterested in, unsupportive of, and uninfluenced by the Religious Right.

We examine in table 6 survey data on conservative Protestant views on specific kinds of laws, which may indicate degrees of support for basic rights as well as degrees of tolerance and compassion for those who are socially different and vulnerable. The evidence is mixed. It shows that self-identified evangelicals are more likely to believe current laws and regulations that protect freedom of speech go too far. Yet fundamentalists and denominationally measured conservative Protestants do not differ from other Americans on this issue. Evangelicals and fundamentalists are more likely to think laws protecting the rights of women go too far; but, again, denominationally measured conservative Protestants are not. Only fundamentalists and denominationally measured conservative Protestants are more likely to think the laws protecting minorities and immigrants go too far. Evangelicals are not. All groups are more likely to believe laws protecting the welfare of children to too far.[8] Yet, while fundamentalists are not more likely to think laws protecting the rights of the disabled go too far, they are significantly *less* likely than other Americans to think that the disabled have too many rights. The bottom half of table 6 compares the views of self-identified evangelicals and fundamentalists with those of other Americans about support for "hate crime" laws. The analysis reveals that neither evangelicals nor fundamentalists support nor oppose more than other Americans laws that would impose extra penalties on people whose assaults are motivated by racial, religious, or ethnic animosity, whose crimes are specifically directed against gays and lesbians, or who vandalize sacred sites.

It appears, then, that conservative Protestants as a whole—with the exception of evangelicals on the topic of the rights of the disabled (and bracketing the contentious issue of human zygotes, embryos, and fetuses)—do not distinguish themselves as leading champions of the rights of the disadvantaged and vulnerable. Typically, at least as the questions are framed here, they either oppose the extent of these groups' rights, or they remain indistinguishable from other Americans on these rights and on "hate crime" laws. At the same time, a look at

TABLE 6 Conservative Protestant Views on Laws, Compared to All Other Americans

(percent)[1]

	Self-Identified Evangelicals	Self-Identified Fundamentalists	All Other Americans	Members of Conservative Protestant Denominations
Today's laws and regulations that protect the following go too far:				
Freedom of speech	29	n.s.[2]	18	
			19	n.s.
Rights of women	23	15	5	
			7	n.s.
Rights of minorities	n.s.	35	23	
			23	29
Welfare of children	16	18	9	
			9	14
Rights of immigrants	n.s.	57	40	
			39	49
Rights of the disabled	2	n.s.	8	
			8	n.s.
"Hate crime" laws that impose extra penalties on the following are a good idea:				
People who assault someone on account of the victim's race, religion, or ethnic group	n.s.	n.s.	60	NA[3]
People whose crimes are directed against gay men and lesbians on account of their sexual orientation	n.s.	n.s.	41	NA
People who vandalize synagogues, churches, mosques, or cemeteries	n.s.	n.s.	15	NA

Source: Southern Focus Poll, Spring 1996; Southern Focus Poll, Fall 1996.

1. Controlling for age, sex, race, education, income, region, marital status, and urban residence, using multiclassification analysis; dichotomous dependent variable means converted to percentages.

2. n.s. = logistic regression procedures show differences between groups are not statistically significant at the $p < .05$ level.

3. NA = variable not available on dataset.

the numbers themselves shows that—excepting fundamentalists on the rights of immigrants—the majority (almost always between 70 and 85 percent) of conservative Protestants do *not* believe that laws and regulations protecting the rights of free speech, women, minorities, children, immigrants, and the disabled go too far. We also see that the majority of evangelicals and fundamentalists do support laws particularly punishing bigoted violence against racial, ethnic, and religious groups. And about 40 percent of evangelicals and fundamentalists support laws aimed at protecting gays and lesbians. The least support of all is given to "hate crime" laws protecting religious meeting houses.

Finally, in table 7 we review conservative Protestants' views about which groups in America do and do not have too much social influence. We treat this as a proxy measure of their perceptions of the threat of out-groups. The findings are straightforward. Conservative Protestants, measured both denominationally and theologically, are more likely than other Americans to think that gay rights groups, liberals, feminists, and atheists have too much influence in America. They are not more likely than other Americans, however, to think the same of Hollywood movie studios, whites, blacks, Jews, Hispanics, or Asians. Conservative Protestants measured theologically are *less* likely than other Americans to think that the Catholic Church, fundamentalist Christians, the Religious Right, or conservatives have too much influence. Measured denominationally, conservative Protestants do not differ from other Americans on their assessment of the influence of any of these groups, except conservatives. The groups who conservative Protestants do seem to feel threatened by are homosexuals, liberals, feminists, and atheists.

Nevertheless, we see that the majority of conservative Protestants do *not* believe that liberals, feminists, and atheists have too much influence. Only gay rights groups evoke this concern from a majority. Comparatively, it is Hollywood movie studios by far who most Americans, including conservative Protestants, think have too much influence. Furthermore, as a group against which people feel hostility, fundamentalist Christians rank relatively high. Among all other Americans, fundamentalist Christians raise almost as much concern as feminists and atheists, and more concern than blacks, Jews, Hispanics, and Asians. Feelings of threat and out-group hostility, in other words, clearly run in both directions.

TABLE 7   Groups Regarded as Having Too Much Influence, Conservative Protestants Compared to All Other Americans
(percent)[1]

	Members of Conservative Protestant Denominations	All Other Americans	Conservative Protestants Theologically
Gay rights groups	68	43	
		42	57
Liberals	45	33	
		32	43
Feminists	39	29	
		28	38
Atheists	43	29	
		26	41
Hollywood movie studios	n.s.[2]	74	
		75	n.s.
Whites	n.s.	28	
		28	n.s.
Blacks	n.s.	19	
		18	n.s.
Jews	n.s.	12	
		12	n.s.
Hispanics	n.s.	9	
		10	n.s.
Asians	n.s.	8	
		9	n.s.
Catholic Church	n.s.	25	
		28	20
Religious Right	n.s.	28	
		33	17
Fundamentalist Christians	n.s.	23	
		27	14
Conservatives	13	22	
		25	13

Source: 1996 Religious Right Survey.
   1. Controlling for age, sex, race, education, income, region, marital status, and urban residence, using multiclassification analysis; dichotomous dependent variable means converted to percentages.
   2. n.s. = logistic regression procedures show differences between groups are not statistically significant at the p < .05 level.

TOLERANCE, DISTANCE, AND DISCRIMINATION

Another area of concern about conservative Protestants is their possible or assumed intolerance of social, ideological, racial, and religious differences in other groups. Tables 8 through 13 report survey data that address this question.

Table 8 reports the relative readiness of conservative Protestants to restrict or censor the expressed views of homosexuals, atheists, racists, militarists, and communists. Overall, we see that in almost one-half of the cases, conservative Protestants are not significantly different from other Americans on these issues; in the rest of the cases, conservative Protestants are more likely to support restrictions and censorship. In no case are conservative Protestants more likely to oppose restrictions. Denominationally defined conservative Protestants and self-identified evangelicals are the most likely to be more amenable than other Americans to supporting censorship, usually with an increased margin of between 7 and 15 percentage points. By contrast, in most cases, self-identified fundamentalists are no more likely than other Americans to support censorship. In general, conservative Protestants seem the most tolerant of controversial speakers in communities, and the least tolerant of deviant books in public libraries.[9]

However, two points should qualify any general conclusion that conservative Protestants are predisposed toward right-wing censorship of opposing views. First, conservative Protestants' readiness to impose restrictions is consistent across different kinds of unconventional viewpoints. This means that conservative Protestants are not ideologically selective in their censorship. Indeed, the group that elicits the greatest overall opposition is those who would abolish elections and set up a military dictatorship. Insofar as authoritarian military regimes are notorious enemies of civil freedoms, in this case conservative Protestants can be viewed as the most prepared to take preemptive steps in defense of freedoms of speech, of the press, of assembly, and so on. The same could conceivably be argued regarding communists. At the same time, conservative Protestants overall display some of the least enthusiasm for the repression of those who we might think would threaten them most directly: people who are against all churches and religion. Second, in only two out of twenty-two instances of greater conservative Protestant support for censorship (evangelicals on militarists and communists teaching college) do the majority of conservative Protestants support that censorship. In all of the other twenty cases, only a minority of

TABLE 8 Conservative Protestant Views on Disallowing Conflicting Opinions, Compared to All Other Americans
(percent)[1]

Opposition to:	Self-Identified Evangelicals	Self-Identified Fundamentalists	All Other Americans	Members of Conservative Protestant Denominations
One who admits to being a homosexual				
Making a speech in one's community	25	n.s.[2]	15/14	25
Teaching in a college or university	37	31	20/20	31
Having a book in a public library	47	37	27/26	38
One who is against all churches and religion				
Making a speech in one's community	n.s.	n.s.	25/24	n.s.
Teaching in a college or university	n.s.	n.s	41/40	49
Having a book in a public library	50	n.s.	28/27	41
One who believes blacks are genetically inferior				
Making a speech in one's community	n.s.	n.s.	37/36	43
Teaching in a college or university	n.s.	n.s.	48/51	n.s.
Having a book in a public library	50	n.s.	33/32	44
One who advocates doing away with elections and letting the military run the country				
Making a speech in one's community	43	n.s	34/33	n.s.
Teaching in a college or university	62	n.s.	47/47	n.s.
Having a book in a public library	50	n.s	40/39	46
One who admits to being a communist				
Making a speech in one's community	n.s.	n.s.	33/32	39
Teaching in a college or university	54	n.s.	38/38	n.s.
Having a book in a public library	43	n.s.	31/30	40

Source: 1996 General Social Survey.

1. Controlling for age, sex, race, education, income, region, marital status, and urban residence, using multiclassification analysis; dichotomous dependent variable means converted to percentages.

2. n.s. = logistic regression procedures show differences between groups are not statistically significant at the p < .05 level.

TABLE 9   Groups Not Wanted as Neighbors, Conservative Protestants
           Compared to All Other Americans
           (percent)[1]

	Members of Conservative Protestant Denominations	All Other Americans	Conservative Protestants Theologically
Homosexuals	59	38	
		38	51
Atheists	43	29	
		27	39
Catholics	n.s.[2]	3	
		3	n.s.
Asians	n.s	9	
		9	n.s.
Hispanics	n.s.	9	
		9	n.s.
Blacks	n.s.	11	
		11	n.s.
Jews	n.s.	4	
		5	n.s.
Fundamentalists	n.s.	11	
		12	4

Source: 1996 Religious Right Survey.
  1. Controlling for age, sex, race, education, income, region, marital status, and urban residence, using multiclassification analysis; dichotomous dependent variable means converted to percentages.
  2. n.s. = logistic regression procedures show differences between groups are not statistically significant at the $p < .05$ level.

conservative Protestants support censorship. Even regarding restrictions on expressions of homosexual views—where conservative Protestants most consistently support restrictions—typically only an average of one-third of them support censorship. On average, two-thirds do not.

Table 9 shows comparative attitudes toward different groups that people may not want to have as neighbors—another proxy measure for social distance and discrimination. Consistent with the findings in preceding tables, conservative Protestants report at considerably higher rates than other Americans that they would not want homosexuals or atheists for neighbors. The majority object to homosexual neighbors; only large minorities object to atheist neighbors. Conservative Protestants do not differ from other Americans, however, when it comes to objecting to Catholics, Asians, Hispanics, blacks, and Jews as neighbors. And theologically defined conservative Protestants find the idea of living next door to a fundamentalist less objectionable than do other Americans. Indeed, we see that "all other" Americans would prefer to live next to Hispanics, Asians, Catholics, or Jews, than to live next door to fundamentalists.

Reporting a different measure of social distance, table 10 compares percentages who say they feel "far" or "very far" from specific racial, religious, and lifestyle groups. Again, the majority of conservative Protestants do feel distant from gays and atheists. A minority of theologically defined conservative Protestants also feel far from feminist groups. However, conservative Protestants are not more likely than other Americans to feel distant from Muslims, Asians, Hispanics, Jews, Catholics, or blacks. Indeed, denominationally defined conservative Protestants are actually less likely than other Americans to feel far-removed from blacks. Conservative Protestants are also less likely to feel distant from fundamentalists, Religious Right activists, and the Christian Coalition. Overall, with the exception of gays and atheists, the majority of conservative Protestants do not feel especially socially distant from these different groups. And, interestingly, about as many conservative Protestants feel distanced from fundamentalists, Religious Right activists, and the Christian Coalition as all other Americans feel removed from blacks, Jews, and Hispanics.

Finally, table 11 approaches the issue of discrimination in terms of voting for political office. The question was "If your party nominated a generally well-qualified person for president and that person happened to be _____, would you vote for that person, or not?" Consistent with results reported in previous tables, conservative Protestants, measured both denominationally and theologically, are more likely to say they would not vote for an atheist or homosexual. Denominationally measured—though not theologically measured—conservative Protestants are also more likely to say they would not vote for a Muslim, a woman, or a Catholic. Neither differs from other Americans when it comes to an Asian or a Hispanic. And theologically measured conservative Protestants are less likely than other Americans to say they would not vote for a black, a Jew, a fundamentalist Christian, or a supporter of the Religious Right.

Viewed in absolute terms, the solid majority of conservative Protestants are predisposed to discriminate against an atheist or homosexual presidential candidate. Only small minorities of conservative Protes-

TABLE 10 Groups Conservative Protestants Feel "Far" or "Very Far" From, Compared to All Other Americans
(percent)[1]

	Members of Conservative Protestant Denominations	All Other Americans	Conservative Protestants Theologically
Homosexuals	63	48	
		45	60
Atheists	n.s.[2]	51	
		46	66
Feminist Groups	n.s.	29	
		28	37
Muslims	n.s.	34	
		35	n.s.
Asians	n.s.	20	
		20	n.s.
Hispanics	n.s.	14	
		15	n.s.
Jews	n.s.	12	
		13	n.s.
Catholics	n.s.	8	
		8	n.s.
Blacks	4	12	
		12	n.s.
Fundamentalists	13	29	
		31	18
Supporters of the Religious Right	12	27	
		30	13
Supporters of the Christian Coalition	11	23	
		25	14

Source: 1996 Religious Right Survey.

1. Controlling for age, sex, race, education, income, region, marital status, and urban residence, using multiclassification analysis; dichotomous dependent variable means converted to percentages.

2. n.s. = logistic regression procedures show differences between groups are not statistically significant at the $p < .05$ level.

tants would discriminate against any other type of candidate (except in the case of a Muslim nominee). In most cases tested, conservative Protestants do not differ statistically from other Americans on this question of presidential voting. In a few cases, including black or Jewish presidential candidates, conservative Protestants are actually less

TABLE 11   Discrimination Regarding Political Office, Conservative
            Protestants Compared to All Other Americans
            (percent)[1]

Would Not Vote for Presidential Candidate Who Is	Members of Conservative Protestant Denominations	All Other Americans	Conservative Protestants Theologically
Atheist	65	44	
		40	63
Homosexual	67	41	
		37	62
Muslim	47	32	
		30	n.s.[2]
Female	14	5	
		6	n.s.
Catholic	13	4	
		6	n.s.
Asian	n.s.	11	
		14	n.s.
Hispanic	n.s.	9	
		10	n.s.
Black	n.s.	8	
		8	3
Jewish	n.s.	5	
		8	3
Fundamentalist Christian	n.s.	17	
		19	12
Supporter of the Religious Right	n.s.	22	
		26	12

Source: 1996 Religious Right Survey.
  1. Percent who would not vote for candidate if respondent's party nominated a generally well-qualified person for president, and that person happened to be . . . ; controlling for age, sex, race, education, income, region, marital status, and urban residence, using multiclassification analysis; dichotomous dependent variable means converted to percentages.
  2. n.s. = logistic regression procedures show differences between groups are not statistically significant at the $p < .05$ level.

likely not to vote for them. Finally, again, we see that fundamentalist Christians rank among the more discriminated against by all other Americans. Opposed as presidential contenders by nearly 20 percent, fundamentalists are viewed with more distrust by other Americans than any other racial or religious group tested, except Muslims.

One final word on religion and tolerance: we have reason to believe that any significant religious differences with regard to tolerance are artifacts of the measurements employed, not a reflection of actual relationships. Political scientist Beverly Busch, in one of the most sophisticated analyses of religion and tolerance to date,[10] using measures of religion and tolerance better than those of most previous studies, has shown that religion is not in fact related to political tolerance; that religion is not related to the predispositions that do effect political tolerance; and that political tolerance is explained primarily by psychological traits and political attitudes not related to religion. This kind of analysis should again caution us about placing too much confidence in what surveys on these matters appear to tell us.

OTHER RELIGIONS AND RACES

Do survey data suggest that conservative Protestants are more hostile to or prejudiced against people of other faiths and races? According to the Religious Right Survey and General Social Survey data reported in tables 12 and 13, they are not.

Table 12 shows that conservative Protestants do not differ from other Americans on a host of measures attempting to test prejudicial attitudes towards members of other religions. With single exceptions in either direction, they do not show greater levels of distrust or animosity toward people of different faiths. This holds true for both denominationally and theologically defined conservative Protestants. One exception is that those in conservative Protestant denominations are less likely to say that members of Eastern religions like Hinduism and Buddhism can fit into American society just like others. Whether or not to interpret this as personal antagonism toward Eastern religions, or rather as a descriptive evaluation of the permeability of American society, is not possible to determine with certainty from the question as written. On the other hand, conservative Protestants are about twice as likely as other Americans to view contemporary Jews as still God's chosen people (likewise, the exact implication of such a claim we cannot ascertain from the question as written). Otherwise, only minorities of conservative Protestants express prejudice toward other religions, and never more than that expressed by other Americans.

Similarly, table 13 reports indicators of social distance from and prejudice against American blacks by white conservative Protestants. In no case do the views of white conservative Protestants differ from

TABLE 12   Conservative Protestant Views on Other Religions, Compared to All Other Americans

(percent)[1]

	Members of Conservative Protestant Denominations	All Other Americans	Conservative Protestants Theologically
It is essential to promote racial, religious, and ethnic understanding and tolerance in the U.S.	n.s.[2]	41 40	n.s.
Immigrants harm American society by bringing in strange customs and beliefs	n.s.	18 17	n.s.
Those who practice Eastern religions like Hinduism and Buddhism can fit into American society just like others (disagree)	29	17 19	n.s.
Because of their religion, Muslims in the U.S. are less patriotic than other Americans	n.s.	41 40	n.s.
It is possible for Jews and Christians to live together in peace and harmony, despite their religious differences	n.s	92 91	n.s.
Jews and Christians share the same basic moral values, despite their religious differences	n.s.	87 88	n.s.
Now, as in the past, Jews are God's chosen people	45	26 21	44
Now, as in the past, Jews must answer for killing Christ	n.s.	10 10	n.s.
Jews are more willing than others to use shady practices to get what they want	n.s.	11 13	n.s.
When it comes to choosing between people and money, Jews will choose money	n.s.	20 20	n.s.

Source: 1996 Religious Right Survey.

1. Controlling for age, sex, race, education, income, region, marital status, and urban residence, using multiclassification analysis; dichotomous dependent variable means converted to percentages.

2. n.s. = logistic regression procedures show differences between groups are not statistically significant at the $p < .05$ level.

TABLE 13   White Conservative Protestant Racial Separatism, Compared to All Other White Americans
(percent)[1]

	Self-Identified Evangelicals	Self-Identified Fundamentalists	All Other White Americans	Members of Conservative Protestant Denominations
Whites have the right to keep blacks out of their neighborhoods if they want, and blacks should respect that	n.s.[2]	n.s.	4 4	n.s.
Respondent supports laws against marriages between blacks and whites	n.s.	n.s.	12 12	n.s.
Respondent would object to sending own children to school where half of the children are black	n.s.	n.s.	17 17	n.s.
Nobody in family brought home a black friend for dinner in the past few years	n.s.	n.s.	40 40	n.s.
Respondent lives in a neighborhood where no blacks live	n.s.	n.s.	63 63	n.s.

Source: 1996 General Social Survey.

1. Controlling for age, sex, education, income, region, marital status, and urban residence, using multiclassification analysis; dichotomous dependent variable means converted to percentages.

2. n.s. = logistic regression procedures show differences between groups are not statistically significant at the $p < .05$ level.

those of other white Americans. Like other white Americans, only small minorities of white conservative Protestants support residential racial segregation, would legally oppose interracial marriages, or would object to sending their kids to a completely racially integrated school. Also like other white Americans, a majority report that, in the past few years, someone in their family brought home for dinner a friend who was black. Like other white Americans, about one-third of white conservative Protestants report that they live in a racially mixed neighborhood. Thus, insofar as survey data tells us anything valid or reliable, we find no evidence suggesting that conservative Protestants feel significantly greater distance from or prejudice against people of other religions or races.

EMOTIONAL AND MENTAL HEALTH

Finally, we briefly review the 1996 General Social Survey data on religion and emotional and mental health. Some of the literature critical of American fundamentalists and evangelicals suggests either implicitly or explicitly that these are people who must be particularly angry, resentful, unhappy, or repressed. These writings intimate themes from the older psychological and sociological literature on "frustration-aggression," "the authoritarian personality," "status anxiety," and so on. They suggest that the social, religious, and political views and activities of publicly visible conservative Protestants must be the expression of displaced anger, emotional repression, irrepressible anxiety, or some other unhealthy emotional or mental condition.[11] I reiterate that survey data are severely limited in their ability to investigate such claims. Nevertheless, relevant data do exist, and are worth examining here.

According to table 14, conservative Protestants are hardly different from other Americans when it comes to emotional and mental health. Self-identified evangelicals are significantly more likely than other Americans to say they are very happy, that life is exciting, and (of those who are married) that their marriages are very happy. On the other hand, self-identified evangelicals are 8 percent more likely than other Americans to say they are afraid to let people know their feelings. Whether to interpret this as an indicator of emotional repression, or of a reflective self-awareness indicating greater emotional health, we cannot say. Besides these few differences, neither evangelicals nor fundamentalists nor denominational conservative Protestants show significant differences from other Americans in emotional and mental health. According to these data, members of these three groups are not especially unsuccessful in their family or work lives, encounter more negative or fewer positive emotions in the course of a week, repress their emotions more, become more violent or vengeful when angry, or are especially likely to have a history of mental health problems. Indeed, although usually statistically insignificant at the $p < .05$ level, the (un-

TABLE 14 Emotional and Mental Health of Conservative Protestants, Compared to All Other Americans
(percent)[1]

	Self-Identified Evangelicals	Self-Identified Fundamentalists	All Other Americans	Members of Conservative Protestant Denominations
Respondent is very happy	43	n.s.[2]	29	
			29	n.s.
Life is exciting	70	n.s.	48	
			48	n.s.
Marriage is very happy	81	n.s.	60	
			60	n.s.
Family life is very or completely successful	n.s.	n.s.	52	
			53	n.s.
Work life is very or completely successful	n.s.	n.s.	47	
			46	n.s.
Average number of days in a week respondent feels negative emotions[3]	n.s.	n.s.	1.6	
			1.6	n.s.
Average number of days in a week respondent feels positive emotions[4]	n.s.	n.s.	4.5	
			4.5	n.s.
Keeps emotions to themselves	n.s.	n.s.	42	
			44	n.s.
Does not let people know when angry	n.s.	n.s.	28	
			28	n.s.
Afraid to let people know feelings	29	n.s.	21	
			21	n.s.
Yells or hits something to vent anger	n.s.	n.s.	8	
			8	n.s.
Thinks about revenge when angry	n.s.	n.s.	6	
			6	n.s.
Has ever had mental health problems	n.s.	n.s.	8	
			8	n.s.

Source: 1996 General Social Survey.

1. controlling for age, sex, race, education, income, region, marital status, and urban residence, using multiclassification analysis; dichotomous dependent variable means converted to percentages.

2. n.s. = logistic regression procedures show differences between groups are not statistically significant at the $p < .05$ level.

3. Total number of days in previous seven days respondent reported feeling sad, blue, ashamed, lonely, fearful, worried about little things, anxious and tense, restless, mad or angry at someone; divided by number of negative emotion questions answered; using OLS regression to test significance.

4. Total number of days in previous seven days respondent reported feeling calm, happy, excited, overjoyed, contented, at ease, or proud of something accomplished; divided by number of positive emotion questions answered; using OLS regression to test significance.

reported) calculated means show that, if anything, conservative Protestants exhibit tendencies toward greater happiness, success in life, positive emotional experiences, and forthright processing of negative emotions than do other Americans.

Finally, the absolute values of the numbers themselves show that the majority of married conservative Protestants say that their marriages are very happy and that their family lives are very or completely successful. About one-half of conservative Protestants view life as exciting, and consider their work lives very or completely successful. Only a minority say they keep their emotions inside, not letting others know their true feelings. And very few conservative Protestants say they become violent or vengeful when angry, or have ever suffered mental health problems. Thus, if conservative Protestants are especially emotionally or mentally disturbed or repressed, the available survey evidence reviewed here fails to reveal that. On the whole, conservative Protestants look pretty much like most other Americans—if not somewhat more happy and content.

SUMMARY

Popular accounts—and sometimes scholarly ones as well—frequently portray conservative Protestants as encapsulated in a well-bounded and homogeneous subculture of orthodoxy, authority, and conservativism. They are sometimes linked with certain unsavory features of the Christian Right, and then viewed as a regimented mass of like-minded devotees, predisposed toward culturally imperialistic views that violate cultural pluralism, social tolerance, and liberal democracy. At the extreme, conservative Protestants—usually referred to en masse as "fundamentalists"—are characterized as a dogmatic, fanatical, and bigoted lot.

The available survey evidence, however, suggests a more equivocal picture. Even as oversimplifying and homogenizing as surveys tend to be, the survey data portray no simple, consistent story about conservative Protestants. On some issues, certain groups of conservative Protestants (but often not others) exhibit signs of religious exclusivism, moral imperialism, and social intolerance. But in numerous other ways they do not. Some conservative Protestants do tend toward greater social distance from and prejudice against certain outside groups, relative to other Americans. But often those tendencies are reflected among only a minority of conservative Protestants. The bulk of conservative Protestants do not share those views. And usually those tendencies are in fact not directed toward the groups one might expect, given the portrayal of conservative Protestants in some of the literature.

On morality, religion, public life, and politics, majorities of conservative Protestants are much more likely than other Americans to emphasize America's Christian roots; to hold a nonrelativistic view of morality; and to view religion as publicly relevant, not merely a private matter. Majorities of conservative Protestants also stand out in wanting to see Christian morality directly influence American legal norms, and wanting the federal government to promote traditional values in society. They are notably more publicly activist about their faith, wanting to see religion more explicitly present in the political process and in public schools. Conservative Protestants are also more likely to oppose much of what they think feminism represents. And minorities of conservative Protestants are more likely than other Americans to support and be influenced by the Religious Right.

At the same time, however, large majorities of conservative Protestants do not think women belong in the home; do believe that people have the right to live by their own morality, whether Christian or not; do oppose Christian social activism that would cause social conflict; do not believe public schools should teach Christian values and morals, or require spoken Christian prayers in the classroom; do not think there is only one Christian view on most political issues; do not support a constitutional amendment declaring the United States a Christian nation; do not support the Religious Right and are not influenced by it when it comes to voting; do agree that criticisms of the Religious Right are valid; do not believe that America's laws that protect freedom of speech, the welfare of children, or the rights of women, minorities, immigrants, or the disabled go too far; and are not soft on racially, religiously, or ethnically bigoted "hate crimes." In all of these ways, the majority of conservative Protestants seem to emerge as supporters of pluralism, tolerance, and human rights.

Regarding issues of social distance and discrimination, the most consistent substantive finding is that many conservative Protestants feel distant from and opposed to the influence of homosexuals. The majority of conservative Protestants think gay rights groups have too much influence, feel far-removed from homosexuals, and would not want a homosexual for a neighbor or a president. And a substantial minority of conservative Protestants—generally with a margin of 10 to 15 percent over other Americans—would be willing to censor the public speeches, university teaching, and public library books of a homosexual. This evidence is robust and clear. Even so, table 6 shows that neither evangelicals nor fundamentalists would be less supportive than other Americans of "hate crime" laws designed specifically to protect gay men and lesbians.

Beyond that, conservative Protestants are also noticeably opposed to atheists, although somewhat less consistently so than to homosexuals. Substantial minorities of conservative Protestants believe atheists have too much influence and would not want one for a neighbor or a president. Some kinds of conservative Protestants also indicate opposition to atheist books in public libraries, and admit feelings of social distance from atheists. Still, other kinds of conservative Protestants do not. Finally, conservative Protestants exhibit less than full acceptance of feminists, women's rights advocates, liberals, and—at least when it comes to presidential voting—Muslims and Catholics; even so, more than two-thirds of conservative Protestants say that they do not feel far-removed from feminist groups. Conservative Protestants (excluding fundamentalists) appear willing to take steps to censor the expressed views of racists, militarists, and communists. And conservative Protestants appear at least marginally more receiving than "other Americans" of blacks, Jews, and the disabled.

On matters of hostility toward people of other religions and races, conservative Protestants appear essentially no different from the rest of Americans. They are no more likely than other Americans to reject the presence of Muslims, Hindus, Buddhists, or Jews in American society. Nor are white conservative Protestants more likely to express particularly racist attitudes toward blacks. Regarding Catholics, Asians, Hispanics, blacks, and Jews, the vast majority of conservative Protestants would be happy to have them as neighbors, do not feel distant from them, and would vote for one for president. Moreover, the majority of conservative Protestants do not think immigrants harm American society; do believe that followers of Eastern religions can fit into American society; do not view Muslims as less patriotic than other Americans; do think Christians and Jews can live in peace and harmony; do not espouse traditional anti-Semitic views; and do not oppose interracial neighborhoods, marriages, or schools.

CONCLUSION

None of this evidence suggests that conservative Protestants are pace-setting advocates for multiculturalist diversity, tolerance, racial integration, or absolute freedom of speech. They clearly are not, if survey data are to be believed. But neither are conservative Protestants shown to be consistently or militantly exclusivist and intolerant. Conservative Protestants appear the least accepting of homosexuals, on the one hand; but on the other, just as accepting as other Americans of members of other religions and races. The statistics also show that large numbers of conservative Protestants disagree among themselves over most of these questions. Finally, in and through even these "flat" numbers, one senses traces of—or at least consistency with—the kinds of tension, ambivalence, and hesitation among conservative Protestants wrestling with these issues that we have seen throughout this book.

Notes

INTRODUCTION: THE BIG EVANGELICAL QUESTION

1. Scholars generally agree that conservative Protestants represent about 25 to 30 percent of the American population. Narrow measurements based on religious self-identification reveal smaller numbers, while those based on broad theological beliefs can yield much larger numbers. See the discussion in the introduction, "Defining 'Evangelical.'"

2. See for instance, Haiven 1984; Casanova 1994: 135–66; Ide 1986; also see Pierard 1984; Reichley 1987; Averill 1989; Wuthnow 1983.

3. See for instance, Watt 1991; Hollinger 1983; Marsden 1987; Quebedeaux 1974; Ellingsen 1988; Fowler 1982; also see Jorstad 1993; Witten 1995; Hunter 1987b; Sweet 1984; Bendroth 1984; Numbers 1984; Wells and Woodbridge 1975.

4. See for instance, Hunter 1983, 1987a; Smith et al. 1998; Shibley 1996.

5. For a detailed account of this project, see Smith et al. 1998: 221–289.

6. See Smith et al. 1998: 226–231.

7. When I pointed out that the majority of evangelicals I interviewed see themselves not as powerful, but as excluded and trivialized, she replied, "But don't you see? Claiming that you are a victim is just another way to get more power." When I suggested that universities are a marketplace for all sorts of contending ideas that students must evaluate, and that perhaps parents could trust their children to make good decisions on religious as well as other important matters—such as political philosophy, sexual lifestyle, personal ethics, etc.—she said, "Some kids can handle it, but some can't. If I knew that a university was allowing evangelicals to proselytize, I would not send my daughters there."

8. See Smith et al. 1998: 120–144.

9. Quoted in *Washington Post* 1994: A22.

10. Walker 1992.

11. Wilkie 1995; also see Yoachum and Tuller 1996; Jones 1995; Rich 1995f, 1996a, 1997.

12. Leo 1994; Jeffrey Birnbaum wrote in a 1995 *Time* magazine cover story (1995: 32) on Ralph Reed that the Christian Coalition—which "despite its increasing sophistication and secularization . . . remains insular, distrustful, and eager to impose what it sees as a Bible-backed morality on the public at large"—had organized satellite downlinks of an hour-long program, "Christian Coalition Live," hosted by Reed, to "more than 200 conservative evangelical churches."

13. Gomes 1996. For examples of mainstream journalism that attempt to defend evangelicalism, see, for instance, *Washington Post* 1994; Meacham 1993; Leo 1994, 1997.

14. Herman 1997: 4, 10, 199–200.

15. Diamond 1995: 162, 177, 312; also see Faludi 1991: 229–235.

16. Fowler 1982; Skillen 1990; also see Rich 1995d.

17. Reported in a September 24, 1979 *U.S. News and World Report* story (p. 37), quoted in Crawford 1980: 161.

18. See for instance, Skillen 1991; 1990: 181–212; Mouw 1992; Marsden 1997; 1994: 429–444.

19. Hollinger 1983: 2.

20. Lienesch 1993: 21.

21. Williams and Blackburn 1996.

22. Jorstad 1993.

23. Darnell and Sherkat 1997; theonomists and fundamentalists, incidentally, are two very different religious creatures.

24. Witten 1995. Likewise, Linda Kintz's *Between Jesus and the Market: The Emotions That Matter in Right-Wing America* (1997) is based on her interpretation of the writings of authors like Tim and Beverly LaHaye, Stu Weber, George Gilder, Newt Gingrich, and Rush Limbaugh.

25. Weisskopf 1993: A10. Compare that to journalist Bruce Bawer's view (1997: 8) of "fundamentalist, evangelical, and charismatic Christianity": "their success . . . owes everything to American missionary work among the poor and undereducated. In their suspicion of the intellect and their categorical assertion that the Bible contains all truth, these kinds of Christianity reflect the American distrust of mind described by Richard Hofstadter in his book, *Anti-Intellectualism in American Life*; indeed, they can be understood as ways of avoiding the obligation to *think*—and, especially, to think for oneself."

26. See for instance, Rothenberg and Newport 1984; Hunter 1983; Kellstedt et al. 1996a.

27. In fact, as survey researchers know well, even identifying basic items, such as survey respondents' race, religion, income, and occupation, can be fraught with difficulty.

28. Furthermore, as surveys have become a routine part of daily American life, and as surveyors tend to replicate question wordings for consistency across

time, many of the standard survey questions and answer categories may actually have come to shape the very ways that ordinary people think about issues—or even think about which issues *are* issues.

29. Wald 1987; Smith 1997: 5.

30. See Smith et al. 1998: 76–77.

31. See Hart 1996; Sewell 1992; Berger 1981.

32. Hart 1996.

33. Regnerus and Smith 1998b.

34. Indeed, the human capacity for denied duplicity and self-deception appears great; see, for instance, Kleinman 1996; Hochschild 1989; Gilkey 1966.

35. Examples of this practice are myriad, but see, for instance, Ide 1986; Provenzo 1990; Hunter 1983.

36. See Woodberry and Smith 1998.

37. The 1996 Religious Identity and Influence Survey data shows a 10.6 percent overlap between charismatic self-identification and membership in a pentecostal denomination. Smidt et al. (1996) report that only 12.2 percent of self-identified charismatics also identify themselves as pentecostal (and that this overlap group comprises .8 of one percent of the total American population).

38. Dayton 1991: 245; see Dayton and Johnson 1991; Marsden 1984; Smith 1980; Ellingsen 1988; Webber 1978: 25–34.

39. Woodberry and Smith 1998: 45–46; Smidt et al. 1996; Rozell and Wilcox 1995; Oldfield 1996.

40. See Schogol and Remsen 1998.

41. Even Martin Marty, American religious historian at the University of Chicago, has treated evangelicals not as a distinct religious movement, but as an expression of fundamentalism. In a brief recounting of the American fundamentalist experience in the twentieth century, Marty (1989: ix–x) writes that post-1920s fundamentalists seemed "to slink away, to live on in hillbilly, backcountry, holyrolling, redneck territories," but "by mid-century they were back, in moderate, scrubbed-up, neo-evangelical forms, in the mode of Billy Graham."

42. Smith et al. 1998.

43. Regnerus and Smith 1998a.

44. Regnerus, Sikkink, and Smith 1999.

45. These were the assumptions that informed the classic studies of, for example, Ruth Benedict on the Zuni, Margaret Mead on the Samoans, Bronislaw Malinowski on the Trobriands, Edward Evans-Prichard on the Nuer, and Clifford Geertz on the Balinese.

46. Sewell 1997; also see Smelser 1992; Scott 1985; Clifford 1988; Clifford and Marcus 1986; sociologists who have also taken this approach include Erikson 1976 and Merelman 1984.

1. MAKING SENSE OF "CHRISTIAN AMERICA"

1. Briggs 1998: A4.

2. Briggs 1998: A4.

3. On a different topic somewhat related to the question of Christian America—namely, who or what groups in America today may be actively opposed or hostile to Christians—evangelicals tended to speak very similarly. This will be discussed later.

4. Individual evangelicals sometimes gave multiple meanings in a single interview, such that the total of all percentages per meaning reported here exceeds 100 percent.

5. In fact, scholars (though not all evangelicals or other Americans) know that the early American colonies varied in their toleration of religious diversity—from the relatively intolerant Puritan Congregationalist colony of Massachusetts, to the quite tolerant colonies of Pennsylvania, Delaware, and Maryland (see, for instance, Frost 1990; McLoughlin 1991). Contemporary evangelical talk about "religious freedom" as the meaning of "Christian America" does not refer to, for example, the Bay Colony's Puritan definition of religious freedom ("Freedom for us, but not for Quakers or Baptists"); but rather to the more broad, cultural notion that each person was and should be free to worship whoever, however, whenever, and for whatever reason they so choose.

6. The argument is based on the premise that the faithful practice of Christianity and the level of a nation's social problems are causally linked. The full but simple logic runs like this: America was once a nation of faithful Christians, and consequently there were fewer moral, social, and political problems. The historical decline of Christian faith and practice has resulted in an increase in these problems. These problems are a bad thing. Therefore, America as a nation should return to its previous, higher level of faithful Christian living.

7. An Assemblies of God man from Ohio, for example, stated: "Well, now, I'm not an historian, but if you get into looking at our past presidents where they used to get up and pray, and used to write in their letters about praying to God, talking about Christianity, and everything, if you look at where the nation came from, you can bring that from the beginning of time when America was a Christian nation."

8. A Pentecostal man from Georgia shared: "Who was that guy who signed the Declaration of Independence? Oh, John Quincy Adams. As a fourteen-year-old [he] was sent to the Queen of Russia as a spokesman for the United States, because of his wisdom. He never read any text except the Bible. He learned to read, count numbers, learned equations, and learned science from the Bible. Those people had wisdom because it was all godly wisdom from the Bible. It started as a godly nation in the beginning. They would pray before they would pass a bill or new law. They would pray, see if they could find scripture to base it by. So, it did start out a godly nation."

9. A Baptist man from Pennsylvania noted: "There is no doubt in my mind that you can go back and find that some of our founding fathers were maybe even immoral in some of their lifestyles, but they as a collective whole founded our nation as 'one nation under God.' They believed in a supreme being. They believed in God Almighty. And they wanted our nation to espouse those values and beliefs. They put it into our Constitution, the Declaration of Independence, they put it on our currency. They made it an indelible imprint on our society."

10. Besides the meanings commonly mentioned by evangelicals under discussion here, individual interviewees occasionally mentioned others that are not detailed in this text. One (and only one) evangelical man, for example, claimed that America was a Christian nation in the past because its founding was part of God's providential purpose in history.

11. See Smith et al. 1998: 187–203; Emerson and Smith (2000).

12. To maintain the interviewees' anonymity, their names have been changed in this text; however, the other identifying information (sex, religious tradition, state of residence, family information, etc.) remains the same.

13. Among evangelicals, "to witness" means to exemplify a good Christian life and to share one's faith with nonbelievers.

14. Similarly, a Pentecostal woman from Washington state maintained: "I don't approve of that. That is my own personal opinion. I can't go around and preach what I do and don't believe in. People have to live their lives the way they want to live. All we can do is express our opinion. We can't do it loudly and be boisterous. You are not going to accomplish anything by going down to City Hall and holding up a sign. Sometimes the best protest you are going to get is doing a quiet protest. Praying for those people. That is the best way you can deal with it. Talking to other people. Educating those other people. It says in the Bible you can't be having sex with a person of the same sex. It is against God's laws to do that, you know. But when you have that chance to talk to somebody about Christ, then that is when you talk to them. You have to be able to see that person and say, well, maybe I can talk to them. You can't tell them they are going to hell."

15. See Hunter 1983, 1987; Wells 1993; Schaeffer 1984.

16. See Noll 1995.

17. See, for instance, Wallis 1976; Hauerwas and Willimon 1989.

18. See Schwalbe and Mason-Schrock 1996.

19. Tannen 1990.

20. See Smith et al. 1998. This process is not uniquely evangelical, by any means. I have observed uncannily similar dynamics at work, for example, in the interactions of a university socialist association, where I once gave a presentation. What appeared on the surface to be strategy and accomplishment talk was really functioning as leftist/progressive identity maintenance talk. There was clearly no pragmatic interest in actually shaping the external world; the purpose was to validate an insular collective moral identity. One would suspect these kinds of identity processes to be widespread among many social groups. See also Kleinman 1996; Taylor and Whittier 1992.

21. David Sikkink originally suggested this interpretation to me.

22. For present purposes, the authenticity and proper interpretation of the following biblical passages is less relevant than their scriptural authority for ordinary evangelicals.

23. See Yoder 1972.

24. Consider also the theology of the Hebrew scriptures, which Christians call the Old Testament. Many associate the Old Testament with a wrathful, arbitrary, and judging God. But arriving at this view requires selective reading of the texts. In the Hebrew Bible, Yahweh is depicted above all as a God of mercy

and love, who bears with the sins of his people, patiently withholding judgment and searching for every opportunity to achieve redemption and reconciliation (see, for instance, Ex 34:6–7; Ps 86:15; Ps 103:6–18; Is 1:2–18; Jer 30:4–22; Joel 2:12–14; Neh 9:16–21; Zech 10:6–12). When Adam and Eve sin, God provides for their needs and for their future salvation (Gen 3:15, 21). The same is true when Cain murders Abel (Gen 4:13–16). After the Flood, God promises never to destroy the earth, no matter how evil it becomes (Gen 9:8–17). Later, Yahweh commands his people to be kind and just to the foreigners who live in their land, although they do not share the covenant promises (Ex 22:21; Lev 24:22). And, eventually, Yahweh's plan of salvation is extended to all the nations of the earth, as it is his purpose to bless all peoples (e.g., Ps 67; Ps 72:17; Is 51:4–5, 60:1–3).

25. See Hart 1996.
26. See Mouw 1992.
27. Briggs 1998: A4.

2. THE PROBLEM OF PLURALISM

1. Other probes included: "What do you say to people who say 'There is one true God and one morality that applies to everyone for their own good, whether they know it or like it, or not. So those morals, and not others, should govern our society'?" "What do you say to people who say 'Everyone has to decide for themselves how to live; nobody can force another to believe or live a certain way; it has to come from each individual's heart'? Do you agree or disagree? Why?" "What do you say to people who say 'I don't believe in God or the Bible, so don't tell me how I have to live'?" and "To what extent should Christian morality be made into *laws*? Are there aspects of Christian morality that should *not* be made into laws?"

2. Sometimes, a realistic acceptance clearly moderated what otherwise would be a commitment to Christian cultural hegemony. A pentecostal woman from Washington State commented, "I think there's a morality that applies to everybody and it's God's laws, and Christians hold that very dear: that God's laws is the law that we need to follow. But I think it's very difficult in society to impose that on people who have come from different cultures. I think once you're living in a country that has certain standards, you [should] just automatically have to fit in. And I think this is what a lot of the problem is: [in the United States] you can retain your culture and still be a part of the larger society."

3. He continued: "Now you don't have to socialize with these people. And probably just from the way these things evolve, they are not going to want to be around you anyway. You can walk away from an off-color joke. You can tell people where you are going and what you are doing: 'My family and I are going on a church retreat.' 'Cause you have to work with them everyday. You just have to treat them nice. You can socialize with them, but there again I am not ever trying to beat something into them."

4. It is an interesting phenomenon that members of a religious subculture continue to believe that the world is generally hostile toward them when per-

sonal experience tells them otherwise. I will not explore that riddle here, since I have written about it elsewhere (Smith et al. 1998).

5. Similarly, one Southern Baptist woman from Missouri said: "Islamic groups may be hostile toward Christians. As individuals I think they're good. I can accept them, and they're people, God's people. Now how they choose to go from there—but just to say all Islamics—no, I do not have a prejudice against them." And a nondenominational man from Minnesota observed, "Islam has competing beliefs, but I don't think they hate Christians. They're just very zealous in what they believe, so therefore that's part of the process, you know. It's them or us."

6. Some readers may think that these people cannot be evangelicals if they hold these views. I reiterate that they either belong to churches widely recognized in their areas as evangelical churches, or they identified themselves as "evangelical" in our telephone survey. Furthermore, the view that holding certain opinions considered unevangelical automatically excludes someone from the ranks of evangelicalism systematically deprives us from ever seeing the diversity that actually exists within the evangelical world.

7. Likewise, another independent charismatic man from North Carolina said, "My belief in hell is not most of what motivates me to have the degree of conversation that I have with people about becoming Christians. It's more my desire for them to have the experience and enjoyment and the benefit of their spiritual relationship with God. If they are not saved they could go to hell. But that's not usually what triggers an involvement or desire to introduce them to something in conversation. It's not something that I say to the person. Because it is an offensive thing to say. It makes more of a difference to me if it's someone I know really well. Then my concern level is much greater. And I might say something in the context, for example, of a close relative. It's not something I introduce repeatedly."

8. See, for instance, C. S. Lewis's *The Great Divorce* (Macmillan Publishing 1946) and *The Last Battle* (Collier Books 1956).

9. He continued, "My beliefs are constantly evolving. God has said there is a time for us to know things and some things we should never know. And what that means is that you and I will never achieve perfect knowledge on this earth, and maybe never."

10. Similarly, a pentecostal woman from Pennsylvania observed: "I think about it if someone dies and wonder if they had a chance to accept the Lord before they went. Other than that I don't know that I think that much about it. I try not, especially if a person has heard the truth and has rejected it, that's been their decision. We can't force them, we can't make them. When you grab someone by the throat, you show no respect. They're not going to listen to you that way. So forget it. You have to use respect. I don't know that there's any necessarily pat method of how to share the gospel. But I agree that Jesus Christ has got to be shared."

11. One charismatic woman from North Carolina, for example, stated: "Well, I have an obligation to honor a person who may have helped to create that stereotype that is uncomfortable for me. You know, you don't choose your siblings and your family of origin, and you're identified [with them]. Those are

my brothers and sisters in the context of the Christian family. I might not choose to behave the way they do, but you know, they are as much a part of the family as I am."

12. A Vineyard church woman from Colorado, for example, argued: "I think that the church and Christians have not been as solid as they should have been—you know, do one thing and say another. With political things, there have been a lot of times when we just haven't stood up for our rights. We just let things slide through. Kind of live-and-let-live-type attitude, where we really should have been standing up against certain things. I don't think people see what they should see when they look at Christians."

3. THE LIMITS OF POLITICS

1. Conway and Siegelman 1984: 9, 11. The authors noted that the Holy Terror is also spreading among conservative Catholics and orthodox Jews.

2. Quoted in Willoughby 1981: 3.

3. Maguire 1982: 2.

4. Haiven 1984: 16, 218. Haiven also writes (1984: 18, 212, 214, 217) that "the born-agains are mysteriously silent on love [and] charity"; that the typical born-again Christian reflects "a natural suspicion of anything different, . . . knee jerk reaction to 'secular' authority, . . . an equally automatic obedience to religious leaders, . . . [and] racial [and] religious intolerance"; that "it is difficult to escape the conclusion that the born-again leaders . . . are, quite simply, dangerous men. Flip your television dial any Sunday morning from one televangelist to the next and you'll hear litanies of hatred and intolerance"; and that there now exists "an imperialism born of fear, of blind reaction, of paranoia, and of righteous anger. . . . The born-again movement is one of the largest engines that drive this new train of thought in American politics." By contrast, Haiven suggests (1984: 219) that "the humanist movement still possesses one genuine virtue which the born-again New Right is unlikely ever to acquire— namely, the spirit of charity."

5. Ide 1986: 183–184.

6. Himmelstein 1990: 203.

7. Goodstein 1996; also see Brownstein 1996; Rich 1995a, 1995b, 1995c.

8. Part of this man's reluctance to legislate Christianity stems from knowing that it could work against Christians as well: "As soon as someone is voted in or out, that legislation can change. And I would hate to have Christianity banished or additional roadblocks [erected] for Christians as a reaction by someone else [newly] voted in."

9. The "Spirit-filled" evangelicals we interviewed were perhaps the most emphatic about getting Christians in office. A pentecostal man from North Carolina, for example, argued: "If there's not Christians standing there [in politics], and there's four hundred [politicians] getting ready to vote, [they will] kill the nation, destroy the nation, for whatever reason. What I'm saying is there is no one there with religious beliefs. And he makes a decision for me and my family. Understand? And there's no God in him. He don't fear the Lord.

While I'm sleeping, they're up making a decision over my life and my dollar and what will take place in my home and community? I don't think so. I want somebody there that's at least going to pray, to consult God. If all of our politicians were Christians, what would we have to fear? If there was a problem, when they spoke we would be quick to listen, quick to follow. But when they speak now, who really listens? [*So the most important thing is to have godly people in positions of power, so they can make the right decisions?*] Positions of power, that's right."

One charismatic woman from North Carolina told us that Christians need to pray about political groups such as the National Organization of Women and gay rights organizations; we asked her exactly what Christians should be praying. She replied: "To make it very, very simple: 'Dear God, in Jesus' name, bad ones out and good ones in. Bad ones out of Congress, mayors, schools, professors. Good ones in.'"

10. See, for instance, Briner 1996; Woodbridge 1995; Bela 1999.

11. She continued: "The same with abortion. I don't agree with abortion for me, but I don't know another person in their footsteps and what they're going through, I have no clue to be able to judge that person for the decision they're making, I don't know. The same with suicide, I'm not in that person's shoes. People say a person who commits suicide has committed a terrible sin, they've taken a life, their own life. I don't know where that person was at when they committed suicide. You don't know what drove 'em to that, what pain they felt. You don't know that they didn't make their amends with God before they died, you know. I can't judge that. I can't say that I wouldn't kill someone under the right conditions if I was protecting someone, that I wouldn't do that, but yet I don't feel it's right. I don't know. It's hard to say, I'm probably not who you want to do this interview with! I'm pretty liberal in some of my thinking."

12. Again, to maintain the interviewee's anonymity, his name in the text has been changed; however, the other identifying information (sex, religious tradition, state of residence, family information, etc.) remains the same.

13. Fitzgerald 1981.

4. EVANGELICALS ON EDUCATION

1. McLaren 1987: review of Alan Peshkin's *God's Choice: The Total World of a Fundamentalist Christian School* (Chicago: University of Chicago Press, 1986).

2. Page and Clelland, 1978; Apple 1996.

3. Reese 1982, 1985.

4. Bates 1993; Gaddy, Hall, and Marzano 1996; Hunter 1991; Provenzo 1990.

5. Provenzo 1990.

6. Rose 1988: 10, 26. "At the same time," writes Rose (1988: 26), "they rally to support the political and economic supremacy of American, for they are concerned with protecting or improving their economic position in a society where it is eroding away." Also see Manatt 1995.

7. Rose 1990: 99; also see Lorentzen 1980.

8. Our interview schedule included the following questions on education: What are the most important things for kids to get out of their elementary and high school education? How do you think public schools are doing these days? [If problems are mentioned:] What are the problems? What are the causes of those problems? To what extent are public schools hostile to your faith, values, or beliefs? How would you like to see your faith and values reflected in or respected by public schools? Can you give me some specific examples of what that would look like? Should Christian morality be taught in the schools, or just in the home? [If in the school:] Which Christian morals exactly? Should Christians be trying to "redeem" the public schools, to make them more Christian? [If yes,] Why? How should Christians be trying to do that? By what means?

9. Smith et al. 1998.

10. Smith et al. 1998.

11. Calhoun 1995; Habermas 1983; Sikkink 1998.

12. Regnerus and Smith 1998a; Sikkink 1998.

13. Nord 1995; Nord and Haynes 1998.

14. Casanova 1994.

5. MALE HEADSHIP AND GENDER EQUALITY

1. Niebuhr 1998: A1–2.

2. Moulton 1998. Marc Cooper (1995) commented in an article published in *The Nation* that popular evangelical psychologist and family activist James Dobson's "talent for shrouding his group's militant and harsh political agenda (antichoice, pro-censorship, antigay) into a folksy approach that oscillates between schmaltz and New Age" has built an organizational "empire employing 1,100 people"—whose employees express an "almost cultlike fealty"—"with an annual budget of $100 million." See also Anti-Defamation League (1994)

3. Quoted in Leo 1997.

4. Bellant 1995.

5. Novosad 1996.

6. Swomley 1996b: 39; 1996a: 35.

7. Conason, Ross, and Cokorinos 1996; also see Rich 1996d.

8. In a similar way, this Evangelical Free man from Minnesota reflected: "We have different strengths and different weaknesses. I am not equal to my wife in childbearing, or in her abilities. She has different abilities and talents that God has given her; and she's not equal to me in some other areas. But together, we come together and decisions are really made on an equal basis. When I know there's a decision to be made, and she has much more ability in those areas than I do, I listen to her and agree with her, and we go ahead with it. And she does the same thing with me. And we are not equal. We're complimentary. But then in reality, as far as love, if you have to draw a line, yeah, we're equal and I believe that's very biblical, but God wants somebody to lead, somebody still has to lead, and in some families the man has relinquished that

leadership to the wife, but that doesn't mean that she's better or more than he is or vice versa. But somebody has to lead. You just can't have two people steering the boat. It isn't gonna work. Somebody has to lead and God has ordained man to lead in that area."

9. Likewise, one Congregational woman from California emphasized equality in God's sight and the need for improved understanding between the sexes: "I think in God's eyes we're equal, totally equal, and I think mutuality has to be one of communicating well. I think that many women and men have not communicated well, and therefore they tend to make a lot of assumptions which aren't so, about their roles and about their importance in marriage and everything. I think we have a long ways to go in terms of understanding. I think that the big issue of mutuality and equality is just that [better understanding], and I think if we can really get a hold of each respecting the other we'll go a long way toward dealing with problems in the family."

10. In fact the possible meanings of the original Greek word for "head" (*kephal*) in the biblical passage (Eph. 5:21–28) are multiple, and which is its best interpretation is contested. *Kephal* can mean (1) literally, the head of a physical body, (2) figuratively, having a position of priority or authority, or (3) figuratively again, "source" or "origin," as in the head of a river or fountain (see Kittel and Friedrich 1985). Evangelical egalitarians endorse the third possible meaning, suggesting that—in the context of marriage as an equal and mutually submissive partnership—husbands serve as sources of life for their wives when they lay down their own lives for their spouses as Christ laid down his for the church. This, they argue, suggests an antithetical meaning to husbandly rule and authority.

11. Hochschild 1989.

12. A Missouri Synod Lutheran woman from California explained that her husband's headship was a decision they made through mutual deliberation in which she had full say: "It isn't that I never told my husband what to do, you understand. But it boiled down to the fact that we discussed it, and would decide, and it was just decided. He didn't lay down the law necessarily or anything like that. But it was just decided through discussion what would be a good way to do."

13. A Congregational woman in Massachusetts also observed: "The husband should be the head of the house as Christ is head of the church. That doesn't mean that he's a dictator by any means. But he should be providing for the family. Providing, or—just all sorts of things, you know. Christian training, kind of guiding the family." And an evangelical Free man from Minnesota said, "It's just like in the human body you only have one head, and ultimately the husband is the head of the family and he carries that responsibility. But again, it's not, you know, in a demeaning sort of way."

14. One possible interpretation, of course, is that the lack of ultimate "showdowns" in evangelical marriages simply reflects the preemptive power that the husbands enjoy: evangelical wives never push any issues to "final say" situations because they know they will lose, and so always capitulate much earlier in the process. This is a potentially reasonable explanation, which our data cannot conclusively confirm or refute; further research along these lines is necessary. However, four considerations suggest that this interpretation may not

explain much of the difference here. First, in a separate quantitative analysis Lundquist (1999) has shown that, although evangelicals are much more likely than other religious Americans to endorse headship ideology, they are not significantly different from others regarding which spouse has more "say-so" and which "gives in" more on the issues of major financial decisions, working outside the home, child rearing, and how to spend leisure time. The only way in which evangelicals were different in practice, despite their endorsement of headship ideology, was that they are more likely than other churchgoing Protestants to say it is the husband who "takes the lead in spiritual matters." Second, although most of our interviewees spoke openly and honestly about personal matters, in none of our interviews did evangelical wives even hint that they gave in early on contentious issues because they knew they would lose in the end. If this were in fact the primary explanation for the apparent absence of "final-say" scenarios among evangelicals, we would have heard at least some traces of it in our interviews—barring absolutely extraordinary levels of evangelical false consciousness on the matter. Third, we have already seen that, for the majority of evangelicals, headship does not mean the right of husbands to dominate their wives, but an obligation to love and serve them. Therefore, if husbands in fact do exert authority over their wives by exercising the final say, it is just as likely to derive from a continuing patriarchy in the general culture as from evangelical headship ideology specifically. A wide spectrum of American husbands, and not just evangelicals, may be guilty of this form of domination. Finally, Arlie Hochschild's (1989) in-depth study of middle-class marriages suggests that couples' professing an egalitarian ideology does not guarantee that they practice an egalitarian marriage. Indeed, often merely talking about equality appears to satisfy their need to *believe* they are egalitarian, and apparently relieves them of the obligation to live out equality in daily life. This disjunct between ideology and practice parallels in reverse what we find in this study: evangelicals typically endorse a non-egalitarian ideology, but live more egalitarian marriages in practice than their ideology would predict. It is not unreasonable to believe that the effect here is a case of "regression toward the mean" in practice, away from the more ideological extremes at both ends.

15. Gallagher and Smith 1999.
16. Lundquist, Smith, and Zellers 1999.
17. Many of our findings were anticipated in important ethnographic works, including Ammerman 1987, Griffith 1997, and Brusco 1995; also see Gallagher and Smith 1999.

CONCLUSION: DEMYTHOLOGIZING THE ANGEL/DEMON

1. Fitzgerald 1981.

APPENDIX: WHAT SURVEYS TELL US

1. The 1996 Religious Identity and Influence Survey is a cross-sectional, nationally representative, random-digit-dial telephone survey, conducted from

January to March 1996 by FGI, a national survey research firm based in Chapel Hill, North Carolina. Survey Sampling, Inc. provided the randomly generated sample, which was designed to represent all telephones in the continental United States. The research design included at least ten calls for each number, and at least three callbacks to convert refusals. In order to randomize responses within households, and so to ensure representativeness by age and gender, interviewers asked to speak with the person in the household whose birthday was next. The sample population was Americans over seventeen years of age, with an oversample of churchgoing Protestants. A total of 2,591 interviews were completed. Weighting procedures have been applied to all logistic regression and multiclassification analyses to adjust for household size and the survey's oversample of churchgoing Protestants, in order to represent proportionately the population of the contiguous United States. The survey's response rate was 69 percent. A more detailed description of the survey's methods can be found in Smith et al. 1998.

2. The 1996 American Jewish Committee's Religious Right Survey was designed in collaboration by the American Jewish Committee and the Gallup Organization International Institute (George Gallup and Corinne Kyle), with advice from academic experts John Green (University of Akron), Tom W. Smith (National Opinion Research Center, University of Chicago), and Christian Smith (University of North Carolina at Chapel Hill). The survey was conducted during May and June 1996, under the direction of the Gallup International Institute, using a random sample of telephone numbers supplied by Genesys. It was designed to be representative of adults living in households having telephones in the United States. Within households, respondents were selected according to the following rule: "Ask for the youngest male living in the household who is age eighteen or older. If not available, ask for the oldest female living in the household." A total of 1,010 interviews were conducted, with an oversample of people aligned with the Religious Right, determined through a set of initial screen questions about social, political, and theological views. Weighting procedures have been applied to all logistic regression and multiclassification analyses to adjust for the survey's oversample of Religious Right aligners, in order to represent proportionately the population of the contiguous United States. See T. Smith 1997.

3. The 1996 General Social Survey represents a full probability, national sample of English-speaking persons eighteen years of age or older, living in noninstitutionalized arrangements within the United States. The interviews, which were conducted in person within households, lasted a median length of one and a half hours. The total N for 1996 is 2,904. For more detailed information regarding General Social Survey methods, see National Opinion Research Center 1996.

4. The two 1996 Southern Focus Polls (Spring and Fall) analyzed here were conducted as telephone interviews by the Institute for Research in Social Science (IRSS) at the University of North Carolina at Chapel Hill between February 11 and March 26, 1996, and between September 22 and November 13, 1996. Each represents a random sample of English-speaking persons eighteen years of age or older living in the United States in households with telephones,

with an oversample of residents of Southern states. The sample was obtained from Genesys Sampling Systems. A total of 1,200 interviews were completed for each survey. In order to randomize responses within households, and so to ensure representativeness by age and gender, interviewers asked to speak with the person in the household whose birthday was next. Weighting procedures have been applied to all logistic regression and multiclassification analyses here to adjust for the survey's oversample of Southerners, as well as for household size, in order to represent proportionately the population of the contiguous United States. For detailed information on Southern Focus Poll methods, see UNC IRSS documents *Survey Methodology, Southern Focus Poll, Fall 1996* and *Survey Methodology, Southern Focus Poll, Spring 1996.*

5. For details on multiclassification analysis, see Andrews, Morgan, and Sonquist 1969. For other works that use multiclassification analyis in this way, see Kellstedt and Smidt 1996 and Guth et al. 1996.

6. Tables should be read comparing different groups across rows on the *same* line. "All other Americans" often has different comparison groups (e.g., self-identified versus denominationally measured versus theologically measured conservative Protestants) for identical questions. These are separated out in the tables by their placement in rows in different lines for the same question. In table 1, for example, 87 and 82 percent of self-identified evangelicals and fundamentalists, respectively, believe that the United States was founded as a Christian nation, compared to only 66 percent of all other Americans. But measured denominationally (one line below and to the right), only 77 percent of conservative Protestants believe this, compared to 66 percent of all other Americans (i.e., *not* in conservative Protestant denominations).

7. For a broader discussion of this subject, see Nord 1995.

8. It is possible that the inclusion of the loaded word "welfare" on this item increased opposition to children's rights in this case, since conservative Protestants are known to be particularly opposed to government-based welfare programs.

9. Perhaps because they feel that the use of their tax dollars to purchase and house these books materially implicates them in the offense, in a way that allowing speeches does not.

10. Busch 1998.

11. Carol Flake (1984: 3) even cites a sociological study that purports to show that evangelicals have lower IQs than other Americans.

References

Ammerman, Nancy. 1987. *Bible Believers*. New Brunswick, N.J.: Rutgers University Press.

Andrews, Frank, James Morgan, and John Sonquist. 1969. *Multiple Classification Analysis*. Ann Arbor: Institute for Social Research.

Anti-Defamation League. 1994. *The Religious Right: The Assault on Tolerance and Pluralism in America*. New York: The Anti-Defamation League.

Apple, Michael. 1996. *Cultural Politics and Education*. New York: Teachers College Press.

Averill, Lloyd. 1989. *Religious Right, Religious Wrong: A Critique of the Fundamentalist Phenomenon*. New York: Pilgrim Press.

Bates, Stephen. 1993. *Battleground*. New York: Poseidon Press.

Bawer, Bruce. 1997. *Stealing Jesus: How Fundamentalism Betrays Christianity*. New York: Crown Publishers.

Bellant, Russ. 1995. "Mania in the Stadia: The Origins and Goals of Promise Keepers." *Free Inquiry* 16 (1): 28–31

Belz, Joel. 1999. "Not the Church's Business: We Dilute Our Message, and We Confuse the World." *World*, 29 May, 7.

Bendroth, Margaret. 1984. "The Search for 'Women's Role' in American Evangelicalism, 1930–1980." In *Evangelicalism and Modern America*, edited by George Marsden. Grand Rapids: Eerdmans.

Berger, Bennett. 1981. *The Survival of a Counterculture: Ideological Work and Everyday Life among Rural Communards*. Berkeley: University of California Press.

Birnbaum, Jeffrey. 1995. "The Gospel according to Ralph." *Time*, 15 May, 29–35.

Briggs, David. 1998. "Evangelicals Return to Grassroots to 'Reclaim America.'" *Durham Herald-Sun*, 12 April, A3.

Briner, Bob. 1996. *Deadly Detours: Seven Noble Causes That Keep Christians from Changing the World*. Grand Rapids: Zondervan.

Brownstein, Ronald. 1996. "Evangelicals Found to Hold Largest Share of GOP Base." *Los Angeles Times*, 25 June, A8.

Brusco, Elizabeth. 1995. *The Reformation of Machismo*. Austin: University of Texas Press.

Busch, Beverly. 1998. "Faith, Truth, and Tolerance: Religion and Political Tolerance in the United States." Ph.D. diss., University of Nebraska.

Calhoun, Craig. 1995. *Critical Social Theory: Culture, History, and the Challenge of Difference*. Cambridge: Blackwell.

Casanova, Jose. 1994. *Public Religions in the Modern World*. Chicago: University of Chicago Press.

Chusmir, Leonard and Christine Koberg. 1988. "Religion and Attitudes toward Work: A New Look at an Old Question." *Journal of Organizational Behavior* 9: 251–262.

Clifford, James. 1988. *Predicament of Culture: Twentieth-Century Ethnography, Literature, and Art*. Cambridge: Harvard University Press.

Clifford, James and George Marcus. 1986. *Writing Culture: The Poetics and Politics of Ethnography*. Berkeley: University of California Press.

Conason, Joe, Alfred Ross, and Lee Cokorinos. 1996. "The Promise Keepers Are Coming: The Third Wave of the Religious Right." *The Nation* (7 October) 263 (10): 11–17.

Conway, Flo and Jim Siegelman. 1984. *Holy Terror: The Fundamentalist War on America's Freedoms in Religion, Politics and Our Private Lives*. New York: Dell Publishing.

Cooper, Marc. 1995. "God and Man in Colorado Springs: Salvation City." *The Nation* (2 January) 260 (1): 9–13.

Cox, Harvey. 1995. "The Warring Visions of the Religious Right." *The Atlantic Monthly*, November, 59–69.

Crawford, Alan. 1980. *Thunder on the Right: The "New Right" and the Politics of Resentment*. New York: Pantheon Books.

Darnell, Alfred and Darren Sherkat. 1997. "The Impact of Protestant Fundamentalism on Education." *American Sociological Review* (April) 62 (2): 306–315.

Dayton, Donald. 1991. "Some Doubts about the Usefulness of the Category 'Evangelical.'" In *The Variety of American Evangelicalism*, edited by Donald Dayton and Robert Johnson. Knoxville: University of Tennessee Press.

Dayton, Donald and Robert Johnson. 1991. *The Variety of American Evangelicalism*. Knoxville: University of Tennessee Press.

Diamond, Sara. 1995. *Roads to Dominion: Right-wing Movements and Political Power in the United States*. New York: Guilford Press.

Doerr, Edd. 1993. "Church-State Separation Still Endangered." *The Humanist* (July-August) 53 (4): 40–42.

Ellingsen, Mark. 1988. *The Evangelical Movement: Growth, Impact, Controversy, Dialog*. Minneapolis: Augsburg.

Emerson, Michael and Christian Smith. 2000. *Divided by Faith: Evangelical Religion and the Problem of Race in America*. New York: Oxford University Press.

Erikson, Kai. 1976. *Everything in Its Path*. New York: Simon and Schuster.

Faludi, Susan. 1991. *Backlash: The Undeclared War against American Women*. New York: Crown Publishers.

Fitzgerald, Frances. 1981. "Reporter at Large: A Disciplined Charging Army." *The New Yorker* (18 May) 57 (5): 53–141.

Flake, Carol. 1984. *Redemptorama: Culture, Politics, and the New Evangelicalism*. New York: Penguin.

Fowler, Robert Booth. 1982. *A New Engagement: Evangelical Political Thought, 1966–76*. Grand Rapids: Eerdmans.

Frost, J. William. 1990. *A Perfect Freedom: Religious Liberty in Pennsylvania*. University Park, Penn.: Pennsylvania State University Press.

Gaddy, Barbara, William Hall, and Robert Marzano. 1996. *School Wars: Resolving Our Conflicts over Religion and Values*. San Francisco: Jossey-Bass Publishers.

Gallagher, Sally and Christian Smith. 1999. "Symbolic Traditionalism and Pragmatic Egalitarianism: Contemporary Evangelicals, Family, and Gender." *Gender and Society* 13: 211–233.

Galloway, Paul. 1995. "Evangelicals a Force, but Who Are They?" *Chicago Tribune*, 26 May, C2.

Gilkey, Langdon. 1966. *Shantung Compound: The Story of Men and Women under Pressure*. New York: Harper and Row.

Goldstein, Steve. 1997. "Poll: Americans Ignorant about Constitution Provisions." *Durham Herald-Sun*, 16 September, A7.

Gomes, Peter. 1996. "The New Liberation Theology." *Harvard Magazine* (November–December) 99 (2): 34–36.

Goodstein, Laurie. 1996. "White Evangelicals 'a Powerful' Bloc." *Washington Post*, 25 June, A6.

Griffeth, Marie. 1997. *God's Daughters*. Berkeley: University of California Press.

Guth, James, Cleveland Fraser, John Green, Lyman Kellstedt, and Corwin Smidt. 1996. "Religion and Foreign Policy Attitudes: The Case of Christian Zionism." In *Religion and the Culture Wars*, edited by John Green, James Guth, Corwin Smidt, and Lyman Kellstedt. Lanham, Md.: Rowman and Littlefield.

Habermas, Jurgen. 1983. *The Theory of Communicative Action*. Boston: Beacon Press.

Haiven, Judith. 1984. *Faith, Hope, No Charity: An Inside Look at the Born-Again Movement in Canada and the United States*. Vancouver: New Star Books.

Hamilton, William. 1994. "The Demographics of a Movement." *Campaigns and Elections* (September) 15 (9): 28–30.

Hart, Stephen. 1996. *What Does the Lord Require?* New Brunswick, N.J.: Rutgers University Press.

Hauerwas, Stanley and William Willimon. 1989. *Resident Aliens: Life in the Christian Colony.* Nashville, Tenn.: Abingdon Press.

Herman, Didi. 1997. *The Antigay Agenda: Orthodox Vision and the Christian Right.* Chicago: University of Chicago Press.

Himmelstein, Jerome. 1990. *To the Right: The Transformation of American Conservatism.* Los Angeles: University of California Press.

Hochschild, Arlie. 1989. *The Second Shift: Working Parents and the Revolution at Home.* New York: Viking Press.

Hollinger, Dennis. 1983. *Individualism and Social Ethics: An Evangelical Syncretism.* Lanham, Md.: University Press of America.

Hunter, James Davison. 1983. *American Evangelicalism: Conservative Religion and the Quandary of Modernity.* New Brunswick, N.J.: Rutgers University Press.

———. 1987a. *American Evangelicals: The Coming Generation.* Chicago: University of Chicago Press.

———. 1987b. "The Evangelical Worldview since 1890." In *Piety and Politics: Evangelicals and Fundamentalists Confront the World,* edited by Richard John Neuhaus and Michael Cromartie. Washington, D.C.: Ethics and Public Policy Center.

———. 1991. *Culture Wars: The Struggle to Define America.* New York: Basic Books.

Ide, Arthur. 1986. *Evangelical Terrorism: Censorship, Falwell, Robertson, and the Seamy Side of Christian Fundamentalism.* Irving: Scholars Books.

Jones, Alan. 1995. "Beware the Christian 'Revolution.'" *San Francisco Chronicle,* 24 July, A19.

Jorstad, Erling. 1993. *Popular Religion in America: The Evangelical Voice.* Westport, Conn.: Greenwood.

Kagay, Michael. 1996. "Growth Area Seen for Religious Right." *The New York Times,* 10 August, A11.

Kellstedt, Lyman and Corwin Smidt. 1996. "Measuring Fundamentalism: An Analysis of Different Operational Strategies." In *Religion and the Culture Wars,* edited by John Green, James Guth, Corwin Smidt, and Lyman Kellstedt. Lanham, Md.: Rowman and Littlefield.

Kellstedt, Lyman, John Green, James Guth, and Corwin Smidt. 1996a. "Grasping the Essentials: The Social Embodiment of Religion and Political Behavior." In *Religion and the Culture Wars,* edited by John Green, James Guth, Corwin Smidt, and Lyman Kellstedt. Lanham, Md.: Rowman and Littlefield.

———. 1996b. "Religious Voting Blocs in the 1992 Election: The Year of the Evangelical?" In *Religion and the Culture Wars,* edited by John Green, James Guth, Corwin Smidt, and Lyman Kellstedt. Lanham, Md.: Rowman and Littlefield.

Kintz, Linda. 1997. *Between Jesus and the Market: The Emotions That Matter in Right-Wing America.* Durham: Duke University Press.

Kittel, Gerhard and Gerhard Friedrich. 1985. *Theological Dictionary of the New Testament,* translated and abridged in one volume by Geoffrey W. Bromiley. Grand Rapids: Eerdmans.

Kleinman, Sherryl. 1996. *Opposing Ambitions: Gender and Identity in an Alternative Organization*. Chicago: University of Chicago Press.

Leo, John. 1994. "Who Gets Invited to the Table?" *U.S. News & World Report* (18 July) 117 (3): 18.

———. 1997. "Cultural Left Draws a Bead on Promise Keepers." *Durham Herald-Sun*, July 20, A19.

Lienesch, Michael. 1993. *Redeeming America: Piety and Politics in the New Christian Right*. Chapel Hill: University of North Carolina Press.

Lorentzen, Louise. 1980. "Evangelical Life Style Concerns Expressed in Political Action." *Sociological Analysis* 41 (2): 144–54.

Lundquist, Melinda. 1999. "Gender Roles and Marital Decision-Making among American Evangelicals: Negotiating Ideology and Practice." MA thesis, University of North Carolina at Chapel Hill.

Lundquist, Melinda, Christian Smith, and Tara Zellers. 1999. "Religion and Women's Workforce Participation." Paper presented at the 1999 meeting of the Society for the Scientific Study of Religion, Boston, Mass., November.

Maguire, Daniel. 1982. *The New Subversives: Anti-Americanism of the Religious Right*. New York: Continuum.

Manatt, Richard. 1995. *When Right IS Wrong: Fundamentalists and the Public Schools*. Lancaster, Penn.: Technomic Publishing.

Marsden, George M. 1984. *Evangelicalism and Modern America*. Grand Rapids: Eerdmans.

———. 1987: *Reforming Fundamentalism: Fuller Seminary and the New Evangelicalism*. Grand Rapids: Eerdmans.

———. 1994. *The Soul of the American University: From Protestant Establishment to Established Nonbelief*. Oxford: Oxford University Press.

———. 1997. *The Outrageous Idea of Christian Scholarship*. Oxford: Oxford University Press.

Marty, Martin. 1989. Introduction to *Religious Right, Religious Wrong*, by Lloyd Averill. New York: The Pilgrim Press.

McLaren, Peter. 1987. "Schooling for Salvation: Christian Fundamentalism's Ideological Weapons of Death." *Journal of Education* 169 (2): 132–139.

McLoughlin, William. 1991. *Soul Liberty: The Baptists' Struggle in New England, 1630–1833*. Hanover: University Press of New England.

Meacham, Jon. 1993. "What the Religious Right Can Teach the New Democrats: Extremists Aside, America's Evangelicals Have a Message We All Need to Hear." *Washington Monthly* (April) 25 (4): 42–48.

Merelman, Richard. 1984. *Making Something of Ourselves*. Berkeley: University of California Press.

Moulton, Kristen. 1998. "Author Tells Baptists to Defend Righteousness." *The Chattanooga Times*, 12 June, A13.

"Moderate Evangelicals Worry about Being Tied to Religious Right." 1995. *Church and State* (April) 48 (4): 15.

"Most Mainline Protestants Are Going to Hell, Pat Robertson." 1995. *Church and State* (July-August) 48 (7): 14–16.

Mouw, Richard. 1992. *Uncommon Decency: Christian Civility in an Uncivilized World*. Downers Grove, Ill.: Inter-Varsity Press.

National Opinion Research Center. 1996. *General Social Surveys, 1972–1996: Cumulative Codebook*. Chicago: National Opinion Research Center.

Niebuhr, Gustav. 1998. "Baptists Declare Wives Should Obey Husbands." *Durham Herald-Sun*, 10 June, A1–2.

Noll, Mark. 1995. "The Rise and Long Life of the Protestant Enlightenment in America." In *Knowledge and Belief in America*, edited by William Shea and Peter Huff. Cambridge: Cambridge University Press.

Nord, Warren. 1995. *Religion and American Education: Rethinking a National Dilemma*. Chapel Hill: University of North Carolina Press.

Nord, Warren and Charles Haynes. 1998. *Taking Religion Seriously across the Curriculum*. Nashville, TN: First Amendment Center.

Novosad, Nancy. 1996. "God Squad: The Promise Keepers Fight for a Man's World." *The Progressive* (August) 60 (8): 25–28.

Numbers, Ronald. 1984. "The Dilemma of Evangelical Scientists." In *Evangelicalism and Modern America*, edited by George Marsden. Grand Rapids: Eerdmans.

Oldfield, Duane. 1996. *The Right and the Righteous: The Christian Right Confronts the Republican Party*. Lanham, Md.: Rowman and Littlefield.

Page, Ann and Donald Clelland. 1978. "The Kanawha County Textbook Controversy: A Study of the Politics of Life Style Concern." *Social Forces* 57 (1): 265–81.

Pierard, Richard. 1984. "The New Religious Right in American Politics." In *Evangelicalism and Modern America*, edited by George Marsden. Grand Rapids: Eerdmans.

Provenzo, Eugene. 1990. *Religious Fundamentalism and American Education: The Battle for the Public Schools*. Albany: State University of New York Press.

Quebedeaux, Richard. 1974. *The Young Evangelicals*. New York: Harper and Row.

Reese, William. 1982. "Public Schools and the Great Gates of Hell." *Educational Theory* 32 (1): 9–17.

———. 1985. "Soldiers for Christ in the Army of God: The Christian School Movement in America." *Educational Theory* 35 (2): 175–94.

Regnerus, Mark and Christian Smith. 1998a. "Selective Deprivatization among American Religious Traditions: The Reversal of the Great Reversal." *Social Forces* (June) 46 (4): 1347–1372.

———. 1998b. "Who Gives to the Poor? The Role of Religious Tradition and Political Location in the Personal Generosity of Americans toward the Poor." *Journal for the Scientific Study of Religion* (September) 37 (3): 481–493.

Regnerus, Mark, David Sikkink, and Christian Smith. 1999. "Who Votes With the Christian Right?: Contextual and Group Patterns of Electoral Influence." *Social Forces* 78 (1).

Reichley, A. James. 1987. "The Evangelical and Fundamentalist Revolt." In *Piety and Politics: Evangelicals and Fundamentalists Confront the World*, edited by Richard John Neuhaus and Michael Cromartie. Washington, D.C.: Ethics and Public Policy Center.

Reynolds, Barbara. 1995. "Christian Coalition a Model for Unchristian Conduct." *USA Today,* 26 May, A15.

Rich, Frank. 1995a. "Bait and Switch." *The New York Times,* 2 March, A23.

————. 1995b. "Bait and Switch II." *The New York Times,* 16 April, A31.

————. 1995c. "Connect the Dots." *The New York Times,* 30 April, 4, 15.

————. 1995d. "Breach of Faith." *The New York Times,* 28 May, 4, 11.

————. 1995e. "The God Patrol." *The New York Times,* 12 July, A17.

————. 1995f. "The Other Perot." *The New York Times,* 16 August, A25.

————. 1995g. "Christian Coalition Chutzpah." *The New York Times,* 20 December, A21.

————. 1996a. "Dole's Unpaid Debt." *The New York Times,* 9 March, A23.

————. 1996b. "Stealth Attack on the Y." *The New York Times,* 20 April, A21.

————. 1996c. "Happy New Year?" *The New York Times,* 18 September, A21.

————. 1996d. "'Thank God I'm a Man.'" *The New York Times,* 25 September, A21.

————. 1997. "The New World Order." *The New York Times,* 27 April, 4, 15.

Risen, James and Judy Thomas. 1998. *Wrath of Angels: The American Abortion War.* New York: Basic Books.

Rose, Susan. 1988. *Keeping Them Out of the Hands of Satan: Evangelical Schooling in America.* New York: Routledge.

————. 1990. "Gender, Education, and the New Christian Right." In *In Gods We Trust,* edited by Thomas Robbins and Dick Anthony. New Brunswick, N.J.: Transaction.

————. 1993. "Christian Fundamentalism and Education in the United States." In *Fundamentalisms and Society,* edited by Martin Marty and R. Scott Appleby. Chicago: University of Chicago Press.

Rothenberg, Stuart and Frank Newport. 1984. *The Evangelical Voter: Religion and Politics in America.* Washington, D.C.: Institute for Government and Politics of the Free Congress Research and Education Foundation.

Rozell, Mark and Clyde Wilcox. 1995. *God at the Grassroots.* Lanham, Md.: Rowman and Littlefield.

Schaeffer, Francis. 1984. *The Great Evangelical Disaster.* Westchester, Ill.: Crossways.

Schogol, Marc and Jim Remsen. 1998. "Promise Keepers' Formidable Foes." *The Philadelphia Inquirer,* 12 July, H7.

Schwalbe, Michael and Douglas Mason-Schrock. 1996. "Identity Work as Group Process." *Advances in Group Processes* 13: 113–47.

Scott, James. 1985. *Weapons of the Weak: Everyday Forms of Peasant Resistance.* New Haven: Yale University Press.

Sewell, William. 1992. "A Theory of Structure: Duality, Agency, and Transformation." *American Journal of Sociology* (July) 98 (1): 1–29.

————. 1997. "The Concept(s) of Culture." Paper presented at the 1997 meeting of the American Sociological Association, Toronto, Canada, August.

Shibley, Mark. 1996. *Resurgent Evangelicalism in the United States: Mapping Cultural Change since 1970*. Columbia: University of South Carolina Press.

Sikkink, David. 1998. "'I Just Say I'm a Christian': Symbolic Boundaries and Identity Formation among Church-going Protestants." In *Reforming the Center: American Protestantism, 1900 to the Present*, edited by Douglas Jacobsen and Vance Trollinger. Grand Rapids: Eerdmans.

Sikkink, David and Mark Regnerus. 1996. "For God and the Fatherland." In *Disruptive Religion*, edited by Christian Smith. New York: Routledge.

Skillen, James W. 1990. *The Scattered Voice: Christians at Odds in the Public Square*. Grand Rapids: Zondervan.

———. 1991. *Political Order and the Plural Structure of Society*. Atlanta: Scholars Press.

Smelser, Neil. 1992. "Culture: Coherent or Incoherent." In *Theory of Culture*, edited by Richard Munch and Neil Smelser. Berkeley: University of California Press.

Smidt, Corwin, John Green, Lyman Kellstedt, and James Guth. 1996. "The Spirit-Filled Movements and American Politics." In *Religion and the Culture Wars*, edited by John Green, James Guth, Corwin Smidt, and Lyman Kellstedt. Lanham, Md.: Rowman and Littlefield.

Smith, Christian, with Sally Gallagher, Michael Emerson, Paul Kennedy, and David Sikkink. 1998. *American Evangelicalism: Embattled and Thriving*. Chicago: University of Chicago Press.

Smith, Timothy. 1980. *Revivalism and Social Reform: American Protestantism on the Eve of the Civil War*. Baltimore: Johns Hopkins University Press.

Smith, Tom. 1997. "The Social and Political Views of the Religious Right." Paper presented to the World Association for Public Opinion Research, Edinburgh, Scotland. September.

"Speaking of Evangelicals." 1994. *Wall Street Journal*, 30 June, A10.

Stan, Adele. 1997. "Why I Became a Born-Again Republican." *Ms. Magazine* (January-February) 7 (4): 22.

Sweet, Leonard. 1984. "The 1960s: The Crises of Liberal Christianity and the Public Emergence of Evangelicalism." In *Evangelicalism and Modern America*, edited by George Marsden. Grand Rapids: Eerdmans.

Swomley, John. 1996a. "Promises We Don't Want Kept." *The Humanist* (January–February) 56 (1): 35–37.

———. 1996b. "Cashing in for Christ." *The Humanist* (September-October) 56 (5): 39–42.

———. 1997. "New Strategies, New Groups." *The Humanist* (March-April) 57 (2): 41–43.

Tannen, Deborah. 1990. *You Just Don't Understand: Women and Men in Conversation*. New York: Ballantine Books.

Taylor, Verta and Nancy Whittier. 1992. "Collective Identity in Social Movement Communities." In *Frontiers in Social Movement Theory*, edited by Aldon Morris and Corol Mueller. New Haven, Conn.: Yale University Press, 104–129.

"Those Troublesome Christians." 1994. *The Washington Post*, 22 July, A22.

Trescott, Jacqueline. 1993. "Group Claims NEA Endorses Pornography: Explicit Sexual Films Cited as Evidence." *The Washington Post,* 10 September, G2.

Wald, Kenneth. 1987. *Religion and Politics in the United States.* New York: St. Martins Press.

Walker, Ruth. 1992. "'Stealth' Candidates in American Politics." *The Christian Monitor,* 2 December, 19.

Wallis, Jim. 1976. *Agenda for Biblical People.* New York: Harper and Row.

Warren, James. 1994. "Enemies of the Right: Even Conservatives Incur the Wrath of the Christian Action Network." *Chicago Tribune,* 11 September, sec. 5, p. 2.

Watt, David Harrington. 1991. *A Transforming Faith: Explorations of Twentieth-Century American Evangelicalism.* New Brunswick, N.J.: Rutgers.

Webber, Robert. 1978. *Common Roots: A Call to Evangelical Maturity.* Grand Rapids: Zondervan.

Weisskopf, Michael. 1993. "Energized by Pulpit or Passion, the Public Is Calling." *The Washington Post,* 1 February, A1–11.

Wells, David. 1993. *No Place for Truth: Or Whatever Happened to Evangelical Theology?* Grand Rapids: Eerdmans.

Wells, David and John Woodbridge. 1975. *The Evangelicals.* Nashville: Abingdon.

Wilkie, Curtis. 1995. "Christian Right Takes Control of Iowa GOP." *Boston Globe,* 9 October, 1.

Williams, Rhys and Jeffrey Blackburn. 1996. "Many Are Called but Few Obey: Ideological Commitment and Activism in Operation Rescue." In *Disruptive Religion,* edited by Christian Smith. New York: Routledge.

Willoughby, William. 1981. *Does America Need the Moral Majority?* Plainfield, N.J.: Haven Books.

Witten, Marsha. 1995. "'Where Your Treasure Is': Popular Evangelical Views of Work, Money, and Materialism." In *Rethinking Materialism,* edited by Robert Wuthnow. Grand Rapids: Eerdmans.

Woodberry, Bob and Christian Smith. 1998. "Fundamentalism et al." *Annual Review of Sociology* 24:25–26.

Woodbridge, John. 1995. "Culture War Casualties: How Warfare Rhetoric Is Hurting the Work of the Church." *Christianity Today* (6 March) 39 (3): 20–27.

Wuthnow, Robert. 1983. "The Political Rebirth of American Evangelicals." In *The New Christian Right,* edited by Robert Liebman and Robert Wuthnow. New York: Aldine.

Yoachum, Susan and David Tuller. 1996. "Right Makes Might in Iowa: Religious Conservatives Hold Key to Today's Caucuses." *San Francisco Chronicle,* 12 February, A1–3.

Yoder, John Howard. 1972. *The Politics of Jesus.* Grand Rapids: Eerdmans.

Index

abortion, 52, 54, 55, 94, 121, 200, 201, 237; rights, 4, 39; clinic protests, 43, 52; clinic shootings, 44, 109; pro-choice activists, 51, 54, 52; pro-life activism, 44, 50, 106; right to life, 51
African Americans. *See* blacks
African-American studies, 146
AIDS, 42
Air Force, 113
American Civil Liberties Union (ACLU), 39, 92
American Revolution, 23
American Jewish Committee, 3, 197, 241
Anglicanism, 13, 57
animal rights, 108
anti-Semitism, 5, 226
Antichrist, 112
Arabs, 129
Articles of Confederation (United States), 23
Asian-Americans, 129, 211, 212, 215, 216, 217, 218, 226
astrology, 148
atheists, 102, 134, 150, 211, 212, 213, 215, 217, 218, 226
authoritarian personality theory, 222

Bakker, Jim and Tammy, 8, 90
Baptists, 232
Bawer, Bruce, 230n25
Bellant, Russ, 161
Benedict, Ruth, 231n45

Bible, 10, 13, 14, 16, 29, 30, 33, 38, 45, 48, 51, 63, 76, 93, 95, 105, 106, 108, 112, 122, 125, 134, 144, 148, 160, 177, 178, 179, 180, 230, 232, 233; biblical literalism, 10, 13
big government, 112
Bilezekian, Gilbert, 190
Bill of Rights (United States), 29, 92, 162
birth control, 142, 190
Blackburn, Jeffrey, 8
blacks/African-Americans, 129, 211, 212, 214, 215, 216, 217, 218, 219, 221, 226; black churches, 13, 14
Boone, Pat, 8
born again, 1, 5, 10, 15, 70, 92, 236
Boston Globe, 5
Boy Scouts/Girl Scouts, 143
Bryant, Anita, 8
Buchannan, Pat, 48, 115, 121
Buddha 73, 75
Buddhism, 67, 75, 76, 78, 79, 80, 219, 220, 226
Busch, Beverly, 219

capitalism, 55
Carter, President Jimmy, 1
Catholicism, 13, 57, 89, 215, 216, 217, 218, 226, 236; Catholic Church 211, 212; Catholic groups, 24
censorship, 93, 213
Center for Public Justice, 7
"character education", 144

charismatics, 14, 16, 17, 230, 231
Christian Science Monitor, 4
Christian schools, 137
Christian Right, 5, 6, 8, 16, 21, 25, 27,
  28, 57, 76, 90, 99, 104, 122, 123,
  124, 126, 127, 130, 195, 198, 223
Christian Coalition, 4, 11, 18, 99, 120,
  122, 123, 125, 126, 216, 230
Christianity Today, 7
Christmas, 103, 148
civil disobedience, 43, 109
Cokorinos, Lee, 162
Colson, Charles, 7
Columbus, Christopher, 31
communists, 213, 214, 226
Conason, Joe, 162
condoms, 133, 142
Confucius, 73, 75
Congress (United States), 109, 237
conservative, 11, 16, 18, 101, 195,
  212
Constantine, (Roman) Emperor, 66
Constitution (United States), 23, 26, 29,
  35, 36, 232
Conway, Flo, 92
Cooper, Marc, 238n2
Coral Ridge Presbyterian Church, *Coral
  Ridge Hour*, 21
corruption, political, 113, 114
creationism, 4, 149, 150, 158
crime, 27
Crusades, the, 195
culture, 18, 19
culture wars, 48, 98, 131, 133, 134,
  148, 157, 159, 193

Darnell, Alfred, 8
Dayton, Donald, 14
Declaration of Independence (United
  States), 23, 50, 232nn8, 9
Delaware, 232n5
Democratic Party, 102
"demon possession", 71
demonstrations, political, 43, 111
Diamond, Sarah, 6
disabled, 210, 211, 225, 226,
divine providence, 152
divorce, 59, 139, 162, 169
Dobson, James, 7, 30, 76, 109, 160,
  238n2
drinking (alcohol), 46, 101, 112
drugs, 27, 46, 77, 101, 116, 123, 138
Duke, David, 205, 206
Dutch Reformed Calvinists, 14

earthquakes, 116
Easter, 103, 148

Eastern Baptist Theological Seminary,
  160
economic pressures, on families, 162,
  169
"economy of responsibility", 169, 177,
  181
Eden, garden of, 116
education, basic, 145, 146, 152, 158
"end-times", 112
"engaged orthodoxy", 131
English language, 63, 68
Enlightenment, the, 56, 57
environmentalism, 51, 102, 146
"equal time" for Christian views, 142,
  147, 149, 151, 158
ethnography, 10
evangelical elites, 7
evangelion, 72
Evans, Tony, 39
Evans-Prichard, Edward, 231n45
evolution, 149, 150, 151, 152; teaching
  in schools, 130
exorcism, 71

Falwell, Jerry, 8, 92, 123, 124
family values, 2, 124, 166, 169
family breakdown, 139, 140, 162, 164,
  165, 166, 167
feminism, 39, 45, 162, 189, 198, 200,
  211, 212, 217, 225, 226
Fitzgerald, Frances, 127, 194
Flake, Carol, 242n11
Focus on the Family, 30, 99, 109, 153
Franklin, Ben, 22
Free Inquiry, 161
freedom of speech, 67, 103, 108, 210,
  211, 213, 225
"frustration-aggression" theory, 222
Fuller Theological Seminary, 7
fundamentalism, 2, 8, 15, 129, 231n41;
  fundamentalist, 5, 13, 14, 15, 16, 17,
  18, 30, 47, 88, 93, 107, 130, 201,
  202, 203, 204, 205, 208, 209, 210,
  211, 212, 214, 215, 216, 217, 218,
  221, 222, 223, 230nn23, 25

Gallagher, Sally, 186
"Gallup scale", 10, 16, 17
Gallup International Institute, 197,
  241n2
Gallup, George, 241n2
gangs, 116, 148
gays/lesbians, 50, 99, 209, 210, 211,
  216; gay and lesbian rights, 2, 53, 94,
  211, 212, 225, 237. *See also* homosexuals
Geertz, Clifford, 231

General Social Survey, 3, 197, 219, 221, 222, 223, 241n3
German Lutherans, 14
Germany, 69
Gilder, George, 230
Gingrich, Newt, 4, 230
global economy, 64
God: judgment, 198; Spirit, 124, 125, 186; Word, 27; providence, 33. See also Holy Spirit
Golden Rule, 102
Gomes, Peter, 5
good government activists, 101
Goodstein, Laurie, 93
GQ, 161
Graham, Billy, 231n41
Green, John, 241n2
Guatemala, 125, 127
gun violence, 109
Gundry, Patricia, 190

Haiven, Judith, 93
Hardesty, Nancy, 190
Hart, Stephen, 11
Harvard University, 5, 28
Harvard Magazine, 5
hate crime laws, 209, 210, 211, 225, 226
Hebrew scriptures, 233n24
hell, 42, 71, 75, 81–87, 118, 233n14, 235n7
Herman, Didi, 6
Himmelstein, Jerome, 93
Hinduism, 75, 219, 220; Hindus, 226
Hispanics, 211, 212, 215, 216, 217, 218, 226
Hochschild, Arlie, 169
Hofstadter, Richard, 230n25
Holiness-Methodists, 13
Hollinger, Dennis, 7
Hollywood, 47, 52, 89, 211, 212
Holocaust, 92
Holy Spirit, 84, 105, 184; gifts of, 14
"Holy Terror", 92, 236n1, Holy Terror, 92
home schooling, 132
homosexuals, 4, 39, 40, 41, 45, 47, 49, 51, 52, 53, 93, 106, 133, 162, 213, 214, 215, 217, 218, 225, 226, 233n14; same-sex marriage, 12. See also gays/lesbians
Humanist, The, 161
humanists, 45. See also secular humanism

Ide, Arthur, 93
immigrants, 62, 210, 211, 220, 225

India, 148
Institute for Research in Social Science (University of North Carolina at Chapel Hill), 197, 241n4
interest-group politics, 102
Iowa, 5
IQ scores, 242n11
Islam, 5, 75 235n5. See also Muslims
Italian-Americans, 62

Japanese, 148
Jefferson, Thomas, 31, 32
Jewish, 21, 75, 148, 218; Jews, 4, 21, 129, 211, 212, 215, 216, 217, 219, 220, 226; Orthodox, 236n1
Jorstad, Erling, 8
Journal of Education, 129
Judgment Day, 54, 55, 58, 109, 169
juvenile delinquency, 165

Keener, Craig, 190
Kennedy, James, 8, 21, 25, 22, 30, 48, 60, 123
Kintz, Linda, 230n24
Koresh, David, 90
Kroeger, Richard and Katherine, 190
Kyle, Corinne, 241n2

LaHaye, Beverly and Tim, 8, 230n24
Leno, John, 5
Lewis, Clive Staples, 85, 235n8
liberals, 2, 11, 55, 102, 150, 162, 193, 195, 198, 205, 206, 211, 212, 226
liberation theology, 125
Lienesch, Michael, 7
Limbaugh, Rush, 230n24
Lincoln, Abraham, 31
Little House on the Prairie, 35
lobbying, political, 115
Lord's Prayer, 35
Louisiana, 205

Madison, James, 32
Maguire, Daniel, 92
Malinowski, Bronislaw, 231n45
Marsden, George, 7
Marshall, Peter, 30
Marty, Martin, 41
Maryland, 232n5
mass media, 47, 51
Massachusetts, 232n5
Mayflower, 31
McCarthy Era, 92
McCartney, William (Bill), 161
McLaren, Peter, 129, 130
Mead, Margaret, 231n45
mental health, 222, 223

Mexican-Americans, 62
militarists, 212, 226
Mohler, Jr., R. Albert, 160, 162
Montt, General Rios, 125
Moral Majority, 1, 15, 92, 97, 122, 123
Mormons, 76
Mott, Stephen, 7
Mouw, Richard, 7
MTV, 52
Muhammad, 73, 75
multiclassification analysis, 198, 242n5
Muslims, 40, 63, 74, 75, 77, 78, 103,
    216, 217, 218, 220, 226. *See also*
    Islam

Nation, The, 162, 238n2
National Rifle Association, 99
National Opinion Research Center
    (NORC), 197, 241n3
National Organization of Women, 49,
    237n9
Nazis, 161
New Age, 39, 40, 45, 51, 238n2
New York Times, 92
Nixon, President Richard M., 32
North, Gary, 7
Notre Dame University, 7
Novosad, Nancy, 161

Operation Rescue, 8, 49, 93
Oregon Citizens Alliance, 53

Paine, Thomas, 22
Patterson, Paige, 160, 162
Pennsylvania, 232n9
Pentagon, 113
pentecostals, 13, 14, 15, 16, 17, 231
Peshkin, Alan, 237n1
Pew Charitable Trusts, 197
Pilgrims, 31, 32, 151
Planned Parenthood, 44
Pledge of Allegiance, 35, 140
poor people, 123
prayer/pray, 4, 53, 83, 87, 91, 107, 114,
    138, 156, 159, 204, 206, 232n7,
    233n14, 236n9; healing 71; in public
    schools, 1, 52, 94, 122, 130, 131,
    134, 141, 152, 153, 158, 203, 204,
    205, 206, 225
Princeton University, 28
Progressive, The, 161
Prohibition, 5
Promise Keepers, 15, 118, 161
prophesy, 112
Protestantism: mainline and liberal de-
    nominations, 17; measuring conserva-
    tive, 198

public libraries, 213, 214, 226
Puritan, 232n5

Quakers, 232n5

race, 14; racists, 5, 213, 226; racial seg-
    regation, 5; racial minorities, 210, 225
rationality, 12
Reed, Ralph, 109, 230
Religious Right Survey, 3, 197, 217,
    218, 219, 220, 241
Religious Right, 1, 2, 4, 11, 13, 93, 130,
    141, 162, 206, 208, 211, 212, 216,
    217, 218, 225, 236n4, 241n2
Religious Identity and Influence Survey,
    16, 24, 197, 231n37, 240n1
Republican Party, 1, 5, 6, 55, 93, 102
Revelation, Book of, 74
Robertson, Pat, 7, 8, 15, 25, 113, 125,
    126, 127
Robinson, James, 8
Roman government, 122
Roosevelt, President Franklin D., 117
Rose, Susan, 130
Rosh Hashanah, 148
Ross, Alfred, 162
Rushdoony, R.J., 8
Russian Mennonites, 14

Saint Paul, 23, 169
Satan, 71, 79
Scanzoni, Letha, 190
school: private, 131, 134, 138; PTAs,
    154
science, 12
secular, 136, 138, 140, 141, 150; secu-
    larists, 55, 77; secularity, 137, 157;
    secularization, 2
secular humanism, 55, 102, 108, 132,
    139, 198, 203, 204
Seculo, Jay, 30
self-esteem, 146
Senate (United States), 205
Sewell, William, 19
sex: outside of marriage, 123; immoral-
    ity, 116; education, 133, 141, 142,
    150, 153, 203
Sherkat, Darren, 8
Siegelman, Jim, 92
sin, 30
Skillen, James, 7
Smith, Tom W., 241n2
social ethics, 11
sociologists, 55
Southern Baptist Theological Seminary,
    160
Southern Baptist, 160, 162, 190, 191

Southern Baptist Faith and Message Statement, 160, 169, 191
Southern Focus Poll, 197, 241n4
Soviet Union, 25
Spanish language, 63
Spanish Inquisition, 118
spiritual gifts, 13; spirit-filled, 15; speaking in tongues, 13, 14
Star of David, 103
status anxiety theory, 222
"strategic relationalism", 45, 67
suicide, 88, 237n11
Sunday school, 89, 135; the Sabbath, 27
Super Bowl, 60
Supreme Court (United States), 60
survey research, 9, 10
Swedish Baptists, 14
Swiss Mennonites, 14
Swomley, John, 161

Tannen, Deborah, 56
technology, 144
televangelists, 43; sex scandals, 52
Ten Commandments, 33, 102, 144, 153
Terry, Randall, 8, 48
theocracy, 129, 162
Third World, 25

Thomas Road Baptist Church, 127
totalitarianism, 102
two-income families, 162, 164

U.S. News and World Report, 5

Valdez oil spill, 146
Valley Forge (PA), 135
Village Voice, The, 161
violence, 43, 46, 138; in schools 133
voting, 109, 115, 236nn8, 9

Wallis, Jim, 7
Washington, George, 31, 32, 135
Washington Post, 8, 93
Weber, Stu, 230n24
Weisskopf, Michael, 8
welfare, 124, 210, 225, 242n8
White House, 109, 113
Wilkie, Curtis, 5
Williams, Rhys, 8
Witten, Marsha, 8
"women's lib", 47, 169; women's rights, 5, 210, 226; women's studies, 146
world peace, 103, 106

xenophobia, 129

Text: 10/13 Sabon
Display: Univers Light Condensed
Composition: Binghamton Valley Composition
Printing and binding: Maple-Vail